# TEACHING NUMBER IN THE CLASSROOM

## WITH 4–8 YEAR-OLDS

# TEACHING NUMBER IN THE CLASSROOM WITH

## 4-8 YEAR-OLDS

**Robert J. Wright, Garry Stanger,
Ann K. Stafford, Jim Martland**

Paul Chapman Publishing

First published 2006
Reprinted 2006 (three times)

Paul Chapman Publishing
A SAGE Publications Company
1 Oliver's Yard
55 City Road
London EC1Y 1SP

SAGE Publications Inc
2455 Teller Road
Thousand Oaks, California 91320

SAGE Publications India Pvt Ltd
B-42, Panchsheel Enclave
Post Box 4109
New Delhi 110 017

Photographs provided by Carole Cannon, Joan McCarthy, Jim Martland and Ann K. Stafford

**Library of Congress Control Number: 2005905282**

A catalog record for this book is available from the British Library

ISBN 10 1-4129-0757-8
ISBN 10 1-4129-0758-6 (pbk)
ISBN 13 978-1-4129-0757-6 (hbk)
ISBN 13 978-1-4129-0758-3 (pbk)

Typeset by Pantek Arts Ltd, Maidstone, Kent
Printed and bound by Athenaeum Press, Gateshead, Tyne & Wear
Printed on paper from sustainable resources

*To: Eli and Millie*
*Eliana*
*Dillon*
*James A. Wheldon*

# Contents

List of Figures                                                                          xi
List of Photographs                                                                      xii
List of Tables                                                                           xiii
Contributors                                                                             xiv
Acknowledgments                                                                          xvii
Series Preface                                                                           xviii
Preface                                                                                  xx

Introduction                                                                             1

PART I
1   Approaching, Organizing and Designing Instruction                                    5

2   General Introduction to Part II                                                       20

PART II
3   Number Words and Numerals                                                            29
    Assessment Task Groups                                                               33
        A3.1:      Forward Number Word Sequences                                         33
        A3.2:      Number word after                                                     33
        A3.3:      Backward number word sequences                                        35
        A3.4:      Number word before                                                    35
        A3.5:      Numeral identification                                                35
        A3.6:      Numeral recognition                                                   36
        A3.7:      Sequencing numerals                                                   37
        A3.8:      Ordering numerals                                                     38
        A3.9:      Locating numbers in the range 1 to 100                                39
    Instructional Activities                                                             40
        IA3.1:     Count Around                                                          40
        IA3.2:     Numbers on the Line                                                   40
        IA3.3:     Stand in Line                                                         41
        IA3.4:     Secret Numbers                                                        41
        IA3.5:     Can You See Me?                                                       42
        IA3.6:     Make and Break Numbers                                                43
        IA3.7:     The Joke Is On You                                                    43
        IA3.8:     Counting Choir                                                        44
        IA3.9:     Take Your Place                                                       44
        IA3.10:    What Comes Next?                                                      45

4   Early Counting and Addition                                                          47
    Assessment Task Groups                                                               51
        A4.1:      Comparing small collections                                           51
        A4.2:      Increase and decrease in the range 1 to 6                             52
        A4.3:      Establishing the numerosity of a collection                           52
        A4.4:      Establishing a collection of specified numerosity                     53
        A4.5:      Establishing the numerosity of two collections                        53

|  |  |  |
|---|---|---|
| A4.6: | Additive tasks involving two screened collections | 54 |
| A4.7: | Counting and copying temporal sequences and temporal patterns | 54 |
| Instructional Activities |  | 55 |
| IA4.1: | Domino Addition | 55 |
| IA4.2: | Addition Dice | 56 |
| IA4.3: | Counters in a Row | 57 |
| IA4.4: | On the Mat | 57 |
| IA4.5: | Where Do I Go? | 58 |
| IA4.6: | Toy Box | 59 |
| IA4.7: | Teddy Bear Walk | 60 |
| IA4.8: | Chains | 61 |
| IA4.9: | Give Me Five | 62 |
| IA4.10: | Pass It On | 62 |

**5   Structuring Numbers 1 to 10** — 64

| Assessment Task Groups |  | 68 |
|---|---|---|
| A5.1: | Making finger patterns for numbers in the range 1 to 5 | 68 |
| A5.2: | Making finger patterns for numbers in the range 6 to 10 | 69 |
| A5.3: | Naming and visualizing domino patterns 1 to 6 | 70 |
| A5.4: | Naming and visualizing pair-wise patterns on a ten frame | 70 |
| A5.5: | Naming and visualizing five-wise patterns on a ten frame | 71 |
| A5.6: | Partitions of 5 and 10 | 71 |
| A5.7: | Addition and subtraction in the range 1 to 10 | 72 |
| Instructional Activities |  | 73 |
| IA5.1: | Bunny Ears | 73 |
| IA5.2: | The Great Race | 74 |
| IA5.3: | Quick Dots | 75 |
| IA5.4: | Make Five Concentration | 76 |
| IA5.5: | Five and Ten Frame Flashes | 77 |
| IA5.6: | Memory Game | 78 |
| IA5.7: | Domino Flashes | 79 |
| IA5.8: | Domino Fish | 80 |
| IA5.9: | Domino Snap | 80 |
| IA5.10: | Make Ten Fish | 81 |

**6   Advanced Counting, Addition and Subtraction** — 82

| Assessment Task Groups |  | 86 |
|---|---|---|
| A6.1: | Additive tasks involving two screened collections | 86 |
| A6.2: | Missing addend task involving two screened collections | 86 |
| A6.3: | Removed items task involving a screened collection | 88 |
| A6.4: | Missing subtrahend task involving a screened collection | 88 |
| A6.5 | Comparative subtraction involving two screened collections | 89 |
| A6.6: | Subtraction with bare numbers | 89 |
| Instructional Activities |  | 90 |
| IA6.1: | Calculator Counting | 90 |
| IA6.2: | Class Count-on and Count-back | 91 |
| IA6.3: | One Hundred Square Activities | 91 |
| IA6.4: | Activities On a Bead Bar or Bead String | 92 |
| IA6.5: | Bucket Count-on | 92 |

| | | |
|---|---|---|
| IA6.6: | Bucket Count-back | 93 |
| IA6.7: | Number Line Count-on | 94 |
| IA6.8: | Numeral Track Activities | 95 |
| IA6.9: | Under the Cloth | 97 |

**7  Structuring Numbers 1 to 20    98**

Assessment Task Groups    105

| | | |
|---|---|---|
| A7.1: | Naming and visualizing pair-wise patterns for 1 to 10 | 105 |
| A7.2: | Naming and visualizing five-wise patterns for 1 to 10 | 105 |
| A7.3: | Naming and visualizing pair-wise patterns for 11 to 20 | 106 |
| A7.4: | Naming and visualizing five-wise and ten-wise patterns for 11 to 14 | 107 |
| A7.5: | Naming and visualizing ten-wise patterns for 15 to 20 | 108 |
| A7.6: | Addition using doubles, fives and tens – addends less than 11 | 108 |
| A7.7: | Subtraction using doubles, fives and tens – subtrahend and difference less than 11 | 109 |
| A7.8: | Addition using doubles, fives and tens – one addend greater than 10 | 109 |
| A7.9: | Subtraction using doubles, fives and tens – subtrahend or difference greater than 10 | 110 |

Instructional Activities    111

| | | |
|---|---|---|
| IA7.1: | Double Decker Bus Flashes | 111 |
| IA7.2: | Getting On and Off the Bus | 112 |
| IA7.3: | Bus Snap | 113 |
| IA7.4: | Make Combinations to Twenty Fish | 113 |
| IA7.5: | Using Ten-plus Combinations | 114 |
| IA7.6: | Five and Ten Game | 116 |
| IA7.7: | Chocolate Boxes | 116 |
| IA7.8: | Double Ten Frame Facts | 117 |
| IA7.9: | Bead Board | 118 |

**8  2-digit Addition and Subtraction: Jump Strategies    120**

Assessment Task Groups    126

| | | |
|---|---|---|
| A8.1: | Forward and backward number word sequences by 10s, on and off the decade | 126 |
| A8.2: | Adding from a decade and subtracting to a decade | 126 |
| A8.3: | Adding to a decade and subtracting from a decade | 127 |
| A8.4: | Incrementing and decrementing by 10s on and off the decade | 128 |
| A8.5: | Incrementing flexibly by 10s and ones | 129 |
| A8.6: | Adding 10s to a 2-digit number and subtracting 10s from a 2-digit number | 130 |
| A8.7: | Adding two 2-digit numbers without and with regrouping | 131 |
| A8.8: | Subtraction involving two 2-digit numbers without and with regrouping | 132 |
| A8.9: | Addition and subtraction using transforming, compensating and other strategies | 132 |

Instructional Activities    134

| | | |
|---|---|---|
| IA8.1: | Leap Frog | 134 |
| IA8.2: | Bead String with Ten Catcher | 136 |
| IA8.3: | Add or Subtract 11 | 137 |
| IA8.4: | Add to or Subtract from 49 | 138 |
| IA8.5: | Calculator Challenge | 138 |
| IA8.6: | Jump to 100 | 139 |
| IA8.7: | Jump from 100 | 140 |
| IA8.8: | Target Number | 141 |

|  | IA8.9: | Walk-about Sequences | 141 |
|  | IA8.10: | Non-standard Measurement Plan | 142 |
| 9 | 2-digit Addition and Subtraction: Split Strategies | | 144 |
|  | Assessment Task Groups | | 148 |
|  | A9.1: | Higher decade addition and subtraction without and with bridging the decade | 148 |
|  | A9.2: | Partitioning and combining involving 2-digit numbers | 149 |
|  | A9.3: | Combining and partitioning involving non-canonical forms | 149 |
|  | A9.4: | Addition involving two 2-digit numbers without and with regrouping | 150 |
|  | A9.5: | Subtraction involving two 2-digit numbers without and with regrouping | 150 |
|  | Instructional Activities | | 151 |
|  | IA9.1: | Follow the Pattern | 151 |
|  | IA9.2: | Ten More or Ten Less | 151 |
|  | IA9.3: | Counting-by-Tens | 152 |
|  | IA9.4: | Add or Subtract Tens | 152 |
|  | IA9.5: | Adding Tens and Ones Using Money | 153 |
|  | IA9.6: | Screened Subtraction Task | 153 |
|  | IA9.7: | Split the Subtrahend (Multiples of 10) | 154 |
| 10 | Early Multiplication and Division | | 155 |
|  | Assessment Task Groups | | 162 |
|  | A10.1: | Counting by 2s, 5s, 10s and 3s | 162 |
|  | A10.2: | Repeated equal groups –visible | 162 |
|  | A10.3: | Repeated equal groups –items screened and groups visible | 163 |
|  | A10.4: | Repeated equal groups –groups screened and items screened | 163 |
|  | A10.5: | Multiplication and division using arrays | 164 |
|  | A10.6: | Word problems | 165 |
|  | A10.7: | Relational thinking using bare number problems | 165 |
|  | Instructional Activities | | 167 |
|  | IA10.1: | Count Around – Multiples | 167 |
|  | IA10.2: | Trios for Multiples | 168 |
|  | IA10.3: | Quick Draw Multiples | 168 |
|  | IA10.4: | Rolling Groups | 169 |
|  | IA10.5: | Lemonade Stand | 170 |
|  | IA10.6: | Array Flip | 171 |
|  | IA10.7: | Duelling Arrays | 172 |
|  | IA10.8: | Mini Multo | 173 |
|  | IA10.9: | Four's a Winner | 174 |
|  | IA10.10: | I Have … Who Has … | 175 |

PART III

| 11 | The Teacher as a Learner | 177 |

| Glossary | 193 |
| Bibliography | 197 |
| Index | 200 |

# List of Figures

| | | |
|---|---|---|
| 1.1 | *Teaching and Learning Cycle* | 13 |
| 1.2 | *The Empty Numberline: Child A* | 16 |
| 1.3 | *The Empty Numberline: Child B* | 17 |
| 1.4 | *The Empty Numberline: Child C* | 17 |
| 1.5 | *The Empty Numberline: Child D* | 17 |
| 1.6 | *The Empty Numberline: Child E* | 18 |
| 1.7 | *Five-wise and Pair-wise settings for 6* | 18 |
| 1.8 | *Ten plus cards* | 19 |
| 1.9 | *Near ten plus cards* | 19 |
| 2.1 | *Two digit addition using a Jump Strategy* | 27 |
| 2.2 | *Two digit subtraction using a Jump Strategy* | 27 |
| 2.3 | *Using a split strategy for 27 + 45* | 28 |
| 2.4 | *Using a split strategy for 82 −28* | 28 |
| 3.1 | *What number could this be?* | 42 |
| 3.2 | *Arrow cards* | 43 |
| 3.3 | *Numeral track* | 45 |
| 4.1 | *Comparing small collections cards* | 51 |
| 4.2 | *Domino addition* | 55 |
| 4.3 | *Counters in a row* | 57 |
| 4.4 | *Where do I go?* | 59 |
| 4.5 | *Teddy Bear Walk* | 60 |
| 5.1 | *Great Race game board* | 75 |
| 5.2 | *Pattern cards* | 76 |
| 5.3 | *Five frame cards* | 77 |
| 5.4 | *Five frame minibus* | 78 |
| 5.5 | *Using ten frame and ten frame minibus* | 78 |
| 5.6 | *Pair-wise dot cards* | 79 |
| 5.7 | *Five-wise dot cards* | 79 |
| 5.8 | *Five-wise and Pair-wise dot card for 6* | 79 |
| 5.9 | *Domino cards* | 80 |
| 6.1 | *Bead String* | 92 |
| 6.2 | *Number Line Count-on (1)* | 94 |
| 6.3 | *Number Line Count-on (2)* | 94 |
| 6.4 | *Numeral Track Activities (1)* | 96 |
| 6.5 | *Numeral Track Activities (2)* | 96 |
| 7.1 | *Arithmetic rack showing 11* | 99 |
| 7.2 | *Double ten frame showing 11* | 99 |
| 7.3 | *Double Deck Bus Flashes* | 111 |
| 7.4 | *Getting on and off the bus (screened)* | 112 |
| 7.5 | *Double ten cards and numeral cards* | 113 |
| 7.6 | *Making combinations to Twenty Fish (1)* | 114 |
| 7.7 | *Making combinations to Twenty Fish (2)* | 114 |
| 7.8 | *How many on the bus?* | 115 |
| 7.9 | *Ten-plus combinations* | 115 |
| 7.10 | *Five and Ten Game Sheet* | 116 |

| | | |
|---|---|---|
| 7.11 | *Chocolate box* | 117 |
| 7.12 | *Chocolate box cards* | 117 |
| 7.13 | *Double ten frame patterns* | 118 |
| 7.14 | *Ten bead board* | 118 |
| 8.1 | *Using the ENL to record jump strategies* | 122 |
| 8.2 | *Incrementing by Tens and Ones* | 129 |
| 8.3 | *Leap Frog A* | 134 |
| 8.4 | *Leap Frog B* | 135 |
| 8.5 | *Spinner made from pencil and paper clip* | 135 |
| 8.6 | *Bead string with ten catcher* | 136 |
| 8.7 | *Add or subtract 11* | 137 |
| 8.8 | *Add to, or subtract from, 49* | 138 |
| 8.9 | *Calculator challenge* | 139 |
| 8.10 | *Using the ENL to record the solution to 23 + 34* | 139 |
| 8.11 | *Hundreds chart and spinners* | 140 |
| 8.12 | *Non-standard measurement plan* | 142 |
| 10.1 | *Multiplication as repeated equal groups* | 155 |
| 10.2 | *Sharing into equal groups* | 156 |
| 10.3 | *Division as sharing or measuring* | 158 |
| 10.4 | *Numerical composite and abstract composite unit* | 159 |
| 10.5 | *Using arrays in multiplication* | 160 |
| 10.6 | *Commutativity of multiplication using arrays and sets* | 161 |
| 10.7 | *Multiplication and division are inverse operations* | 161 |
| 10.8 | *Strips for rolling groups* | 169 |
| 10.9 | *Using an area model to illustrate 4 groups of 5* | 170 |
| 10.10 | *Using a linear model to illustrate 4 groups of 5* | 170 |
| 10.11 | *Lemonade stand record sheet* | 171 |
| 10.12 | *Layout of array and numerical cards* | 171 |
| 10.13 | *Array and numerical cards* | 172 |
| 10.14 | *Partially screened array card* | 172 |
| 10.15 | *Example of dueling array cards* | 173 |
| 10.16 | *Mini Multo game board* | 173 |
| 10.17 | *Four's a Winner game board* | 175 |
| 10.18 | *I Have ... Who Has ... cards* | 176 |

# List of Photographs

| | | |
|---|---|---|
| 1 | Using the numeral roll for FNWS and NWA (1) | 34 |
| 2 | Using the numeral roll for FNWS and NWA (2) | 34 |
| 3 | Numeral identification | 36 |
| 4 | Sequencing numerals (1) | 37 |
| 5 | Sequencing numerals (2) | 38 |
| 6 | Which tower has more blocks? | 51 |
| 7 | How many counters are there? | 52 |
| 8 | Get me eight counters, please | 53 |
| 9 | Estabishing the numerosity of two collections | 53 |
| 10 | Where do I go? | 58 |

| | | |
|---|---|---|
| 11 | Show me three on your fingers please. | 68 |
| 12 | Show me eight | 69 |
| 13 | Tell me how many dots you see | 70 |
| 14 | Pair-wise patterns on a Ten-Frame | 70 |
| 15 | Five wise patterns on a Ten-Frame | 71 |
| 16 | Partitions of 5 and 10 | 71 |
| 17 | Addition and subtraction settings in the range 1–10 | 72 |
| 18 | Bunny Ears (1) | 73 |
| 19 | Bunny Ears (2) | 73 |
| 20 | Here are four red counters | 87 |
| 21 | I added some green counters and now there are six counters. How many green counters did I add? | 87 |
| 22 | Numeral track activities | 95 |
| 23 | Numeral track: decade crossing | 96 |
| 24 | Adding two numbers on the arithmetic rack | 100 |
| 25 | Showing fourteen on the arithmetic rack | 106 |
| 26 | Naming and visualizing pair-wise image patterns for 11–20 | 107 |
| 27 | Incrementing by Tens | 128 |
| 28 | Uncovering Tasks (1) | 130 |
| 29 | Uncovering Tasks (2) | 130 |
| 30 | Subtracting 10 from a 2-digit number | 130 |
| 31 | Making equal groups | 156 |
| 32 | Counting-by-twos (skip counting) | 157 |
| 33 | Repeated equal groups – items screened, groups visible | 163 |
| 34 | Using arrays | 164 |
| 35 | Using a partially screened array for multiplication (1) | 165 |
| 36 | Using a partially screened array for mutiplication (2) | 165 |
| 37 | Relational thinking | 166 |

# List of Tables

| | | |
|---|---|---|
| 1.1 | Classroom Instructional Framework for Early Number Learning | 9 |
| 1.2 | Design of display chart for four-group rotation model | 12 |
| 1.3 | Design of display chart for three-group rotation model | 12 |
| 2.1 | Contrasting traditional and emerging approaches to number instruction in the first two years of school | 24 |
| 2.2 | Responses of a child with, and a child without, sound knowledge of the ten and ones structure of teen numbers | 26 |

# Contributors

## AUTHORS

**Dr Robert J. Wright** holds the position of Professor in Mathematics Education at Southern Cross University in Australia and is an internationally recognized leader in understanding and assessing young children's numerical knowledge and strategies, publishing many articles and papers in this field. His work in the last 15 years has included the development of the Mathematics Recovery Programme which focusses on providing specialist training for teachers to advance the numeracy levels of young children assessed as low attainers. In Australia, the UK, the USA and elsewhere, this programme has been implemented widely and applied extensively to classroom teaching and to average and able learners as well as low attainers. He has conducted several research projects funded by the Australian Research Council including a current project focusing on assessment and intervention for 8–10-year-olds.

**Garry Stanger** has had a wide-ranging involvement in primary, secondary and tertiary education in Australia. He has held positions of Head Teacher, Deputy Principal and Principal, and has been a Mathematics Consultant with the New South Wales Department of Education. He has also taught in schools in the USA. He has worked with Robert Wright on the Mathematics Recovery (MR) project since its inception in 1992 and has been involved in the development of the Count Me In Too early numeracy project. He currently runs Master's courses in early numeracy at Southern Cross University.

**Ann Stafford**'s academic background includes graduate study at Southern Cross University, Australia, the University of Chicago, and Clemson University. She received a Master's degree from Duke University and an undergraduate degree from the University of North Carolina at Greensboro. Her professional experience includes teaching and administrative roles in K-5 classrooms and supervision in the areas of mathematics, gifted, early childhood, and remedial as well as teaching and research positions at Clemson University. She has led in the writing and development of Early Childhood and Mathematics Curricula for the School District of Oconee County, South Carolina. Ann has received numerous professional awards and grants for outstanding contributions to the region and state for mathematics and leadership. She is currently involved in leading the implementation and classroom applications of Mathematics Recovery in the USA.

**Jim Martland** is a member of the International Board of Mathematics Recovery and Director of Mathematics Recovery Programme (UK) Limited. He is Senior Fellow in the Department of Education at the University of Liverpool. In his long career in education he has held headships in primary and middle schools and was Director of Primary Initial Teacher Training. In all the posts he continued to teach and pursue research in primary mathematics. His current work is with local education authorities in the UK and Canada, delivering professional development courses on assessing children's difficulties in numeracy and designing and evaluating teaching interventions.

## CONTRIBUTORS

**Amy Shiloh Ernst** is a mathematics specialist in Harford County, Maryland. She has been a Mathematics Recovery teacher and leader since 1999. She coordinates the Mathematics Recovery intervention programme in her school. She is involved in several mathematics projects in her district, including curriculum revision, assessment production, staff development, and evaluation of the Everyday Math program. She completed her Master's in Education at Loyola College in Maryland and is continuing graduate work in middle school mathematics at Towson University.

**Kurt Kinsey** is an educational consultant for Mountain States Mathematics, working together with schools and school systems to improve the mathematics educational experience for students. His teaching background includes secondary mathematics, mathematics intervention at the early and middle levels, teacher in-service and graduate-level coursework. Current projects include work as a member of the US Mathematics Recovery Board of Directors and program development for the National American Indian, Alaskan, and Hawaiian Educational Development Center.

**Charlotte Madine** has extensive experience of teaching children from ages 5 to 11 years. She was an advisory teacher before taking up her present post as Numeracy Consultant with Knowsley Council in the North West of England where she works with both teachers and children. While working as a consultant she has contributed to National Numeracy Strategy and other mathematics publications. In addition she contributed to the development of BAFTA-nominated interactive CD-ROMs for mathematics with John Moores University, Liverpool, England. She has a Certificate in the Advanced Study of Education (Mathematics Recovery) from the University of Liverpool, England. She has been training Mathematics Recovery teachers since 2000.

**Lucinda 'Petey' MacCarty** of Sheridan, Wyoming is a consultant for Mountain States Mathematics. A primary focus of her work is Mathematics Recovery Specialist Teacher Training with ongoing coaching and support. Other work includes designing and facilitating professional development for standards-based curricula, writing mathematics frameworks and assessments, and facilitating systemic change for mathematics education in public schools. In addition, she has an active role on the US Mathematics Recovery Council Board of Directors. An M.Ed from Montana State University and a mathematics coordinator position prompted a shift from 6–12 to K-12 mathematics education resulting in an exciting career working with K-12 teachers to improve mathematics teaching and learning.

**Joan McCarthy** is a Numeracy Consultant for the Learning Support Services in Wigan, UK. She has been closely involved with the Mathematics Recovery Programme since its introduction to the UK in 1996 and has worked closely with Jim Martland, Professor Robert J. Wright and Ann K. Stafford, becoming a trainer in 1998. Joan is an experienced primary school practitioner who was instrumental in raising standards in mathematics in Leigh Education Action Zone (1999–2004) and in designing resources for students.

**Dr Penny Munn** is Senior Lecturer in the Department of Childhood and Primary Studies at Strathclyde University in Glasgow, Scotland. She is a Developmental Psychologist whose research interests are the development of numeracy and literacy in children, the professional development of teachers, and the organizational contexts of numeracy teaching and learning. She is course director of the Postgraduate Certificate: Maths Recovery at Strathclyde and delivers short courses on assessing and teaching early numeracy to practicing teachers throughout Scotland.

**Chris Porter** is currently Primary Consultant supporting schools with developing Mathematics teaching for Salford Local Education Authority (LEA) in the North West of England. She has held positions in a range of primary schools. Studying for a further degree in Mathematics Education at Manchester Metropolitan University in the early 1990s kindled her interests into researching children's mathematical development. The training begun with Jim Martland in 1999 with a small group of teachers has grown each year so that the LEA now has MR-trained teachers in many of their schools with teachers asking when they can be trained on Mathematics Recovery.

**Julia Sheridan** has extensive experience of classroom teaching of children from age 5 to 11 years. Additionally, she was a mathematics coordinator and advisory teacher before taking up her present post as Numeracy Consultant with Sefton Children, Schools and Families Service in the North West Region of England where she works with both children and teachers. While working as a consultant she has contributed to National Numeracy Strategy working parties and mathematics publications. She has a Master's Degree (Education) and a Certificate in the Advanced Study of Education (Mathematics Recovery) from the University of Liverpool, England. She has been training Mathematics Recovery teachers since 1999.

**Pam Tabor** is a school-based mathematics specialist in Havre de Grace, Maryland. In this capacity she provides ongoing professional development in mathematics for classroom teachers, para-educators, and parents. She frequently presents at local, regional, and national conferences. She is a certified Mathematics Recovery leader and serves on the US Mathematics Recovery Council Board of Directors. She is currently conducting a classroom teaching experiment as a part of her course of study for a PhD in mathematics education from Southern Cross University in Australia. Her area of specialty is instruction designed to build 2-digit addition and subtraction concepts.

# Acknowledgments

This book is a culmination of several interrelated research projects conducted over the last 15 years, many of which come under the collective label of Mathematics Recovery. All these projects have involved one or more of the authors or contributors undertaking research, development and implementation in collaboration with teachers, schools and school systems. These projects have received significant support from the participating schools and school systems.

The authors wish to express their sincere gratitude and appreciation to all the teachers, students and project colleagues who have participated in, and contributed to, these projects. We also wish to thank the following organizations for funding and supporting one or more projects which have provided a basis for writing this book: the government and Catholic school systems of the north coast region of New South Wales, Australia; the Australian Research Council; the New South Wales Department of Education and Training; the School District of Oconee County and the South Carolina Department of Education in the United States; many other school districts across the United States; the University of Liverpool and Wigan, Sefton, Salford, Stockport, Knowsley and Cumbria Education Authorities in England; Flintshire County Council in Wales; Frontier School Division in the Province of Manitoba, Canada; the Ministry of Education in the Bahamas; the University of Strathclyde; and Glasgow, Edinburgh, and Stirling Education Authorities in Scotland.

We also wish to thank the children and staff in schools in Edinburgh, Flintshire, Wigan and the USA for agreeing to appear in the photographs.

# Series preface

If you ask educationalists and teachers whether numeracy intervention deserves equal attention with literacy intervention the overwhelming answer is 'Yes, it should'. If you then ask whether this happens in their experience the answer is a resounding 'No!' What then are the reasons for this discrepancy? Research shows that teachers tend to regard addressing difficulties in literacy as more important than difficulties in early numeracy. Teachers also state that there is a lack of suitable tools for assessing young children's numeracy skills and knowledge and appropriate programmes available to address the deficits.

The three books in this series make a significant impact to redress the imbalance by providing practical help to enable schools and teachers to give equal status to early numeracy intervention. The books are:

▶   *Early Numeracy: Assessment for Teaching and Intervention, 2nd Edition*, Robert J. Wright, Jim Martland and Ann K. Stafford, available December 2005
▶   *Teaching Number: Advancing Children's Skills and Strategies, 2nd Edition*, Robert J. Wright, Jim Martland, Ann K. Stafford and Garry Stanger, available August 2006
▶   *Teaching Number in the Classroom with 4–8 year-olds*, Robert J. Wright, Garry Stanger, Ann K. Stafford and Jim Martland, available December 2005.

The authors are internationally recognized as leaders in the field of early numeracy intervention. They draw on considerable practical experience of delivering training courses and materials on how to assess young children's mathematical knowledge, skills and strategies in addition, subtraction, multiplication and division. This is the focus of *Early Numeracy*. The revised version contains six comprehensive diagnostic assessment tools to identify children's strengths and weaknesses and has a new chapter on how the assessment provides the direction and focus for teaching intervention. *Teaching Number* sets out in detail nine principles which guide the teaching together with 180 practical, exemplar teaching activities to advance children to more sophisticated strategies for solving numeracy problems. The third book, *Teaching Number in the Classroom with 4–8 year-olds*, extends the work of assessment and teaching intervention with individual and small groups to working with whole classes. In this new text the lead authors have been assisted by expert, primary practitioners from Australia, America and the United Kingdom who have provided the best available instructional activities for each of eight major topics in early number learning.

The three books in this series provide a comprehensive package on

1.   The identification, analysis and reporting on children's numerical knowledge, skills and strategies
2.   How to design, implement and evaluate a course of teaching intervention
3.   How to incorporate both assessment and teaching in the daily numeracy programme in differing class organizations and contexts.

The series is distinctive from others in the field because it draws on a substantial body of recent, theoretical research supported by international, practical application. Because all the assessment and teaching activities portrayed have been empirically tested the books have the additional, important distinction that they indicate to the practitioner ranges of responses and patterns of behavior which children tend to make.

The book series provides a package for professional growth and development and an invaluable, comprehensive resource for both the experienced teacher concerned with early numeracy intervention and for the primary teacher who has responsibility for teaching numeracy in kindergarten to upper junior level. Primary numeracy consultants, mathematics advisers, special education teachers, teaching assistants and initial teacher trainees around the world will find much to enable them to put numeracy intervention on an equal standing with literacy. At a wider level the series will reveal many areas of interest to educational psychologists, researchers and academics.

Find out more about Math Recovery by visiting our website at http://www.mathrecovery.com/index.shtml

# Preface

This book provides a comprehensive approach to the teaching of early numeracy in the classroom. The book complements the authors' other books:

*Early Numeracy: Assessment for Teaching and Intervention* (2000)
*Teaching Number: Advancing Children's Skills and Strategies* (2002)
*Early Numeracy: Assessment for Teaching and Intervention, 2nd Edition* (2006)

Part 1 focusses on approaching, organizing and designing instruction and helping teachers to understand mathematics learning. Part I also includes a detailed overview of traditional and emerging approaches to teaching early numeracy.

Part II consists of eight chapters, each of which focusses on an important topic of early numeracy learning. These topics range over learning about number words and numerals; early and advanced counting strategies; structuring numbers in the ranges 1 to 10 and 1 to 20; strategies for adding and subtracting two 2-digit numbers; and early multiplication and division. Each of the chapters in Part II is organized into three sections: topic overview; assessment tasks and instructional activities. The emphasis on assessment tasks is consistent with the fundamental principle of our approach, that is, that comprehensive assessment precedes instruction. Instruction must be based on a very sound understanding of children's current knowledge and strategies.

Part III focusses on issues related to teachers' professional learning in early numeracy, including teachers' use of videotaped interviews of assessments to support their learning about children's conceptual development.

The book sets out a constructivist, inquiry-based approach to instruction. The approach builds on clear understandings of children's current levels of knowledge, where their learning should progress to, and the means by which children learn early numeracy topics.

The methods presented in this book have been used extensively by practitioners in the United States, the United Kingdom and Australia, as well as in several other countries. The book is of interest to all who are concerned with finding new ways to teach early numeracy and with raising standards of learning in schools. Teachers, advisers, numeracy consultants, mathematics supervisors and learning support personnel, as well as teacher educators and researchers whose work relates to this field, will find much of interest and practical help to develop confidence and skill in the teaching of early numeracy.

# Introduction

The authors of this book have worked extensively on research and development projects in early numeracy for at least the last 15 years. Much of our research in the early 1990s focused on the development of the Mathematics Recovery Programme – a programme of intensive instruction for children encountering significant difficulties in early number learning. From the mid-1990s onward, this programme has been used extensively in the United States, the United Kingdom, Australia and elsewhere. An additional important point is that, in many of the school districts where Mathematics Recovery has been implemented, the programme has provided the basis for major transformations in approaches to teaching early numeracy in the classroom, that is, in teaching early numeracy to all children.

The authors and contributors to this book have spent countless hours on the provision of school-based and system-based professional development and support focussing on early numeracy assessment and instruction. This work has involved many thousands of teachers in a range of countries. The work provides teachers with ways to observe and document children's mathematical activity and thinking, and approaches to instruction that take account of detailed information about children's current levels of knowledge.

The theory and approaches presented in this book have their origins in constructivist-based research into early number learning. This includes Leslie Steffe's constructivist teaching experiment research and Paul Cobb's classroom teaching experiment research, as well as research into early number learning by the first author of this book. This book also draws significantly on approaches to teaching number developed by the Freudenthal Institute.

## PURPOSE OF THIS BOOK

This book has the purpose of providing a detailed and comprehensive guide to the classroom teaching of early numeracy, that is, the teaching of early numeracy to all children. This book complements our earlier two books – *Early Numeracy: Assessment for Teaching and Intervention* and *Teaching Number: Advancing Children's Skills and Strategies* which focus mainly on the provision of specialist, intervention teaching of low-attaining children.

## THE STRUCTURE OF THE BOOK

The book is organized into three Parts. Part I focusses on our general approach to teaching early numeracy, Part II focusses on the teaching of specific topics of early numeracy, and Part III focusses on issues related to teacher professional development in early numeracy.

### Part I

Part I consists of two chapters: Chapter 1 focusses on approaching, organizing and designing instruction and Chapter 2 provides a general introduction to Part II.

Chapter 1 consists of three sections. The first presents nine principles of classroom teaching which have been used extensively by the authors and others as a guide to classroom teaching. Also included in this section is the Classroom Instructional Framework for Early Number (CIFEN) which provides detailed guidance for the development of instructional sequences, that is, sequences of interrelated instructional topics that progressively build an important aspect of children's early number knowledge.

In the second section, scenarios are presented which demonstrate different approaches to classroom organization for instruction. Block scheduling is also discussed. The third section provides a description and illustration of the use of the Teaching and Learning Cycle for designing instruction.

Chapter 2 consists of three sections and provides a detailed overview of Part II. Section 1 sets out the common structure that applies to Chapters 4 to 11. Sections 2 and 3 provide a broad overview of the approaches to teaching number to 4–8-year-olds that are the focus of Chapters 3 to 10. Section 2 focusses on aspects of the teaching of number typical of the earlier years in this range, say 4–6-year-olds, and Section 3 focusses on aspects of the teaching of number typical of the later years in this range, say 6–8-year-olds.

# Part II

Part II of the book is organized into eight chapters, each of which presents an important topic of early numeracy. There is a common structure for these chapters, consisting of three sections – topic overview, assessment task groups, and instructional activities. In each chapter the first section provides a comprehensive overview of the topic of early number learning that is the focus of the chapter.

The second section of each chapter sets out in detail up to nine assessment task groups relevant to the topic of the chapter, which can be used by the teacher to assess comprehensively the extent of children's knowledge of the topic. Assessment in this form provides a crucial basis for instruction. An assessment task group is a group of assessment tasks in which all the tasks are very similar to each other. The tasks in each assessment task group focus on a particular aspect of the number topic in the chapter. Each task group includes details of how to present the assessment tasks and notes on the purpose of the task, children's responses, and so on. Across Chapters 3 to 10 there is a total of 59 assessment task groups.

The third section of each chapter sets out in detail up to ten instructional activities relevant to the topic of the chapter. Each instructional activity has the following five-part format: title, intended learning, description, notes and materials. These activities are designed so that they are easily incorporated into lessons. Across Chapters 3 to 10 there is a total of 75 instructional activities.

## Topics in Chapters 3 to 10

Chapter 3 focusses on children's early learning about number words and numerals. Developing facility with number word sequences and learning to name numerals constitute important aspects of early numeracy, and the view taken in this book is that these aspects are deserving of a renewed emphasis. This chapter presents new information about how children learn these aspects and approaches to instruction that take account of children's learning.

Chapter 4 focusses on the early development of counting, where counting is regarded as an activity oriented to solving an arithmetical task such as figuring out how many items in a collection or how many items in all when two small collections are put together. The chapter provides a detailed description of a progression of counting types of increasing sophistication – emergent, perceptual and figurative counting, and how these types of counting provide the basis for children's early addition strategies.

Chapter 5 focusses on a new and important topic in early numeracy, that is, structuring numbers in the range 1 to 10. This topic relates to children's facility to combine and partition numbers without using counting-by-ones. Instead the child uses an emerging knowledge of doubles, and the five and ten structure of numbers, that is, using five and ten as reference points. Learning this topic provides an important basis for children's early addition and subtraction strategies, and an important basis for moving beyond a reliance on counting-by-ones.

Chapter 6 continues on from Chapter 4 with a focus on the development of more advanced counting-by-ones strategies and the use of these strategies to solve addition and subtraction tasks. These are the strategies of counting-on, which includes counting-up-from and counting-up-to, and counting-back which includes counting-back-from and counting-back-to. The chapter explains clearly the place of these strategies in the overall development of early numeracy.

Chapter 7 extends the focus of Chapter 5 to the topic of structuring numbers in the range 1 to 20. This topic relates to the development and use of non-counting strategies in the range 1 to 20, and provides a crucial basis for the development of mental strategies for addition and subtraction involving 2-digit numbers. This chapter presents new approaches to teaching involving use of materials such as the arithmetic rack or the double ten frame.

Chapters 8 and 9 focus on the development of mental strategies for addition and subtraction involving two 2-digit numbers. Chapter 8 focusses on the development of a range of strategies which are referred to as jump strategies – in the case of addition, the student begins from one addend and goes forward in jumps of tens and ones according the second addend. Chapter 9 focusses on the development of a range of strategies which are referred to as split strategies – in the case of addition, the student splits each of the two addends into tens and ones and then separately combines, tens with tens and ones with ones. The chapters include detailed descriptions of approaches to the development of these two kinds of strategies for addition and subtraction.

Chapter 10 focusses on the early development of multiplication and division knowledge. This includes the emergent notions of repeated equal groups and sharing, the development of skip counting and the use of arrays in teaching multiplication and division. Also explained are the ideas of numerical composite and abstract composite unit – important milestones in the development of numerical thinking, the idea of commutitivity, and the inverse relationship between multiplication and division.

## Part III

Chapter 11 focusses on issues related to teacher professional development in early numeracy. This includes discussion of four examples of children's conceptual difficulties and four examples showing how teachers can use their intuition and creativity to support children's learning. Also explained are teachers' use of videotaped interviews of assessments to support their learning about children's conceptual development and, related to their use of videotaped interviews, the three stages of growth in teachers' reflective conversations with children. Chapter 11 includes a set of six teacher activities that can be the basis of a programme of school-based professional learning focussing on children's early numeracy knowledge. Chapter 11 concludes with a detailed discussion of the role of repeatability and differentiation in early number instruction.

## CONCLUSION

The Glossary lists the main terms used in this book. Each of these terms is printed in bold type in the text at its first occurence. The Bibliography concludes the book.

# PART I

# 1

# Approaching, Organizing and Designing Instruction

## Summary

This chapter consists of three sections. The first presents nine principles of classroom teaching which have been used extensively by the authors and others as a guide to classroom teaching. Also included in this section is the Classroom Instructional Framework for Early Number (CIFEN) which provides detailed guidance for the development of instructional sequences, that is, sequences of interrelated instructional topics that progressively build an important aspect of children's early number knowledge. In the second section, scenarios are presented which demonstrate different approaches to classroom organization for instruction. Block scheduling is also discussed. The third section provides a description and illustration of the use of the Teaching and Learning Cycle for designing instruction.

Section 1 sets out two key elements of our approach to instruction in early number. These are the nine Guiding Principles for Classroom Teaching and the Classroom Instructional Framework in Early Number. Section 2 describes three scenarios which illustrate classroom organization for instruction in early number and also discusses block scheduling. Section 3 sets out the Teaching and Learning Cycle, a blueprint for designing instruction. Section 3 also includes three example lesson plans which draw on instructional activities from Part II (Chapters 3 to 10).

## SECTION 1: APPROACHING INSTRUCTION

The purpose of this section is to set out key ideas in the general approach to teaching number in the classroom that is advocated in this book. These key ideas are presented in the following two topics: (a) Guiding Principles for Classroom Teaching; and (b) the Classroom Instructional Framework for Early Number (CIFEN). This section draws on some of the ideas in our two earlier books: *Early Numeracy: Assessment for Teaching and Intervention* (Wright et al., 2000) and *Teaching Number: Advancing Children's Skills and Strategies* (Wright et al., 2002).

## Guiding Principles for Classroom Teaching

More than ten years ago, in research projects where we worked formally with teachers and school systems, we developed the following set of nine guiding principles of teaching. In the last ten years these principles have been applied extensively to guide the teaching of number in the early years of school:

1. *The teaching approach is inquiry based, that is, problem based. Children routinely are engaged in thinking hard to solve numerical problems which for them are quite challenging.*
2. *Teaching is informed by an initial, comprehensive assessment and ongoing assessment through teaching. The latter refers to the teacher's informed understanding of children's current knowledge and problem-solving strategies, and continual revision of this understanding.*
3. *Teaching is focussed just beyond the 'cutting-edge' of child's current knowledge.*
4. *Teachers exercise their professional judgment in selecting from a bank of teaching procedures each of which involves particular instructional **settings** and tasks, and varying this selection on the basis of ongoing observations.*
5. *The teacher understands children's numerical strategies and deliberately engenders the development of more sophisticated strategies.*
6. *Teaching involves intensive, ongoing observation by the teacher and continual micro-adjusting or fine-tuning of teaching on the basis of her or his observation.*
7. *Teaching supports and builds on children's intuitive, verbally based strategies and these are used as a basis for the development of written forms of arithmetic which accord with the child's verbally based strategies.*
8. *The teacher provides the child with sufficient time to solve a given problem. Consequently the child is frequently engaged in episodes which involve sustained thinking, reflection on her or his thinking and reflecting on the results of her or his thinking.*
9. *Students gain intrinsic satisfaction from their problem-solving, their realization that they are making progress, and from the verification methods they develop.*

Each of these principles is now discussed in more detail.

### Principle 1

*The teaching approach is inquiry based, that is, problem based. Children routinely are engaged in thinking hard to solve numerical problems which for them are quite challenging.*

The inquiry-based approach to teaching number is sometimes referred to as learning through problem-solving or problem-based learning. In this approach the central learning activity for children is to solve tasks that constitute genuine problems, that is problems for which the children do not have a ready-made solution. What follows is that the issue of whether a particular task is appropriate as a genuine problem largely depends on the extent of the children's current knowledge.

### Principle 2

*Teaching is informed by an initial, comprehensive assessment and ongoing assessment through teaching. The latter refers to the teacher's informed understanding of children's current knowledge and problem-solving strategies, and continual revision of this understanding.*

Assessment for providing specific and detailed information to inform instruction is the critical ingredient in our approach to teaching early number. It is essential to conduct a detailed assessment of children's current **number knowledge**, and to use the results of assessment in designing instruction. In each of Chapters 3 to 10, the second section of the chapter contains detailed descriptions of assessment tasks and notes on their use. These have the explicit purpose of informing the design of instruction. The second aspect of this principle, ongoing assessment through observation and reflection, is equally as important as initial assessment.

## Principle 3

*Teaching is focussed just beyond the 'cutting-edge' of the child's current knowledge.*

This principle accords with Vygotsky's notion of zone of proximal development, that is, instruction should be focussed just beyond the child's current levels of knowledge in the areas where the child is likely to learn successfully through sound teaching. This principle is very important in our focus on the teaching of early number. The principle highlights the importance of assessment to inform teaching. Assessment provides the teacher with a profile of children's knowledge and the teacher focusses instruction so that children will be moved beyond their current levels of knowledge.

## Principle 4

*Teachers exercise their professional judgment in selecting from a bank of teaching procedures each of which involves particular instructional settings and tasks, and varying this selection on the basis of ongoing observations.*

This principle highlights the need to develop a bank of instructional procedures and to understand the role of each procedure, in terms of its potential to bring about advancements in students' current knowledge. In each of Chapters 3 to 10, the third section of the chapter includes up to ten examples of learning activities which can be used to develop an appropriate bank of teaching procedures. Also, the second section of each chapter contains an extensive set of assessment tasks. These tasks constitute an additional source of instructional procedures because the tasks are easily adapted for instruction.

## Principle 5

*The teacher understands children's numerical strategies and deliberately engenders the development of more sophisticated strategies.*

This principle highlights the need for teachers to have a working model of children's knowledge of early number and the ways in which children's knowledge typically progresses. In each of Chapters 3 to 10, the first section of the chapter provides a detailed overview of the development of an aspect of **early number** knowledge. Our belief is that teachers can develop an appropriate working model through reading, reflecting and observing, in conjunction with their teaching practice.

## Principle 6

*Teaching involves intensive, ongoing observation by the teacher and continual micro-adjusting or fine-tuning of teaching on the basis of her or his observation.*

This principle highlights the importance of observational assessment in determining children's specific learning needs, and the need for this assessment to be ongoing and to lead to action, that is, the fine-tuning of instruction on the basis of ongoing assessment.

## Principle 7

*Teaching supports and builds on the child's intuitive, verbally based strategies and these are used as a basis for the development of written forms of arithmetic which accord with the child's verbally based strategies.*

This principle highlights that children's initial number knowledge is by and large verbally based rather than involving written forms. Thus we suppose that children's initial counting and calculating strategies mainly involve mentally computing with sound images of number words and number word sequences. The further development of number knowledge involves a gradual process of incorporating written symbols, including but not limited to **numerals**, and linking these symbols to already acquired, verbally based number knowledge.

## Principle 8

*The teacher provides the child with sufficient time to solve a given problem. Consequently the child is frequently engaged in episodes which involve sustained thinking, reflection on her or his thinking and reflecting on the results of her or his thinking.*

In our research and development work in early number learning over the last 20 years and longer, we have always emphasized the importance of sustained thinking and reflection for the learning of mathematics. The topic of early number learning is well suited to significant problem-solving by children. This problem-solving and the mental processes of thinking hard and reflecting during problem-solving are, we believe, a fundamental aspect of early number learning.

## Principle 9

*Children gain intrinsic satisfaction from their problem-solving, their realization that they are making progress, and from the verification methods they develop.*

This principle relates to Principle 8. Our experience in working closely with teachers and students for many years on the topic of early number learning is that when young children work hard at problem-solving and their problem-solving is successful, this is typically a very positive experience for the learner. To go further, we argue that this kind of learning is a kind of cognitive therapy, having intrinsic rewards beyond such processes as teacher affirmation and peer recognition.

# The Classroom Instructional Framework for Early Number

One of the key ideas underlying the approach to teaching early number presented here is that it is important for the teacher to be aware of the longer-term goals of instruction. Thus a yearly or half-yearly programme in early number should not be regarded as a list of topics with little or no connections among the topics. By way of contrast, the programme should be seen as one or more sequences of closely related topics where students' success on each topic depends very much on the extent to which they have developed sound knowledge of foregoing topics. Thus the Classroom Instructional Framework for Early Number (CIFEN) provides detailed guidance for teachers in the development of instructional sequences, where an instructional sequence is a sequence of interrelated, instructional topics that progressively build an important aspect of students' early number knowledge.

Table 1.1 describes the CIFEN. The CIFEN sets out a progression of early number topics that typically would span the first three or four years of school. The listing of the topics in separate columns indicates that the topics are somewhat distinct from each other. Nevertheless, this does not indicate that the topics should necessarily be taught separately from each other. By way of contrast, instructional activities can serve to integrate learning across these distinct topics. Topics are arranged in levels in the table to indicate their order in the progression of teaching. Thus topics appearing around the same level in different columns are intended to be taught in reasonably close proximity, for example, within one-quarter or one-half of a school year. Our intention is that the organization of topics in CIFEN will be interpreted and adapted by teachers in a range of ways according to issues such as the specific curriculum being followed and the availability of resources. Finally, as indicated in Table 1.1, Chapters 3 to 10 (Part II) of this book provide detailed information on the teaching of each of the topics listed in the table.

**Table 1.1** Classroom Instructional Framework for Early Number Learning

| Chapter 3 | Chapter 3 | Chapters 6 and 8 | Chapters 5 and 7 |
|---|---|---|---|
| Number Word Sequences to 10 – Forward and Backward | Numerals to 5 | Emergent Counting<br><br>Perceptual Counting | |
| Number Word Sequences to 30 – Forward and Backward | Numerals to 10<br><br>Numerals to 20 | Figurative Counting | Early Spatial Patterns and Finger Patterns |
| Number Word Sequences to 100 – Forward and Backward | Numerals to 100 | Counting-on and Counting-back | Structuring Numbers 1–10 |
| Number Word Sequences to 1,000 and Beyond | Numerals to 1,000 and Beyond | | Structuring Numbers 1–20 |

| Chapters 8 and 9 | Chapter 10 |
|---|---|
| Structuring Numbers 1 to 100 Using Jump Strategies | Early Multiplication and Division |
| Structuring Numbers 1 to 100 Using Jump, Split and other Strategies | Advanced Multiplication and Division |
| Mental computation involving addition and subtraction with 2- and 3-digit numbers | |

# SECTION 2: ORGANIZING INSTRUCTION

In our work with classroom teachers we have observed a range of successful approaches to classroom organization for instruction. We have also observed teachers who use several approaches to achieve a range of goals. In this section we use scenarios to describe three commonly used approaches that, we believe, provide models which can be informative for teachers.

## Scenario 1

Ms Smith has a class of 25 children. In Ms Smith's class, mathematics is timetabled daily for 70 minutes during the morning session. Ms Smith particularly values whole-class teaching and collaborative learning in her mathematics lessons. Ms Smith uses a range of similar formats for her lessons. Below are two examples of these formats:

Format 1
10 minutes warm-ups
30 minutes of whole-class teaching
20 minutes of seat work
10 minutes of teacher-led discussion.

The initial 10 minutes in Ms Smith's lesson is a fast-paced session focussing on activities to strengthen and consolidate children's knowledge of particular topics. One activity that Ms Smith has been using in the last couple of weeks involves flashing **ten frames**. The children's task is to state quickly the number of dots on the upper row, the number of dots on the lower row, the number of dots altogether, and the number of dots needed to make 10. The second part of this lesson focusses on whole-class teaching. As an example, Ms Smith was working on the topics of strengthening children's facility with number word sequences in the range 1 to 100, reading 2-**digit** numerals and locating numbers in the range 1 to 100. Ms Smith worked with each of these interrelated topics in turn, posing tasks to her children and calling on children to respond and to comment on the responses of others. Ms Smith also led the class in whole-class activities such as counting-on from a given number, reading numerals and arranging a group of numeral cards in numerical order. The third part of this lesson involves children working at their desks on independent learning activities. Some children are working in pairs and others are working individually. This work relates closely to the topics that were taught in the second part of the lesson. In addition, Ms Smith has used independent learning activities at different levels in terms of children's knowledge of the topics of focus. In this way, she is able to differentiate her instruction according to her knowledge of children's current levels of knowledge and learning needs. In the final part of this lesson, Ms Smith leads a whole-class discussion of some of the tasks from the independent learning activities. Several children are called on to explain their solutions and Ms Smith takes every opportunity to explain key ideas and consolidate children's knowledge.

Format 2
10 minutes warm-ups
5 minutes whole-class explanation of activities
40 minutes of group activities involving rotation
15 minutes of teacher-led discussion and consolidation.

In this format, the initial part of Ms Smith's lesson is the same as it is in the first format. The main focus of this lesson is for children to work in groups of four to six children and to rotate through six different workstations. When available, helpers are used at some of the work stations. A helper might be a paraprofessional, a parent helper or a child helper from a higher grade. The activity at each workstation can be varied according to children's particular learning needs. Before the children move to their workstations, Ms Smith spends five minutes explaining any new activities and addressing difficulties with activities that arose in a previous session. In the last part of the lesson, Ms Smith poses questions to the whole class, focussing on the activities of each workstation in turn, and concludes this part with general questions on the topics currently being learned. Typically, Ms Smith uses this format on Thursdays or Fridays, when parent and child helpers are more readily available.

## Scenario 2

In Mr Jorjez's classroom the following format is used:

10 minutes of whole-class teaching
  5 minutes of introducing problems for the day
30 minutes of children working individually or in pairs on inquiry-based learning
25 minutes of whole-class, teacher-orchestrated discussion.

Mr Jorjez has a class of 20 children. He particularly values inquiry-based learning, that is, learning through problem-solving, and thinks it is important for children to be given opportunities to discuss with each other the tasks they are trying to solve. Such discussion he believes can enhance sense-making and the development of more sophisticated mathematical knowledge. The first part of Mr Jorjez's lesson involves teacher-led whole-class activities. These activities are very much like the warm-up activities used by Ms Smith (Scenario 1) and consolidate specific aspects of number knowledge or develop children's automaticity with number facts for example.

The main focus of Mr Jorjez's lesson is for the children to work on developing solutions to tasks which are intended to be genuine problems in the sense that the children do not have a ready-made response. For example, they do not have a procedural or algorithmic method to solve these problems. Before this part of the lesson begins, Mr Jorjez works with the whole class to read the tasks and to briefly discuss them. In this way children begin to think about the tasks and to formulate initial solution methods that might be attempted. During this part, Mr Jorjez gets an initial sense of the ways children might construe the tasks, and the kinds of solution methods they might attempt. In the third part of the lesson, children work to solve the tasks that have been discussed by the teacher and the whole class. Children can choose to work in pairs or singly, and there is opportunity to seek assistance from other children or from the teacher. The lesson involves children working on a relatively small number of tasks, typically no more than four.

The final part of the lesson involves a whole-class, teacher-led discussion of the tasks. This part begins with the teacher reading the first task, and calling on volunteers to go to the whiteboard and explain their solutions. Each child is obliged to listen and to attempt to understand the particular solution method being explained. In this way, the teacher carefully orchestrates discussion of each task in turn. A range of solution methods is developed, and Mr Jorjez takes every opportunity to highlight and emphasize methods that he regards as having potential to lead to more sophisticated number thinking. In this part of the lesson, methods of recording solutions are developed. These methods accord with children's strategies and have an important communicative role.

## Scenario 3

Ms Thompson has a class of 20 children. She particularly values whole-class teaching that is closely aligned to children's current levels of knowledge and that is complemented by seat-work activities that are especially chosen to support her whole-class teaching. She also values independent and collaborative learning activities. The children are organized into four groups of approximately equal numbers of children. In Ms Thompson's class, mathematics is timetabled for one hour per day, in the morning. Children are organized in the groups according to their current progress in learning mathematics. She does not expect that children will remain in the group to which she originally allocated them. Ms Thompson is aware that children progress in mathematics at different rates. She has observed that sometimes children appear to plateau in their learning and at other times they make surprising progress in a relatively short period of time. For these reasons Ms Thompson is continually monitoring children's learning and progress, and reallocating children to their groups accordingly.

Ms Thompson uses a four-group rotation model to organize her mathematics lessons. The mathematics hour is partitioned into four periods of 15 minutes. Ms Thompson uses a display chart like the one shown in Table 1.2 to facilitate her classroom organization and management. A three-group rotation

**Table 1.2** Design of display chart for four-group rotation model

| Period/ Group | 1 | 2 | 3 | 4 | Children |
|---|---|---|---|---|---|
| **Red** | Teacher | Seat work | Learning station | Learning station | Niara, Phyllis, Tynasia, Tre, Bill |
| **Blue** | Learning station | Teacher | Seat work | Learning station | Pam, Dominick, Harry, Addis, Heather |
| **Yellow** | Learning station | Learning station | Teacher | Seat work | Shanea, Devin, Ty-Keisha, Cole, Joline |
| **Green** | Seat work | Learning station | Learning station | Teacher | Jill, Jade, Marissa, Mark, Kim |

model could also be used (Table 1.3). At weekly intervals she will reallocate the groups to each line in the model. This ensures that, for each group, there is variety from week to week, in the order in which children rotate through the four kinds of activities. For example, in Table 1.2, for the red group the rotation is teacher, seat-work, learning station, learning station. In the following week, the groups are rotated upwards in the left-hand column – blue to first row, yellow to the second row, green to the third row and red to the fourth row. Over a period of four weeks, each group has experienced each of the four rotations in the table.

**Table 1.3** Design of display chart for three-group rotation model

| Period/ Group | 1 | 2 | 3 | Children |
|---|---|---|---|---|
| **Red** | Teacher | Seat work | Learning station | Michael, Jalisa, Avery, Thomas, Summer, Bonnie, Amy |
| **Blue** | Learning station | Teacher | Seat work | Ansley, Tanner, Makayla, Horace, Leslie, Janette, Michael |
| **Yellow** | Seat work | Learning station | Teacher | Rick, Jedda, Kalindi, Aaliyah, Sharon, Matthew, Simone |

In the learning station activities children can work individually or in small groups on independent instructional activities such as number games or computer-based activities. During the periods of learning station activities children have opportunities to work with children from a different group and, over the course of four weeks, each group has opportunities to work with any other group.

Ms Thompson's main role is to have a highly interactive teaching session with each group in turn. This involves tailoring the content of each group-teaching session as closely as possible to the learning needs of that group. Also, the seat work involves independent learning activities focussed on the work currently taught in the group-teaching session. In this way, the seat-work period focusses on practice and consolidation that is specific to that group and closely tuned to the content currently being learned by that group. The learning station periods provide opportunities for instructional games and novel learning that differs from and complements the teaching and seat-work sessions.

## Block scheduling

We have seen a diverse range of approaches for organizing mathematics instruction. As well as the approaches exemplified above, we have seen several approaches based on block scheduling and reorganization of classes. Green Hills school, for example, has one third grade, one fourth grade and one fifth grade, with about 30 children in each grade. There is a block schedule of 70 minutes for mathematics, across these grades during the middle session of each day. During this mathematics period, the children are allocated to one of five classes so that each class contains children who have been assessed as being close together in terms of their learning needs in mathematics. This involves scheduling two additional teachers (five teachers in all) during the mathematics period. Additionally, rather than allocate equal numbers of children to each of the five classes, the class of children with the most significant learning needs is allocated a smaller number of children, say 12 to 14. Whereas the class of high-attaining children is allocated a larger number of children, say 24 children.

## SECTION 3: DESIGNING INSTRUCTION

In designing instruction, many teachers have found it useful to use the Teaching and Learning Cycle (Figure 1.1) in conjunction with the Guiding Principles for Classroom Teaching (GPCT) set out earlier in this chapter. The Teaching and Learning Cycle has four key elements for teachers to consider in planning instruction for children.

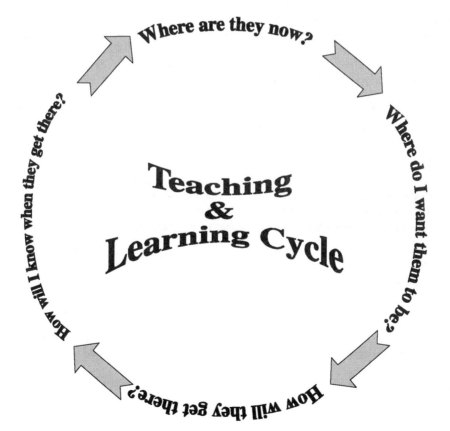

**Figure 1.1** Teaching and Learning Cycle

# The Teaching and Learning Cycle

## Where Are They Now?

Part II of this book (Chapters 3 to 10) contains assessment tasks that enable teachers to establish a clear picture of children's number knowledge. This is an essential phase of the Teaching and Learning Cycle and relates to Principles 2 and 3 in the GPCT.

## Where Do I Want Them to Be?

Part II of this book (Chapters 3 to 10) contains what we regard as the essential number topics in teaching young children. This phase of the Teaching and Learning Cycle relates to Principle 5 in the GPCT.

## How Will They Get There?

Earlier in this chapter we outlined suggestions for organizing classrooms and for using the activities described in Part II (Chapters 3 to 10) in lessons to support children's number development. This phase of the Teaching and Learning Cycle relates to Principles 4, 6, 7 and 8 in the GPCT.

### Characteristics of problem-centred lessons

Consider the following characteristics when selecting number lesson activities.

▶   Activities should require children to use strategic thinking rather than automatic or procedural responses. There are times when you might design activities to enhance factual knowledge but activities should largely involve problematic rather than routine tasks.
▶   Activities should allow children to use their current number knowledge. If the activities are too advanced, there is a risk that children will become frustrated in attempting to undertake the activities.
▶   Children should acquire some mathematical knowledge from engaging in an activity. If the tasks are too simple, children will not have an opportunity to advance their number knowledge.

## How Will I Know When They Get There?

This also refers to the importance of assessment in the Teaching and Learning Cycle, and again we refer you to the assessment tasks and ideas on how they can be used that are outlined in Chapters 3 to 10, and relates to Principle 9 in the GPCT.

The following three lesson plans use instructional activities drawn from Chapters 3 to 10.

# Lesson 1

## Comment

The main activity in this lesson is the *Number Clothes Line*. This might appear to be an activity that requires only routine thinking. However, for many young children, the placement of numerals might require a **strategy**, for example, counting-up or-back from one or from a visible numeral.

## Introductory Activity (Warm-Ups)

**Forward number word sequences:** 1 to 20; 8 to 15.
**Backward number word sequences:** 10 to 1; 12 to 5; 20 to 10.

## Whole-Class Activity

See Instructional Activity IA3.2: Numbers on the Line.
Smallest number is 3 and largest is 17.

▶ Individuals are invited to select a number card and peg it on the line in the correct position.
▶ After each card is pegged, ask the class if it is in the correct position.
▶ When all cards are pegged, say the forward and backward sequences together, pointing to each card.
▶ Have the children close their eyes while the teacher turns a card over. *What number has been turned over? How did you know?*
▶ Observe those children who look at the number before and those who count from the beginning of the sequence.
▶ Repeat this, turning two cards over, then several.
▶ Turn all the cards over except one (for example, 11). Point to other cards before and after the 11 and ask how they found the numbers.
▶ Leave the cards pegged to the line for later in the lesson.

Explain the pairs activity: see Instructional Activity IA4.5: Where Do I Go?
Demonstrate this activity on the floor with class in a circle.

## Pairs – IA4.5: Where Do I Go?

The intention of this activity is to build facility with number word sequences and identifying numerals.
Choose pairs with children of similar levels.
Alter the packs of cards according to the level of the pair. Some pairs could have cards from 1 to 10 and others might have cards from 8 to 17 or 15 to 30.

## Whole-Class Discussion

Use the number clothes line to review children's progress.
Ask some number after and number before questions.

# Lesson 2

## Comment

The activities used in this lesson (Memory Game, Make Ten Fish and Ten Frame Snap) might also appear to be quite routine. It is what the teacher does with an activity and when it is given that are critical to whether or not it is problematic for children. One child might require some strategic thinking to solve a task, whereas for a more advanced child the answer might be automatic.

## Whole-Class Activity

Instructional Activity IA5.1: Bunny Ears
The intention of this activity is to develop finger patterns from six to ten.
The teacher asks the class to: *Make an eight! Make a six!*
Children are selected to show the pattern they made. Some might have a double pattern and others might have a five plus pattern or some other arrangement of the fingers.
The teacher might also ask the class to try to make a double pattern or a five plus pattern.

## Small-Group Activities

The class has been divided into three groups that will rotate through three activities – one per day for the next three days. The groups have been organized by the teacher according to the children's tens combination levels.
Activity A – Instructional Activity IA5.6: Memory Game
Activity B – Instructional Activity IA5.10: Make Ten Fish
Activity C – Ten Frame Snap, a variation of Instructional Activity IA5.9: Domino Snap
Each activity uses ten frame cards.
Each group has a helper to explain the activity and guide the children. The teacher is one of the helpers and the others might be paraprofessionals or parents.

## Whole-class Discussion

The class comes together and the teacher flashes some ten frame combinations on the overhead projector, asking: *What did you see? How many dots?*

# Lesson 3

## Comment

This whole-class lesson is based on addition and **missing addend tasks**. After the introductory tasks, one missing addend task is given. Typically there will be a variety of strategies displayed in children's solutions of the problem.

## Whole-Class Introduction

The class has been using the **empty number line** to solve addition tasks.
The teacher tells a story like: *There are 37 girls in the group and 25 boys. How many children are there altogether?* She asks the class to think about how they would work this out and uses an empty number line to illustrate their thinking. Child A starts at 37 and makes two ten jumps (57) and then counts five ones to get to 62 (Figure 1.2).

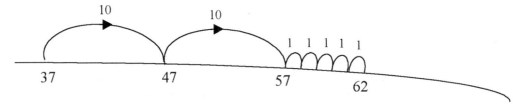

**Figure 1.2** The Empty Numberline: Child A

Child B starts at 37 and also makes two ten jumps (57) and then uses three of the five to make 60 the adds the remaining two to make 62 (Figure 1.3).

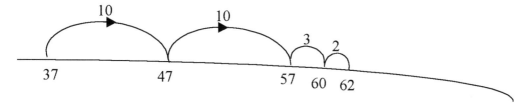

**Figure 1.3** The Empty Numberline: Child B

Child C adds three to make 40, then two to make 42 and then makes two ten jumps 52 then 62 (Figure 1.4).

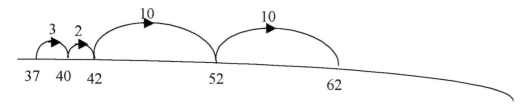

**Figure 1.4** The Empty Numberline: Child C

### Small Group/Individual Activities

The teacher gives the class this problem: there are 28 people on a bus. How many more people can fit on the bus if it can carry a total of 55 passengers?

Children are given ten minutes to solve this task and then they will reassemble and discuss how they solved the problem. They are not directed into groups but are allowed to work in pairs or individually. The teacher walks around the room observing children's solutions and answering questions. After children complete this problem, they are asked to write a similar problem and solve it.

### Whole-Class Discussion

When the class comes together, the teacher asks several children to explain their strategies and asks the class to comment or question these children. Child D jumps 2 to 30, then 5 to 35 and then tens to 55 (Figure 1.5).

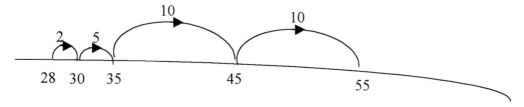

**Figure 1.5** The Empty Numberline: Child D

Child E makes two ten jumps to 48, then 2 to 50 and 5 to 55 (Figure 1.6).

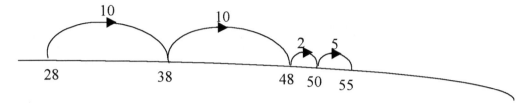

**Figure 1.6** The Empty Numberline: Child E

Child F counts by ones from 28 to 55 and keeps track with fingers and also uses recording to keep track of the tens.

The teacher also asks several questions in order to check whether or not children have understood the various strategies. There were several children who completed the task faster than most of the class members. The teacher directed them to invent a number problem of their own and to show how they solved it.

## Discussion of Lessons 1, 2 and 3

To what extent do these lessons reflect the characteristics of problem-centred lessons as described in this section? Lesson 3 is the most problem-centred of the three lessons. However, in Lessons 1 and 2 the teacher aims to target the activities so that they require inquiry-based thinking rather than using routine procedures. The teacher does this first by understanding where children are in each of the areas being targeted and then by planning activities that will extend each child. Even in an activity such as Ten Frame Snap (Lesson 2), which might not be regarded as a problem-centred activity, the teacher can select the cards to be used that will extend but not be too difficult for the participants. This can be done as follows:

For children that have not learnt the combinations to ten, the teacher could use the cards shown in Figure 1.7.

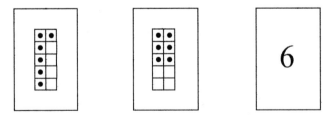

**Figure 1.7** Five-wise and Pair-wise settings for 6

For children who are learning the ten plus and doubles combinations to 20, these cards could be used (Figure 1.8).

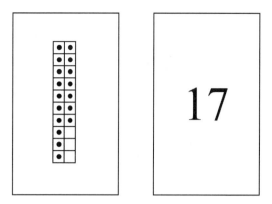

**Figure 1.8** Ten plus cards

For those children who are **facile** with the tens plus combinations, the teacher might decide to use cards with other combinations (near ten combinations for example) as illustrated in Figure 1.9.

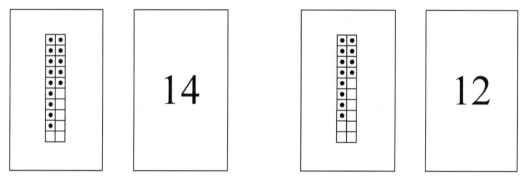

**Figure 1.9** Near ten plus cards

In the activities above, children can be engaged in problem-based learning, if we know their current levels of knowledge, and design activities that will foster advancement of their knowledge.

The instructional activities are not intended to be prescriptive. Some can be used without modification. Others might need modification to be suitable for the children with whom you are working. Our intention is that these activities will serve as models to assist teachers in designing new activities from a variety of situations.

# 2

# General Introduction to Part II

### *Summary*

This chapter consists of three sections and provides a detailed overview of Part II. Section 1 sets out the common structure that applies to Chapters 3 to 10. Sections 2 and 3 provide a broad overview of the approaches to teaching number to 4–8-year-olds that are the focus of Chapters 3 to 10. Section 2 focuses on aspects of the teaching of number typical of the earlier years in this range, say 4–6-year-olds, and Section 3 focusses on aspects of the teaching of number typical of the later years in this range, say 6–8-year-olds.

In Part II (Chapters 3 to 10) we set out a coherent and detailed approach to the teaching of specific number topics to 4–8-year-olds. Chapter 3 focuses on children's initial learning about number words and numerals. Chapter 4 focuses on the development of counting and children's early notions of addition involving the use of counting strategies. Chapter 5 focusses on developing early number knowledge that de-emphasizes the use of **counting-by-ones** and instead emphasizes ways of **combining** and **partitioning** numbers without counting, in the range 1 to 10. Chapter 6 builds on Chapter 4 focussing on the advanced counting-by-ones strategies that children use for solving addition and subtraction problems. Chapter 7 builds on Chapter 5 and focusses on combining and partitioning numbers without counting in the range 1 to 20. Chapters 8 and 9 focus on children's beginning knowledge of place value and addition and subtraction involving two 2-digit numbers. Finally, Chapter 10 focusses on children's early multiplication and division learning.

This chapter consists of three sections. Section 1 sets out the common structure that applies to Chapters 3 to 10. Sections 2 and 3 provide a broad overview of the approaches to teaching number to 4–8-year-olds that are the focus of Chapters 3 to 10. Section 2 focusses on aspects of the teaching of number typical of the earlier years in this range, say 4–6-year-olds, and Section 3 focusses on aspects of the teaching of number typical of the later years in this range, say 6–8-year-olds.

## SECTION 1: STRUCTURE OF CHAPTERS IN PART II

Each of the chapters in Part II (Chapters 3 to 10) has a common structure consisting of three sections: a topic overview, assessment tasks and instructional activities. The first section (topic overview) includes detailed descriptions of the topic and, when relevant, describes its relation to the topics of earlier or later chapters.

## Assessment Task Groups

In each chapter, the second section (assessment tasks) contains from five to nine task groups. There is a total of 59 task groups in these eight chapters. A task group is a group of assessment tasks in which all of the tasks are very similar to each other. Thus each task group focusses on a particular aspect of early number knowledge related to the topic of the chapter. Collectively, the task groups in a given chapter constitute a comprehensive approach to assessing and documenting a child's knowledge related to the chapter topic. For example, the task groups in Chapter 3, provide a comprehensive set of assessment tasks related to the particular aspects of children's early number knowledge that relate to number word sequences and numerals.

## The Rationale for the Assessment Task Groups

One of the basic assumptions underlying this book is that, prior to commencing the teaching of any topic in the early number curriculum, it is critically important to have a very sound understanding of children's current knowledge of that topic. For this reason the assessment task groups appear before the instructional activities rather than after them. The task groups are not intended as prescriptive procedures to be strictly adhered to. Rather, they are intended as examples of assessment tasks that, we believe, can provide a detailed picture of the children's knowledge of the early number topic in question.

## Format of the Assessment Tasks

Throughout the chapters in Part II, the assessment tasks have the following three-part format: materials; what to do and say; and notes. This format is ideally suited for use in a one-to-one interview with a child. Nevertheless, we find this format useful for providing a simple and straightforward explanation of each assessment task that can be easily adapted by teachers to a range of applications. The notes section at the end of each task might refer to any of the following: the purpose of the task; why the task is important; possible variations to the task and possible limits to the variations; descriptions of the responses typical of children; features of children's solutions which should be particularly noted; and possible links to other task groups.

## Ways to Use the Assessment Tasks

There are five important ways that the reader might use or adapt the assessment tasks: (a) observational assessment; (b) large group or whole-class written assessments; (c) individualized assessment; (d) videotaped assessment interview; and (e) as a source of instructional activities. Each of these is described in more detail.

### Observational Assessment

The tasks are intended to provide a context where teachers might advance their knowledge of children's thinking and learning in early number. This might involve using the tasks in informal, opportunistic ways that involve little or no change to the regular classroom routine. This approach constitutes what is often called observational assessment, that is, assessment that involves questioning and observing children at their desks, as opportunities might arise throughout the day. Finally, this approach might include the use of a class or group list to profile children's current levels of knowledge.

### Written Assessment

Although the tasks are written in a ready form for individualized assessment, they could be adapted for administration to groups rather than individuals, for example, many of the tasks could be adapted to a written format for large-group (whole-class) administration.

### Individualized Assessment

The tasks can, of course, be used in individualized assessments conducted by the class teacher or support personnel, with all children in the class or a particular subgroup, for example, those children who seem to have persistent difficulties with a particular topic.

### Videotaped Assessment Interviews

This approach involves using a simple videotaping process (camera on tripod) to record an individualized assessment interview. Incorporating videotaping in this way has several advantages, one of which is that the videotaped assessment interview can be a very rich source of professional learning for teachers. Also, the process of videotaping for later analysis frees the interviewer from the need, during the interview, to describe or categorize the children's responses. This significantly increases the potential for productive observation, interaction and reflection, on the part of the teacher, during the course of the interview.

### Assessment Tasks as a Source of Instructional Activities

Virtually all the assessment tasks are ideally suited for adaptation to instructional activities. Further, because the assessment tasks are organized into task groups, the tasks within a task group or across several groups typically constitute an implied, instructional sequence. Again, although the tasks are presented in a format for one-to-one interaction, they are easily adapted to situations involving small- or large-group instruction. To emphasize this point, in each chapter, the assessment sections are intended to provide the reader with not only a significant source of instructional activities, but also one or more implied instructional sequences. In this way, the assessment tasks complement the set of instructional activities that appear in the final section of each chapter (see below).

## Assessment Tasks as a Source of Teachers' Learning

A final point about the assessment tasks is that we believe the most effective use teachers can make of these, at least initially, is with the deliberate purpose of advancing their professional knowledge and learning. This might involve, for example, a school-based, team-based approach to professional learning. Ideally, this is undertaken with an instructional leader who is expert in the approach to early number learning that is presented in this book.

## The Instructional Activities

In each of Chapters 3 to 10, the third and final section contains up to ten instructional activities related to the early number topic addressed in that chapter. There are a total of 75 instructional activities in these eight chapters. Each instructional activity has the following five-part format: title, intended learning, description, notes and materials.

## SECTION 2: TEACHING NUMBER IN THE EARLY YEARS – CONTRASTING TRADITIONAL AND EMERGING APPROACHES

The traditional approaches to teaching number in the early years were typically organized as follows: (a) an initial focus on a range of topics which are typically referred to as 'pre-number'; (b) learning about numbers and operations (addition, subtraction, and so on.) in the range 1 to 10; and (c) extending this learning to numbers and operations in the range 11 to 20. The topic of pre-number involves activities with everyday materials and simple learning materials (for example, small plastic objects). One such activity focusses on children sorting or classifying objects according to a common attribute, colour, shape, and so on. Another example, matching, involves materials such as cups and saucers. Given, say, six cups and six saucers, the child's task is to match each cup to a saucer. This activity is often referred to as putting items into one-to-one correspondence. Learning about numbers and operations in the range 1 to 10, would typically involve a focus on each number in the range 1 to 10 in turn. So learning about 'six' would include learning to associate the numeral '6', the spoken and written word 'six' and a simple representation of the quantity of six, for example, a dice pattern consisting of two rows of 3 dots. The study of six would also include learning about addition combinations involving six, and perhaps also subtraction and multiplication involving six. Similar approaches would be taken with numbers in the range 11 to 20.

The three topics just described are in large part the focus of children's number work in the first two years of school. The origins of this approach are the reforms in curricula and teaching of mathematics in the early years of school, which occurred in several countries including the United Kingdom, the United States and Australia, in the late 1950s and early 1960s. Piaget's theory of young children's number development was one of the major influences on these earlier reforms.

The pre-number activities (sorting, matching, classifying, and so on) are still regarded as appropriate learning activities for young children because the activities are likely to contribute to the development of logical and numerical thinking. What is no longer accepted is the view that for every child in the first year of school, an extended period focussing on these activities, is essential as a basis for the subsequent development of number knowledge.

In summary, traditional approaches to early number instruction:

▶   began with a topic called pre-number focussing on subjects such as sorting, matching, classifying, and putting objects into one-to-one correspondence;
▶   then focussed on the study of numbers in the range 1 to 10 in turn;
▶   included addition, subtraction, and perhaps multiplication involving each number in turn;
▶   then extended study of numbers to numbers in the range 11 to 20 in turn;
▶   were introduced in several countries around 1960; and
▶   were strongly influenced by Piaget's theory of young children's number development.

Table 2.1 sets out some of the key features of traditional approaches to the teaching of number in the early years of school and contrasts these with emerging approaches. The emerging approaches summarized in Table 2.1 are described in detail in Part II (Chapters 3 to 10).

## SECTION 3: TEACHING PLACE VALUE – A NEW APPROACH

To the extent that it is an important topic in early number learning, place value refers to understanding the tens and ones structure of 2-digit numbers and the hundreds, tens and ones structure of 3-digit numbers. In the middle and upper elementary years, place value knowledge involving 2- and 3-digit numbers is extended to numbers in the thousands, millions and so on, and to decimals.

## Difficulties with Place Value

As stated above, children's initial important ideas about place value relate to 2- and 3-digit numbers, and there are many indications that, in certain contexts in which they do simple arithmetic, older children either have very little knowledge of initial place value, or at least are unable to access their place value knowledge when performing operations (addition, subtraction etc.) on 2- and 3-digit numbers.

**Table 2.1** Contrasting traditional and emerging approaches to number instruction in the first two years of school

| Traditional approaches | Emerging approaches |
|---|---|
| Study of the 'pre-number' topics provides a basis for learning about numbers and should occur before learning about numbers. | Pre-number topics can enhance development of logical and number knowledge but are not necessarily an essential prerequisite for early number knowledge. |
| Children should study numbers in the range 1 to 10 for an extended period before focussing on numbers beyond 10. Similarly, then study numbers in the range 11 to 20. | Teachers should develop children's verbal (in the sense of spoken and heard rather than written) knowledge of number words and their knowledge of numerals, extending beyond 20 and beyond 100 as soon as possible. |
| Children should study each number in turn to learn about its cardinality, its numeral, and number combinations involving the number. | Teachers should take a flexible and open-ended approach to learning about number words and numerals. |
| It is important for children to work with spatial patterns and count the dots in spatial patterns to learn about cardinality in the range 1 to10. | Instructional activities involving flashing spatial patterns can help children learn to combine and partition numbers in the range 1 to 10 without counting by ones. |
| Teaching cardinality and ordinality of numbers in the range 1 to 10 is important. | Teachers should de-emphasize the teaching of ordinality and cardinality. |
| Children should be encouraged to use materials to solve early number problems for as long as they seem to need or rely on the materials. | Teachers should use instructional strategies as soon as possible that help to advance children to levels where they do not rely on seeing materials. |
| When children first learn about numbers in the range 11 to 20 it is important to teach the associated ideas of place value. Similarly for numbers in the range 20 to 100. | Children should learn about the number words and numerals beyond ten, long before they learn about 2-digit place value. |
| Children should learn about place value before they learn about addition and subtraction involving numbers beyond 10. | Children can learn about addition and subtraction involving numbers beyond 10, before they learn about place value. |
| Place value should be formally taught using base-ten materials, before children learn addition and subtraction involving multi-digit numbers. | Place value knowledge should arise from children's developing strategies for addition and subtraction involving 2- and 3-digit numbers. |

## Place Value: a Traditional View

In the last 30 or so years, the prevailing view about place value knowledge has been that it is a necessary foundation for addition and subtraction involving multi-digit numbers (the numbers from 10 onward). Thus children would be taught the place value of teen numbers prior to adding and subtracting in the range 11 to 20 and, similarly, children would be taught place value in the range 20 to 100 prior to addition and subtraction in this range. This view of the teaching of place value arose around the mid-1970s, as part of a broader development involving the use of base-ten materials for the teaching of place value and for the teaching of the standard column algorithms for addition, subtraction and so on. This development in the mid-1970s was part of a broader back-to-basics movement in the teaching of number which, by and large, was a reaction to the overly formal 'new mathematics' of the 1960s and early 1970s. Thus this 'traditional view' of the central role of the teaching of place value, and the use of base-ten materials to teach place value is a relatively recent phenomenon.

## Place Value: an Alternative View

In this book we present an alternative view of when and how place value should be taught. According to this view, children can develop important initial place value knowledge through the operations of addition and subtraction with multi-digit numbers. Therefore, learning addition and subtraction in the range 1 to 20, can lead to a sound knowledge of what we call the 'ten and ones structure of teen numbers' (knowing 14 is 10 and 4 and so on) and similarly, learning addition and subtraction involving two 2-digit numbers can result in a sound knowledge of the tens and ones structure of numbers in the range 20 to 100 (knowing 36 is 30 and 6 and so on). We are not arguing here that base-ten materials have no useful role to play in number learning. Rather, we advocate the use of base-ten materials in ways that differ from the way these materials are used in the traditional approach. This alternative approach to using base-ten materials is the focus of Chapter 9.

## Teaching Place Value through Addition and Subtraction

### The Ten and Ones Structure of Teen Numbers

The notion of sound knowledge of the ten and ones structure of teen numbers is explained in Table 2.2. The table shows three kinds of tasks relating to this topic, and the contrasting responses of two children to these tasks. A child who has little or no knowledge of the ten and ones structure of teen numbers is likely to respond to the three tasks in ways the same as or similar to those described in the third column. The child who has sound knowledge of the ten and ones structure of teen numbers is likely to respond in ways like those shown in the second column. This assumes that the children have not been trained to give the correct response to these tasks. Children who respond in the mature way (as in the second column) on the first and second task only or the first task only, have partially developed knowledge of this topic.

**Table 2.2** Responses of a child with, and a child without, sound knowledge of the ten and ones structure of teen numbers

| Tasks | With sound knowledge of ten and ones structure | Without sound knowledge of tens and ones structure |
| --- | --- | --- |
| 1. Here is a bundle of ten sticks. Here are six more sticks. How many sticks in all? | Spontaneously answers 'sixteen'. | Counts on from ten to sixteen while looking at each of the six sticks in turn or attempts to count all of the sticks from one. |
| 2. Here are four sticks (cover with a screen), and here are 10 more sticks (place out a pile of 10 sticks), how many sticks in all? | Spontaneously answers 'fourteen'. | Counts on from four to fourteen while looking at each stick in the pile of 10 or counts from one to four, while looking at the screen, and then continues to count each of the ten sticks in the pile. |
| 3. Place out a numeral card for '18'. Point to the numeral '1' in '18' and ask the child 'what does this stand for?' | Answers 'ten'. | Answers '1'. |

## An Additive Sense of Place Value

In the discussion above we explain what it means for a child to know the ten and ones structure of the teen numbers and the tens and ones structure of numbers in the range 20 to 100. Our view is that this knowledge constitutes the important initial learning about place value. We refer to this as an additive sense of place value. In the case of 3-digit numbers, for example, an elaborated understanding of place value would include knowing that, for 546: (a) 546 is equal to 500 plus 40 plus 6; (b) 500 is equal to 5 times 100, 40 is equal to 4 times 10, 6 is equal to 6 times one; (c) the place value in the hundreds is 10 times the place value in the tens, and the place value in the tens is 10 times the place value in the ones. The child who has an additive sense of place value knows (a) above but might have little or no sense of (b) and (c).

## Addition, Subtraction and Place Value in the Range 1 to 100

As a general rule, children's knowledge of place value within a range of numbers (for example, 11 to 20, 20 to 100), will develop in association with their development of mental strategies for adding and subtracting within that range of numbers. In particular, the development of knowledge of the ten and ones structure of teen numbers is likely to occur when children develop the strategies described in Chapter 7. In other words, the development of flexible strategies for addition and subtraction in the range 1 to 20, including the use of adding through 5, adding through 10, using doubles and partitioning numbers, will incorporate development of the ten and ones structure of teen numbers. In similar vein, developing flexible strategies for addition and subtraction involving two 2-digit numbers, will incorporate development of the tens and ones structure of 2-digit numbers. The development of these strategies is the focus of Chapter 8 and Chapter 9.

# Learning to Add and Subtract Two 2-digit Numbers

### Formal Algorithms for Adding and Subtracting

Adding and subtracting multi-digit numbers has been and continues to be an important topic in primary mathematics. Approaches in the past emphasized teaching children the formal algorithms for addition and subtraction. The term 'formal algorithms' refers to the standard, written algorithms for addition and subtraction, that is, the procedures in which the numbers are written in columns and one works from right to left adding (or subtracting) in each column. In the approach to teaching number presented in this book, the formal algorithms are still regarded as important, but they are taught after children have developed facile, informal, mental strategies.

### Informal Strategies versus Formal Algorithms

An important reason for delaying the teaching of the formal algorithms is that children's informal strategies typically are significantly different from formal algorithms. In the case of informal strategies children typically work from left to right, and often work with the whole number, rather than one column at a time. When children who have not developed facile informal strategies are taught the formal algorithms, they tend not to develop informal strategies because their learning of the formal algorithms tends to interfere with their development of informal strategies. Because of this, the approaches to this topic presented in this book focus on delaying the teaching of the formal algorithms until children learn facile informal strategies.

Children who can increment and decrement by 10s on and off the decade, and who have facile strategies for addition and subtraction in the range 1 to 20, are ready to extend their knowledge to the development of informal strategies for adding and subtracting two 2-digit numbers. Children who have not been taught the formal written algorithms will use a range of strategies to add and subtract two 2-digit numbers. Many of these strategies fall into two classes of strategies: (a) **jump strategies**, and (b) **split strategies**. The strategies are demonstrated in Figures 2.1, 2.2, 2.3 and 2.4.

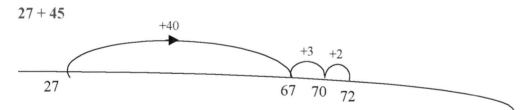

**Figure 2.1** Two-digit addition using a Jump Strategy

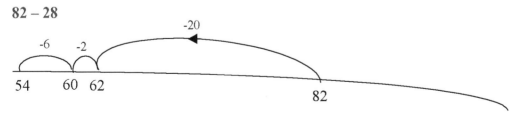

**Figure 2.2** Two-digit subtraction using a Jump Strategy

$$27 + 45: \quad 20 + 40 \longrightarrow 60$$
$$7 + 5 \longrightarrow 12$$
$$60 + 12 \longrightarrow 72$$

**Figure 2.3**  Using a Split Strategy for 27 + 45

$$82 - 28: \quad 80 - 20 \longrightarrow 60$$
$$12 - 8 \longrightarrow 4$$
$$60 - 10 \longrightarrow 50$$
$$50 + 4 \longrightarrow 54$$

**Figure 2.4**  Using a Split Strategy for 82 − 28

In Chapter 8, the focus is on instructional approaches that are particularly suited to developing jump strategies and related kinds of strategies. In Chapter 9, the focus is on instructional approaches that are particularly suited to developing split strategies. We take the view that instruction can focus on one or both of these approaches, and that the focus on jump strategies can precede the focus on split strategies or vice versa.

# PART II

---

# 3
# Number Words and Numerals

## Summary

This chapter focusses on children's early learning about number words and numerals. Developing facility with number word sequences and learning to name numerals constitute important aspects of early numeracy, and the view taken in this book is that these aspects are deserving of a renewed emphasis. This chapter presents new information about how children learn these aspects and approaches to instruction that take account of children's learning.

## TOPIC OVERVIEW

Learning about the names of numbers (number words) and the symbols for numbers (numerals) is a very important part of early number learning.

*Numbers.* Numbers are ideas or concepts. The number six for example, is the idea of 'six-ness'.
*Number words.* Number words are the names for numbers. We can distinguish between names that are spoken or heard and names that are written or read. In this chapter the term 'number words' will usually refer to spoken or heard number words.
*Digits.* The digits are the ten basic symbols in the numeration system (the system of **symbolizing** numbers). The digits are 0, 1, 2, . . . 9.
*Numerals.* Numerals are the written symbols for numbers, for example, 27, 346, 8. The ten digits from 0 to 9 can also be referred to as numerals.

## Learning about Number Words

Young children encounter number words very frequently. For many infants, as soon as they start to make sense of spoken language, number words are commonly used. The infant or young child is likely to encounter number words in senses such as their age or that of a sibling or friend, and the house number in a street. Number words will also be encountered in conversations referring to simple quantities, such as *Bill has two sisters* or *there are three cats*.

### Number Word Sequences

As well as encountering number words, children will also encounter number words in the context of a sequence of words, for example, *one, two, three, … ten*. This is referred to as a forward number word sequence (FNWS) or the FNWS from one to ten. Children might also encounter these words spoken in the reverse order, that is the backward number word sequence (BNWS) from ten to one.

### Facility with FNWSs and BNWSs

The extent to which a child has knowledge of FNWSs is referred as the child's facility with FNWSs. In similar vein, one can refer to the child's facility with BNWSs. Some school entrants, for example, have good facility with the FNWS from one to thirty and beyond, while others may know only the first few words of the sequence (one, two, three). Typically, children will have less facility with BNWSs than with FNWSs, for example, a child might be able to say the FNWS from 'one' to 'twenty-nine' but not be able to say the BNWS from 'eight' to 'one'.

### Number Word After and Number Word Before

Being able to say FNWSs and BNWSs is one important aspect of the young child's emerging facility with number words. A second important facility is being able to say one or two words after or before a given word. For example, when asked to 'say the number after eight', one child might answer immediately, 'nine'. Another child might say the words forward from 'one' and then answer 'nine' (referred to as 'dropping back to one'). A third child might not be able to answer 'nine'.

Learning about number words and number word sequences is a very prominent aspect of early number knowledge, and one of the earliest aspects to emerge. Instruction to develop children's facility with number words is regarded as very important. This is because facility with number words provides an important basis for the development of what are called 'early arithmetical strategies' (the first strategies that children use in additive and subtractive situations).

## Learning about Numerals

As well as learning about number words, another important aspect of early number involves learning about numerals. This includes learning to: (a) identify numerals; (b) write numerals; and (c) recognize numerals, and to learn about **numeral sequences**. Identifying numerals is also referred to as naming numerals or reading numerals, for example, where a teacher displays '10' and the child's task is to say 'ten'. An example of recognizing numerals is that a teacher puts a collection of numeral cards from '11' to '20'on a desk, not in numerical order, and asks the child 'which number is twelve?'. Numeral sequences refers to presenting the numerals in a sequence, for example, the numeral sequence from 11 to 20.

### The Numerals from 1 to 10

Children will typically learn the names of the numerals from 1 to 10 through frequent association of the numeral and its name. This can occur through activities with the numerals individually or with the numeral sequence from 1 to 10. Thus children's early learning of numerals occurs in much the same way as children learn the names of letters. Indeed, in the early stages of learning about numerals, some children might not distinguish very much between numerals and letters.

## The Numerals from 11 to 20

Children can and should learn the names of the numerals from 11 to 20 in much the same way as they learn the names of the numerals to 10, that is by frequent association of the numeral and its name, again through activities with the numerals individually, and with numeral sequences. For several reasons learning the numerals in the teens can be difficult for children. For one thing, their more established knowledge of the number words and numerals from 1 to 10 interacts with their emerging knowledge of teen number words and numerals. Also, the names of the teen numbers are such that they cause difficulties for children learning to associate these names with numerals. This is discussed in more detail below. A final point is that children can and should become skillful at associating number words with numerals in the teens, that is, naming numerals in the teens, long before they understand that the left hand digit ('1') in each of the numerals from 11 to 19 indicates or stands for the number 'ten'. In the same way that children develop a sight vocabulary of very common words – 'and', 'the', and so on – they can develop a sight vocabulary of numerals. In this way children initially associate the name 'fifteen' with the numeral '15' without necessarily understanding why the digits '1' and '5' are used to write the numeral for 'fifteen'.

## The Numerals from 20 to 99

When children start to encounter the numerals from '20' onward, they begin to learn a naming system which is very close to a regular or transparent system. Children can come to know for example, that a 2-digit numeral of the form '6...', has the name 'sixty-', and that the second part of the name of '6...' is the name of the digit in the right-hand place. For most children, learning implicit rules or principles of this kind is not difficult. As in the case of numerals in the teens, children can and should learn the names of numerals from 20 to 99 long before they necessarily know that the left-hand digit in a numeral such as '46' indicates four tens. Learning the place value features of the digits in multi-digit numerals is complex. This can and should be learned much later than when children first learn to name these numerals.

## 3-digit Numerals

An important point about the naming system for 3-digit numerals is that there is a very regular system to the way one deals with the left-hand digit in a 3-digit numeral. In all cases, for example, 461, 207, 117, the numeral is read by simply first saying 'four hundred', 'two hundred', 'one hundred', and so on. Learning this implicit rule or principle is relatively easy for children. Thus, children who have a sound knowledge of numerals and number words in the range 1 to 100 can be taught the names of 3-digit numerals with relative ease, and, as in the case of 2-digit numerals, children can and should learn the names of 3-digit numerals long before they know in detail about the place value features of 3-digit numerals.

## Difficulties with Names of 2-digit Numbers

Many researchers and writers on early number have highlighted difficulties associated with the particular number names. This problem arises in the English language, other European languages, and some other languages but does not arise in certain East Asian languages (for example, Chinese, Japanese, Korean). The problem mainly concerns the number names: 'eleven', 'twelve', … 'nineteen', but also names such as 'twenty', 'thirty', and 'fifty'. In the East Asian languages, the numeral '11' for example, is literally read as 'one ten one', that is, 'one ten one' is the spoken number word for '11'. Similarly, the number word for '15' is 'one ten five', for '20' is 'two ten', and '58' is 'five ten eight'. The system of number words in the East Asian languages is described as transparent. In virtually all languages and cultures, children typically learn the number word system before they learn the numeral system, that is, they learn the spoken sequence of number words before they learn the sequence of numerals.

The important point is that, in English and other languages with the difficulty just described, when children come to learn the numeral system, the non-transparent number naming system can result in significant and persistent difficulties for many children. This arises when children are learning to read numerals, that is, learning to make links from the numeral system to the number word system, which they already know to some extent at least. Consider the case of a child who has been learning the names of numerals in the teens. For example, this child has learned to read '18' by first saying 'eight'. Confronted with the task of reading '27', a typical response for this child is to look at the digit on the right hand side, and say 'seven … ', and after a moment's reflection, to say 'seventy-two'. In similar vein, children who are learning to read numerals in the range '20' to '100' will often have difficulty writing numbers in the teens. The child has the sound 'sixteen' in their mind, so they first write the digit '6', and after some reflection, they might correctly write '1' to the left of the '6'. A final example is that some children seem to have extreme difficulty with associating the numeral '12' and the spoken number word 'twelve'. In this regard '12' typically is much more difficult than '11'. In the case of '11', reversing the order of the digits is not an issue. Children will often read '12' as 'twenty' or 'twenty-one'. If a child is asked to select the larger of two numbers (presented on cards as the numerals '12' and '18'), a child might select '12' because they read '12' as 'twenty-one'.

# ASSESSMENT TASK GROUPS

## List of Assessment task Groups

A3.1: Forward number word sequences
A3.2: Number word after
A3.3: Backward number word sequences
A3.4: Number word before
A3.5: **Numeral identification**
A3.6: **Numeral recognition**
A3.7: Sequencing numerals
A3.8: Ordering numerals
A3.9: Locating numbers in the range 1 to 100

## TASK GROUP A3.1: Forward Number Word Sequences

**Materials:** None.

**What to do and say:** *Start counting from one please. I will tell you when to stop.* Stop the child at 32. *Start counting from 47 please.* Stop the child at 55. And so on.

**Notes:**

▶ Children might have particular difficulties progressing to the next decade, for example, after 29.
▶ Listen carefully for omissions. Children might omit decade numbers or numbers such as 66.
▶ Children who can say the sequence through 99, 100, 101 etc. might say 200 after 109.
▶ Children might confuse the pronunciation of teens and decades, for example *fifty* instead of *fifteen*.

## TASK GROUP A3.2: Number Word After

**Materials:** None.

**What to do and say:** *I am going to say a number and I would like you to say the number that comes after the number I say. What comes after six? After 11?* And so on.

**Notes:**

▶ Children who can say the sequence from one to beyond 10 will not necessarily be successful on these tasks.
▶ Children might need to drop back, to solve these tasks, for example, for *after seven?*, the child says *one, two, three, four, five, six, seven, … eight!*.
▶ Children might confuse decades and teens, for example, *after sixteen?*, they may say *seventy!*.

Using the numeral roll for FNWS and NWA (1)

Using the numeral roll for FNWS and NWA (2)

## TASK GROUP A3.3: Backward Number Word Sequences

**Materials:** None.

**What to do and say:** *Count back from ten please. Count backwards from 23 please.* Stop the child at eight. *Count back from 43.* Stop the child at 36. And so on.

**Notes:**

▶ Children are typically more facile with forward sequences than with backward sequences.

▶ Children who can say the forward sequence to beyond 30 might have difficulty with backward sequences involving the teens.

▶ Children might have difficulties progressing to the next lowest decade, for example, *42, 41, …?*; or *42, 41, 40, …?*.

▶ Children might confuse teens and decades, *23, 22, 21, 20, 90, 80*, and so on.

▶ Children might say the next lowest decade number, *52, 51, 40, 49, 48* and so on, or omit a decade number.

▶ Children might omit a word in the backward sequence which they do not omit in the forward sequence, for example, *sixteen, fifteen, thirteen, twelve*, and so on. This error can be persistent and can result in errors when using the backward sequence for subtraction, for example, 17 – 4 as *sixteen, fifteen, thirteen, twelve!*.

## TASK GROUP A3.4: Number Word Before

**Materials:** None.

**What to do and say:** *I am going to say a number and I would like you to say the number that comes before the one I say. What comes before three? Before eight?* And so on.

**Notes:**

▶ Children who can say the sequence from 10 or more, back to one, will not necessarily be successful on these tasks.

▶ Children might use a dropping back strategy. This involves saying a forward number word sequence to figure out the number word before, (for example: *Before 6?*, the child responds *one, two, three, four, five, six, – five!*).

▶ Children might confuse number word after with number word before.

## TASK GROUP A3.5: Numeral Identification

**Materials:** Set of numeral cards from 1 to 10, not in numerical order. Similarly, a set of numeral cards from 11 to 20, and a set of cards for selected numerals in the range 21 to 100 (about 12 to 15 of these).

**What to do and say:** Display the cards in turn. *Tell me the number on the card please.*

Numeral identification

**Notes:**

▶ Children might say a forward number word sequence. For example, when identifying the numeral 5, the child says *one, two, three, four, five!*

▶ Depending on your sense of the children's level, you can start with the set of cards from 11 to 20.

▶ Children who can easily identify the numerals from 11 to 20 will very likely be able to identify the numerals from 1 to 10.

▶ A common error is to identify 12 as 20 or 21.

▶ Numerals from 13 to 19 might be read as decade numbers. For example, 13 is read as *thirty*.

▶ Children might identify 2-digit numbers incorrectly, for example, saying *seventy-two* for 27. Most likely this arises from applying inappropriately, a method of reading teen numbers (for example 17 is read from right to left *seven* then *teen*) to 2-digit numbers.

## TASK GROUP A3.6: Numeral Recognition

**Materials:** Set of five or more numeral cards, for example, the cards from 1 to 10.

**What to do and say:** Arrange the cards randomly on the desk. *Which number is six? Three?* And so on.

**Notes:**

▶ Children might be able to recognize numerals that they cannot identify. For example, the child cannot identify the numeral 12 (when an individual card with the numeral 12 is displayed) but can successfully respond to a task such as *which number is the 12* (for example, using a set of cards for the numbers from 11 to 20). These children seem to have difficulty in generating a sound image of the word 'twelve'.

## TASK GROUP A3.7: Sequencing Numerals

**Materials:** Sets of numeral cards as follows: 1 to 10; 10, 20, 30, … 100; 46, 47, … 55.

**What to do and say:** Arrange the ten cards from 46 to 55 randomly on the desk. *Put these numbers in order please, starting from the smallest.* Similarly, use the set of cards from 1 to 5, 1 to 10 or the decade cards.

**Notes:**

▶    If the child is not fluent at numeral identification (for example, for the numerals from 46 to 55) then they will probably have difficulty in sequencing the numerals.
▶    A common response is to take account of the 'ones' only: 50, 51, 52, 53, 54, 55, 46, 47, and so on.
▶    An alternative phrasing is to use the term 'least' rather than 'smallest'.

Sequencing numerals (1)

Sequencing numerals (2)

## TASK GROUP A3.8: Ordering Numerals

**Materials:** Sets of four numeral cards such as the following: 8, 12, 18, 31.

**What to do and say:** Arrange the four cards randomly on the desk. *Put these numbers in order please, starting from the smallest.*

**Notes:**

▶   Typically these tasks are much easier for children who are facile at identifying numerals.
▶   The relative difficulty of these tasks depends on the number of numerals to be ordered, for example, ordering three numerals is much easier than ordering six numerals.
▶   Errors of ordering numerals can sometimes result from incorrectly reading (identifying) numerals, for example, the child reads 12 as 'twenty-one' and therefore orders the numerals as follows: 8, 18, 12, 31.

## TASK GROUP A3.9: Locating Numbers in the Range 1 to 100

**Materials:** A strip of cardboard about 20 inches (50cm) long with a number line showing the decade numbers, 0, 10, 20, 30 ... 100, evenly spaced. Numeral cards for numbers in the range 1 to 100 (for example, 6, 13, 22, 25, and so on).

**What to do and say:** Arrange the number line on the desk. *Read the numbers on the line please.* Select one of the numeral cards (22). *Read this number please. Show me where this number would be on the number line.* Similarly with the other numeral cards.

**Notes:**

▶    The number line can include evenly spaced marks for each number. Alternatively these can be omitted.

▶    Children who cannot identify numerals are likely to find this task quite difficult.

# INSTRUCTIONAL ACTIVITIES

## List of Instructional Activities

IA3.1:   Count Around
IA3.2:   Numbers on the Line
IA3.3:   Stand in Line
IA3.4:   Secret Numbers
IA3.5:   Can You See Me?
IA3.6:   Make and Break Numbers
IA3.7:   The Joke Is On You
IA3.8:   Counting Choir
IA3.9:   Take Your Place
IA3.10: What Comes Next?

## ACTIVITY IA3.1: Count Around

**Intended learning:** To extend knowledge of forward number word sequences (FNWSs).

**Description:** Children stand in a circle and count around, each child saying the next number in the sequence. Start the count at one. The child who says the number 12 sits down. The next child begins the count again at one. The activity continues until only one child is left standing.

▶   Extend to crossing decade numbers.
▶   Use shorter or longer sequences.
▶   Vary the range of numbers (for example, start at 45 and sit down on 53).
▶   Extend to backward number word sequences.

**Notes:**

▶   Children might omit numbers, say them in the incorrect order or not be able to give the next number, particularly when crossing a decade number.
▶   Ask questions such as: *Who will sit down next? Who will say five? Who will be left standing?*
▶   Suitable for whole class or groups.

**Materials:** None.

## ACTIVITY IA3.2: Numbers on the Line

**Intended learning:** To sequence numerals.

**Description:** Place a set of numeral cards from 15 to 25 face down on the floor, in a pile, in random order. Ask a child to take a card and peg it on the washing line. Ask a second child to take the next card from the pile and place it appropriately on the line. Continue until all the numbers have been pegged on the line in the correct sequence. Ask children to read the numbers aloud to check. If any numbers are in the wrong place, discuss and ask a child to re-position.

▶ Use shorter or longer sequences.
▶ Vary the range of numbers, for example from 126 to 135.
▶ Read the sequences backward as well as forward.
▶ Extend to non-consecutive numbers for example 46, 48, 51 54, 60.

Notes:

▶ When children are about to place their card, ask questions such as: *Is it more or less than …? Will you place it to the left or right of …? Which two numbers should it go between?*
▶ Vocabulary includes: more, less, higher, lower, before, after.
▶ Suitable for whole class or groups.

Materials: Washing line, pegs, numeral cards.

## ACTIVITY IA3.3: Stand in Line

**Intended learning:** To extend knowledge of backward number word sequences (BNWSs) and numerals.

**Description:** Give each child one card from a set of cards with numerals 1 to 30. Ask a child to come to the front and hold up their card, for example16. Children must look at their own card and decide who has the number before 16 (15). The child holding number 15 stands to the left of the first child (holding number 16). Continue the line until it has six children in it and shows the sequence from 16 to 11.

Each child in turn, displays and says their number. All of the children read the number sequence backwards in unison and then repeat with their eyes closed.

▶ Use a range of starting numbers.
▶ Vary the range of numbers, for example from 57 to 74.
▶ Build sequences forward as well as backward.
▶ Focus on crossing decade numbers forwards and backwards.
▶ When the children are standing in line choose several to turn their cards over. Can the children still say the BNWS correctly?

Notes:

▶ Children might omit numbers, say them in the incorrect order or not be able to give the next number, particularly when crossing a decade number.
▶ Suitable for whole class or groups.
▶ Vocabulary includes: more, less, higher, lower, before, after, larger, smaller, in between.

Materials: Set of numeral cards from 1 to 30.

## ACTIVITY IA3.4: Secret Numbers

**Intended learning:** To order non-sequential numerals.

**Description:** Provide six non-sequential numerals on cards for example 17, 23, 28, 31, 36, 42. Select two children. Give the largest number (42) to one child and the smallest (17) to another. Place the two children with their cards about three metres apart. Select a third child to choose one of the remaining numbers. They must keep their number secret and decide where to stand in between 17 and 42. Ask: *What could the number be?*

Establish that it must be more than 17 and less than 42. Ask the child to reveal their secret number. Continue with a second secret number, then a third and fourth until all the cards are in the correct order.

▶ Vary by using other sets of cards.
▶ Vary the range of numbers used.

**Notes:**

▶ Suitable for whole class or small groups.
▶ Adapt for pairs by providing sets of cards for children to order and record.

**Materials:** Large numeral cards, sets of smaller cards (for working in pairs).

## ACTIVITY IA3.5: Can You See Me?

**Intended learning:** To identify and recognize numerals from 1 to 5.

**Description:** Display a collection of birthday cards. Each card has one of the numerals from 1 to 5. Discuss the cards briefly. From a set of large wooden or plastic numerals, select one secretly, for example 3 (see Figure 3.1). Hide 3 behind a screen (piece of card) and gradually reveal part of it. Ask: *What number could this be? Can you see it on a birthday card?* Take several suggestions and then reveal a little more. Continue until the numeral is fully revealed. Establish that it is the number 3 and ask a child to select a birthday card showing the number 3 from the display. Similarly with other numerals.

▶ Ask the children to draw the numeral in the air, trace it on their partner's hand or back, or write it on a whiteboard.
▶ Have the children find the numeral from a larger collection of numeral cards.
▶ Extend the range of numerals to 9 and include zero.
▶ Ask children: *What number can't this be? Why?*
▶ Use a kangaroo glove puppet with the number hidden in the pouch.
▶ The technique of gradually moving the screen to reveal the numeral can involve moving the screen in one of several ways, for example, moving the screen down, moving the screen to the left.

**Notes:**

▶ Suitable for whole class or small groups.
▶ Use two different numerals together, revealing each more than once, for example 3 and 4.
▶ Use two or three similar numerals, revealing each more than once, for example 2, 3 and 8.
▶ Numeral cards can be used instead of plastic or wooden numerals.

**Figure 3.1** What number could this be?

**Materials:** Collection of birthday cards (one for each numeral) within the required range of numerals (several cards for each numeral), plastic or wooden numerals, card screen.

## ACTIVITY IA3.6: Make and Break Numbers

**Intended Learning:** To combine and partition hundreds, tens and ones.

**Description:** Display a 50 arrow card. Ask the children to say the number. Repeat this for other decade numbers (for example, 70). Now use the two arrow cards to display a 2-digit number (50 and 6 ... 56). Continue in the same way using arrow cards to make 3-digit numbers (600, 30 and 8 ... 638).

Show the class large 2- and 3-digit numerals and select children to demonstrate to the class how these can be made using arrow cards. This could be done using an overhead projector. Repeat the activity with children using their own arrow cards.

Display a numeral (for example, 673) and point to each digit asking: *What number is this? How many hundreds in 673? How many tens in 673? How many ones?* After the children answer, use the arrow cards to confirm the number of hundreds, tens and ones. Have them make 3-digit numbers using their arrow cards. Include examples where the digits are the same (for example 55 and 333) and numerals with a zero on the ones or tens (for example 204, 780).

**Notes:**

▶    The activity can be extended to 4-digit numerals.
▶    Suitable for whole class or groups.
▶    Vocabulary includes: partition, combine.

**Materials:** A set of large arrow cards and sets of arrow cards for individual use. (See Figure 3.2)

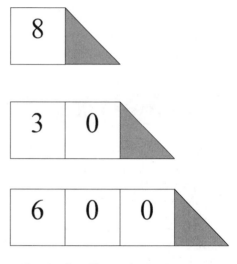

These 3 cards combine to make 638

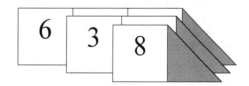

**Figure 3.2** Arrow cards

## ACTIVITY IA3.7: The Joke Is On You

**Intended learning:** To sequence decade numbers (multiples of ten).

**Description:** Write the multiples of ten on blank playing cards (or use decade cards). You will also need a Joker from a pack of cards. Shuffle the cards and give one to each child until all are distributed. Ask the children, one at a time to attach their cards face down on the chalkboard ledge or on the floor or pegged on a string line. The last child reveals their number and finds its correct position in the line. For example, 30 would be placed third in the line. The card occupying that place is given to someone else who must find its correct position in the line. The activity continues until the Joker is revealed. The children are then asked to say which numbers are missing from the sequence. Children then play the game in pairs.

▶    Vary the activity by using any appropriate sequence of numbers for example 35 to 44, or 1 to 15.
▶    Children could continue after the Joker has been found. When the Joker is found, ask a child to turn over the remaining cards and complete the sequence.
▶    When playing in pairs, children can use two or more rows, denoted by different colours (or suits if using playing cards).

**Notes:**

▶    Suitable for whole class, groups or pairs.
▶    Some children might need to go to the beginning of a row and count by ones. Others might use previously turned cards as starting points or clues.
▶    Ask questions such as: *Where do you think this number will go? Which card could help you?*
▶    Any picture card could be used in place of the Joker.

**Materials:** Set of blank playing cards or numeral cards.

## ACTIVITY IA3.8: Counting Choir

**Intended learning:** To count in ones, tens and hundreds.

**Description:** Divide the class into three groups. The teacher takes the role of conductor holding a baton (pointer). The teacher begins the count for example 21, 22, 23, 24 and then points the baton at one of the groups who continue the count in unison for example 25, 26, 27… until the teacher points the baton at another group. This group, in turn, continues the count. The teacher moves the baton from group to group randomly bringing in sections of the choir. Similarly with other starting numbers.

Give one group a card labelled *ONES*, the second group a card labelled *TENS*, and the third labeled *HUNDREDS*. The teacher begins the count again for example *7, 8, 9* and then points to the *ONES* group who continue the count in ones for example *10, 11, 12, 13*. The teacher moves the baton to the *TENS* group who continue the count in tens for example *23, 33, 43, 53*. The teacher then moves the baton to the *HUNDREDS* group who continue the count in hundreds for example *153, 253, 353, 453*. The teacher moves the baton from group to group randomly, bringing in different sections of the choir. Similarly with other start numbers. Vary the activity by counting in ones only, in ones and tens, extending to counting in thousands, or counting backwards by ones, tens or hundreds.

**Notes:**

▶    Suitable for whole class or large group.
▶    Children can be grouped according to their facility in counting by ones, tens and hundreds.
▶    A hundred square can be used to support children counting in ones and tens.
▶    Children might experience difficulty when crossing decade numbers or going beyond 999.

**Materials:** Baton, a set of cards (labeled *Ones, Tens, Hundreds*).

## ACTIVITY IA3.9: Take Your Place

**Intended learning:** To sequence and order numerals.

**Description:** Ask a child to roll two dice to generate a 2-digit number. The child holds up the digit cards to represent that number, for example 26. A second child rolls the dice, takes the digit cards and makes a second 2-digit number for example 34. Ask: *Which is more 26 or 34? Where should 34 stand?* A third child rolls the dice, selects the cards and makes a third 2-digit number for example 21. Ask: *Is it higher or lower than 26? Where should it go?* Roll again to generate a fourth number and ask similar questions. Check that the numbers are in the right order. Ask number 26: *Why are you standing in between 21 and 34?* (Encourage explanations such as *I am more than 21 and less than 34.*) Repeat the activity several times.

▶ Vary the activity by using one die or spinner numbered 1–9 and order 1-digit numbers.
▶ Extend by using two 1–9 dice or spinners.
▶ Progress to using three dice to generate 3-digit numbers.

**Notes:**

▶ Suitable for whole class, groups or pairs.
▶ Children might read 2-digit numerals incorrectly from right to left, for example, 72 is read as 'twenty-seven'.
▶ When doing this activity in pairs, children could be asked to record their numbers.
▶ It is important to ask appropriate questions and encourage explanations from children.
▶ Extend children's vocabulary to include: higher, lower, more, less, larger, smaller.

**Materials:** Two dice (or spinners) numbered 1 to 6, or 1 to 9, sets of digit cards 1 to 9.

## ACTIVITY IA3.10: What Comes Next?

**Intended learning:** To be able to say the number after any given number.

**Description:** Tell the children that you are going to count and that when you stop counting, you want them to say the next number. Say: *One, two, three, four, five.* Children shout, whisper or sing: *Six!*

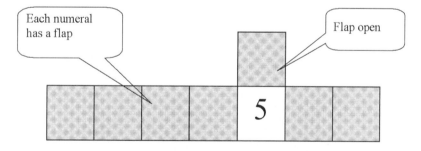

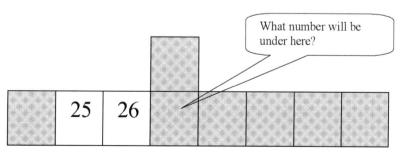

**Figure 3.3** Numeral track

Continue with other number word sequences, for example *seventeen, eighteen, nineteen, twenty* ... . Use shorter sequences for example *twenty five, twenty six,* .... . Display the **numeral track** from 25 to 34. Lift the flaps to show 25 and 26. Say the numbers with the children and ask: What number will be under here (27)? What comes next? Take several responses and then choose a child to lift the flap and reveal the number. Continue, starting with other sequences. Progress to lifting one flap (29) and challenging the children to give the next number (30).

▶      Vary the activity by using other sequences on the numeral track for example 11 to 20 or 95 to 104.
▶      Vary the activity to saying the number before any given number.

**Notes:**

▶      Children might need to count from one, to give the next number.
▶      Some children might have difficulty when shorter sequences are used (for example, two numbers only.
▶      Suitable for whole class or groups.
▶      Vocabulary includes: next number, number after, number before.

**Materials:** Numeral track.

# 4
# Early Counting and Addition

**Summary**

This chapter focusses on the early development of counting, where counting is regarded as an activity oriented to solving an arithmetical task such as figuring out how many items in a collection or how many items in all when two small collections are put together. The chapter provides a detailed description of a progression of counting types of increasing sophistication – emergent, perceptual and figurative counting, and how these types of counting provide the basis for children's early addition strategies.

## TOPIC OVERVIEW

### The Importance of Counting

Counting is regarded as an extremely important aspect of early number instruction. Counting is very prominent in young children's early mathematical activity and seems to be virtually a natural and spontaneous activity for children in the first two or three years of school, and also for many preschoolers. Further, it is well known by teachers and others, that many children in the middle and upper primary years make extensive use of counting when solving arithmetical problems, that is, problems that involve any of the four operations (addition, subtraction and so on.). To make this point another way, counting is a prominent aspect of much of the so-called 'mental arithmetic' or mental computation done by children in the primary years and beyond.

### Levels of Sophistication in Counting

There are various levels in mathematical sophistication of the ways children use counting and it is important for teachers to have some understanding of these. Teachers who have a good knowledge of these are better able to develop instructional approaches focussed on developing more sophisticated arithmetical strategies in their children. The levels of sophistication in counting will be described in detail in this chapter.

### Counting versus Saying a Number Word Sequence

Chapter 3 focussed on children learning about number words including learning to say forward number word sequences (FNWSs) and backward number word sequences (BNWSs). In that section we did not use the term 'counting' as a label for a child's activity of saying a FNWS. This is because we find it useful to distinguish between, on the one hand, the activity of merely reciting the sequence of number words and, on the other hand, the activity of saying the words in a context where the child is purposefully keeping track of items. The latter activity is referred to as counting, and the distinction just described has been highlighted by several researchers and writers (for example, Steffe and Cobb, 1988). This distinction relates to a qualitative difference between the mental activity associated with merely saying an FNWS, and the mental activity associated with counting, where each number word is associated with an item.

## Perceptual Counting

**Perceptual** counting refers to situations in which the items to be counted are available for the child to see. Counting that is not perceptual counting refers to situations in which the child knows how many counters are in a small collection (for example, four) but those counters are screened and not available for the child to see.

### Using Perceptual Counting to Establish Numerosity of a Collection

An example of perceptual counting is when a teacher puts a collection of 15 counters on the desk (the child does not know how many counters there are) and asks the child how many counters there are. Typically, the child would move the counters in turn, or at least point at them one by one, and coordinate each movement or point with a number word. Thus one would say the child uses counting to establish the **numerosity** of a collection of counters.

### Using Perceptual Counting to Establish a Collection of Specified Numerosity

Another example is when a teacher puts a large pile (say 50) of counters on the desk, and asks the child to get eight counters. Again, the child typically would move the counters one by one in coordination with saying the number words from 'one' to 'eight'. In this case one would say the child uses counting to establish a collection of specified numerosity.

### Using Perceptual Counting to Establish the Numerosity of Two Collections

Another example of perceptual counting is when a teacher places out 7 red counters and 5 green counters and asks the child how many counters in all. Typically, the child would begin by counting the counters in one of the collections and continue to count the items in the second collection. For some children, tasks involving counting the items in two visible collections (for example, 7 red and 5 green) seem to be more difficult than tasks involving counting the items in one collection (for example, 12 red counters).

## Beginning Addition through Counting

The activity of perceptual counting is described above. In the case of perceptual counting, the items to be counted are available for the child to see. More advanced levels of counting occur when children count to solve problems involving items which are not available to be seen. Consider a task involving eight counters under one screen and five under a second screen. The two collections are briefly displayed for the child and the child is told how many in each. Also, for ease of demarcation, the first collection comprises red counters and the second comprises green counters. The child's task is to figure out how many counters in all. From an adult perspective this is a trivial arithmetic problem involving addition of two numbers in the range 1 to 10. But from the perspective of the child for whom the task is problematic, this is a task about counters and numbers. The arithmetical idea of addition is currently somewhat remote for the child. The task just described is referred to as an **additive task** involving two screened collections of counters. The counters used in this way constitute a setting in which the child can begin to develop notions of adding numbers.

## Counting-from-one versus Counting-on

Consider a child who is known in advance to be capable of perceptual counting (see above). The child is presented with the additive task involving two screened collections (8 + 5). Typically, young children will respond to this kind of task in one of four ways: the perceptual counter, the **figurative** counter, the counting-on child, the **non-count-by-ones** child. Each of these four types of responses is now explained.

## The Perceptual Counter

The perceptual counter is unable to use counting to solve the task and is the least advanced in terms of arithmetic sophistication. Currently, perceptual counting is this child's most advanced kind of counting.

## The Figurative Counter

The figurative counter looks at the first screen while counting from 'one' to 'eight', and then looks at the second screen while counting from 'nine' to 'thirteen'. This is referred to as figurative counting. The child counts-from-one to solve an additive task where the counters are not available to be seen. We do not use the term 'count-all' because this term does not distinguish between the perceptual and the figurative counter. Both of these would be referred to as 'counting-all'. The difference is that the perceptual counter can use count-all to figure out how many counters in all, only when the two collections are visible. By way of contrast, the figurative counter can use count-all to figure out how many counters in all, when the two collections are screened (not available to be seen).

## The Counting-on Child

The counting-on child looks at the first screen and says 'eight', and then looks at the second screen, and says 'nine, ten, eleven, twelve, thirteen'. This is referred to as counting-on to solve an additive task and is regarded as more advanced than figurative counting. Both counting-on and figurative counting are regarded as more advanced than perceptual counting.

## The Non-count-by-ones Child

This child solves the task by first working out (without counting) the number to be added to 8 to make 10 (2), then partitioning 5 into 2 and 3, then adding 3 to 10 (without counting) to make 13. This strategy is referred to as 'adding to 10', 'adding through 10', and 'bridging to 10'. This child is said to use a non-count-by-ones strategy, and this is regarded as a more sophisticated strategy than counting-on.

## Counting as Coordinating Words and Items

As indicated earlier, we make a distinction between counting and merely saying number words because in the case of counting the child coordinates each number word with an item. Like the perceptual counter, the figurative counter and the counting-on child (see above) are coordinating number words with items. The difference is that the perceptual counter is directly perceiving (seeing) the items (counters), whereas the figurative counter and the counting-on child imagine or visualize the items to be counted. For this reason figurative counting and counting-on as just described are regarded as cognitively and arithmetically more advanced than perceptual counting.

## Emergent, Perceptual and Figurative Counting

This chapter focusses on the first three levels of counting, that is, emergent, perceptual and figurative counting. Perceptual and figurative counting have already been described (see above).

## Emergent Counting

The term 'emergent' is used in cases where the child is not able to count perceptually. Thus the child is unable to count a collection of say, 12 or 15 counters. The child might not know the number word sequence or might not correctly coordinate each number word with an item to be counted. For example, the child might say 'four, five' while pointing at one counter only, or say 'se-ven' and coordinate one counter with 'se' and another with 'ven'.

## Determining the Most Sophisticated Level

It is not uncommon for children to use a level of counting that is less advanced than they are capable of. As teachers, our task is to elicit the most advanced kind of counting that the child can use spontaneously and with certitude. Thus a child is classified as a perceptual counter only when we are convinced that the child is not able to use figurative counting or counting-on to solve a task such as 8 + 5 involving two covered collections. Typically, it is necessary to present the child with several tasks rather than just one, in order to elicit the most advanced kind of counting.

## ASSESSMENT TASK GROUPS

### List of Assessment Task Groups

A4.1: Comparing small collections
A4.2: Increase and decrease in the range 1 to 6
A4.3: Establishing the numerosity of a collection
A4.4: Establishing a collection of specified numerosity
A4.5: Establishing the numerosity of two collections
A4.6: Additive tasks involving two **screened** collections
A4.7: Counting and copying **temporal sequences** and temporal patterns

## TASK GROUP A4.1: Comparing Small Collections

**Materials:** Cards with one, two … six dots (see Figure 4.1). Dots are randomly arranged (not in regular spatial patterns). About 10 cards for each number of dots (60 cards in all).

**Figure 4.1** Comparing small collections cards

**What to do and say:** Place out two cards, for example, 2-dots and 4-dots. *Pick up the card which has more dots.* Repeat with other pairs of cards showing different numbers of dots.

**Notes:**

▶ This task is relatively easy for 5-year-olds and above. Accordingly, the task might reveal a lack of very beginning number knowledge.
▶ Children might spontaneously say a number to indicate how many dots on a card.
▶ Children who are not able to ascribe numerosity to a collection (Task A4.3) might nevertheless be successful on these tasks.
▶ An alternative phrasing is to use the term 'spot' rather than 'dot'.

Which tower has more blocks?

## TASK GROUP A4.2: Increase and Decrease in the Range 1 to 6

**Materials:** About 20 counters all of one color. A container (cup) used to conceal a small collection of counters.

**What to do and say:** Place out two counters. *How many counters?* Place the two counters in the cup and cover the cup. Place two more counters in the cup (4 in all). *How many counters are there in the cup now?* Place one more counter in the cup (5). *How many now?* Remove two counters (3). *How many now?* Continue as follows: add 2 (5); remove 1 (4); add 2 (6); and so on.

**Notes:**

▶   These tasks assess the child's ability to determine the resultant number in a collection in the range 1 to 6, when one or two items are added or removed.

▶   In similar vein to Task Group A4.1, this task is relatively easy for 5-year-olds and above, and might also reveal a lack of very beginning number knowledge.

## TASK GROUP A4.3: Establishing the Numerosity of a Collection

**Materials:** About 30 counters all of one color.

**What to do and say:** Place out a collection of 12 counters. *How many counters are there?* Similarly 15, 18 or 8 counters.

How many counters are there?

Notes:

▶ To succeed at these tasks children need to know the forward number word sequence up to the number of counters in the collection to be counted.

▶ Take note of whether the child spontaneously uses an organized approach to counting. For example, the child might have a 'pull-out' strategy, moving each counter in turn, away from the collection.

▶ Common errors are omitting a number word or incorrectly coordinating number words and items.

▶ Coordination errors include saying one word for more than one item, or saying more than one word for one item.

▶ Take note of whether the child is aware that the last number word is the answer to 'How many?'.

## TASK GROUP A4.4: Establishing a Collection of Specified Numerosity

**Materials:** About 50 counters all of one color.

**What to do and say:** Place out all of the counters in a pile. *Get me eight counters please from this pile.* Similarly 13, 16 counters, and so on.

Notes:

▶ Refer to the notes for Task Group A4.3. Children's success on this Task Group corresponds closely with their success on Task Group A4.3.

Get me eight counters, please

## TASK GROUP A4.5: Establishing the Numerosity of Two Collections

**Materials:** A collection of counters of one color (red) and a collection of another color (green).

**What to do and say:** Place out seven red counters. *Here are seven counters.* Place out five green counters. *Here are five green counters. How many counters altogether?* Similarly with 8 and 3, 10 and 9, 5 and 3, and so on.

Notes:

▶ Some children have difficulty in conceiving of two collections alternatively as one collection whose items can be counted.

▶ Children who are successful on Task Groups A4.1 to A4.4, but have difficulty with these tasks might count each of the two collections separately from one but not count all of the items in the two collections together.

Establishing the numerosity of two collections

## TASK GROUP A4.6: Additive Tasks Involving Two Screened Collections

**Materials:** A collection of counters of one color (red) and a collection of another color (green); two screens of cardboard or cloth.

**What to do and say:** Briefly display and then screen six red counters. *Here are six red counters.* Briefly display and then screen three green counters. *Here are three green counters. How many counters altogether?* Similarly with collections such as 8 red and 2 green, 11 red and 4 green, 5 red and 2 green, and so on.

**Notes:**

▶ The purpose of these tasks is to see if the child uses counting-on.
▶ Some children might solve these tasks by counting from one. They are apparently unable to use counting-on to solve these kinds of tasks.
▶ In the case of children who are not able to solve these tasks, the second collection (green counters) can be unscreened.
▶ The general approach with these tasks is to have the number of counters in the second collection (green counters) typically in the range 2 to 5, and the number in the first collection (red counters) larger than the number in the second collection (green counters). The number in the first collection can be in the range 4 to 20 or beyond 20.

## TASK GROUP A4.7: Counting and Copying Temporal Sequences and Temporal Patterns

**Materials:** None.

**What to do and say:** *I am going to make some claps and I want you to tell me how many times I clap.* Clap three times. *How many times did I clap?* Similarly with six claps, two claps, and so on.

*This time I am going to make a pattern of claps and I want you to copy my pattern.* Make four claps in a 2-2 pattern. *Can you copy my pattern? How many claps was that altogether?* Similarly with patterns such as: 3-3, 3-2, 2-2-2, and so on.

**Notes:**

▶ Ask the child to look away so that they do not observe you making the claps.
▶ Typically, children are less facile at counting temporal sequences than at counting collections, for example, counting a sequence of ten claps versus a collection of ten counters.
▶ Children might be able to copy a temporal pattern but not be able to work out how many items (claps) in the pattern.

# INSTRUCTIONAL ACTIVITIES

## List of Instructional Activities

IA4.1:   Domino Addition
IA4.2:   Addition Dice
IA4.3:   Counters in a Row
IA4.4:   On the Mat
IA4.5:   Where Do I Go?
IA4.6:   Toy Box
IA4.7:   Teddy Bear Walk
IA4.8:   Chains
IA4.9:   Give Me Five
IA4.10:  Pass It On

## ACTIVITY IA4.1: Domino Addition

**Intended Learning:** To add with two collections where the first collection is screened and the number in the second collection is in the range 2 to 5.

**Description:** The teacher has a large blank domino. Four dots are placed in the left square of the domino (see Figure 4.2). The children are asked how many dots they can see. The teacher then uses the flap or card to screen the dots. The children are asked how many dots are under the flap. If the children are unsure, the teacher can unscreen the dots to establish how many, and then screen them. The teacher then places three dots on the right-hand side of the domino and poses the problem: *There are 4 dots under here and we have 3 more. How many dots do we have altogether?* The teacher allows some thinking time and re-poses the question if necessary. The activity can be continued using other numbers for example, 7 and 5, 8 and 3.

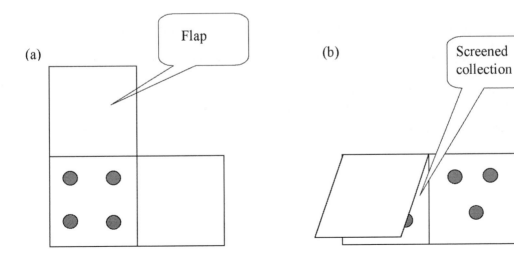

**Figure 4.2** Domino addition

**Notes:**

▶ The numbers chosen for this activity should take account of children's facility with the forward number word sequence (FNWS).

▶ The range of numbers used can be varied. The number used on the left-hand side of the domino can vary in accordance with children's facility with the FNWS. The number on the right-hand side should be in the range 2 to 5, for example 17 + 5. 28 + 2, 46 + 3.

▶ When the first addend is beyond 10, a card can be used to display the number of dots.

▶ When the first addend is large, it is not necessary to put out a corresponding number of dots. Ask children to pretend that there are a given number of dots under the flap.

▶ This activity is suitable for whole class or small groups.

▶ An overhead projector can be used with transparencies and translucent counters.

▶ Vary the activity by using other contexts which are familiar to the children, for example, a house and ants.

**Materials:** Large blank domino with flaps that screen each side. A card can be used to screen the side of the domino.

## ACTIVITY IA4.2: Addition Dice

**Intended learning:** To add when the first addend is given by a number and the second addend is given by a collection in the range 2 to 5.

**Description:** The teacher throws the number die, counts out counters to match the number thrown, and then screens the counters with a piece of card. The child throws the dot die. The teacher asks: *There are 6 dots under here and 3 dots on the die. How many dots are there altogether?* The teacher allows time to solve the problem and might re-pose it, or briefly display the counters under the card. Continue the activity using different numbers generated by the dice. As children become familiar with the activity, counting out the counters from the first throw is not needed. The range of numbers on the number die can be increased.

**Notes:**

▶ The numbers chosen for this activity should take account of children's facility with the forward number word sequence (FNWS).

▶ An extension of this activity is to have two numbered dice with the numbers on the second die restricted to the range 1 to 5.

▶ Activity is suitable for small groups or pairs.

▶ The context can be varied by using, for example, cubes and paper cups.

**Materials:** Number dice or spinner (1 to 6, 7 to 12, 13 to 18), a dot die with the six obscured counters.

## ACTIVITY IA4.3: Counters in a Row

**Intended learning:** To count-on from a given number with visible items in a row.

**Description:** An overhead projector and opaque counters or translucent counters (preferably the same color) are used. The teacher counts out the counters laying them in a line. Children are asked to check the number of counters in the line (counting with the teacher if necessary). The teacher uses a strip of card to screen the collection, then counts out three more counters continuing the line. The teacher poses the question: *There are eight counters under the card and we have three more counters. How many counters are there altogether?* The children write their answers on their whiteboards (or on scrap paper). The teacher asks the children for their answers and are asked to come to the front and explain their answers. The teacher then uses the collections of counters on the screen to talk the children through the calculation, demonstrating counting-on from the number of screened counters.

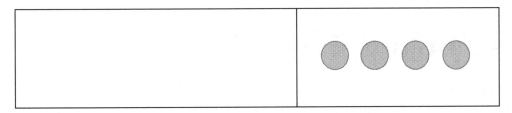

**Figure 4.3** Counters in a row

**Notes:**

▶ The numbers chosen should take account of children's facility with the forward number word sequence (FNWS).
▶ The range of numbers used can be varied.
▶ The activity is suitable for whole class, small group or individuals.
▶ This activity can help children learn to count-on.

**Materials:** Overhead projector and overhead projector counters, strip of card, individual whiteboards and marker pens.

## ACTIVITY IA4.4: On the Mat

**Intended learning:** Counting the number of children in a group.

**Description:** Children walk, run, skip or dance indoors or outdoors. Large mats (or circles) are placed (or drawn) in the area. On the signal, the children move to the nearest mat (or circle) and stand still. They count how many children are in the group. When they agree about the number of children they sit down holding up the correct number of fingers. The teacher asks a volunteer to check each group by touching each child in turn as the class counts together. Repeat.

Variations include:

▶ Fewer mats (or rings) will give larger collections of children to count.
▶ Children could stop when the music stops.
▶ The rule might be: no more than six on a mat.
▶ The teacher could state the number of children to be on each mat or each mat (or ring) could display a different number saying how many children should sit there.
▶ One child from each group could be asked to collect a number card to indicate the number of children on the mat.

**Notes:**

▶ Children might not know the number word sequence.
▶ Children might not coordinate the number words with the children on the mat.
▶ Children might forget to include themselves in the count.
▶ Suitable for whole class or large groups.

**Materials:** Large mats.

## ACTIVITY IA4.5: Where Do I Go?

**Intended Learning:** To count perceptual items correctly and to order numbers correctly.

**Description:** The teacher decides which numbers to use for the game. This will depend on the children's ability to identify numerals and also their forward number word sequence range. For example, a child might be able to say the FNWS to 20 but unable to identify some of the numerals from 1 to 20 and to count collections of up to 20 items. The teacher can decide to work in a range such as: 1 to 5, 1 to 10, 1 to 15 or 1 to 20. If working in the 1 to 10 range, the numerals 1 to 10 are written four times on cards, each time in a different color (for example, red, yellow, green and blue). Four other cards displaying a circle of each of the four colors are also needed. The teacher places the four colored circles in a column, shuffles all the other cards (40 if working in 1 to 10 range), and then places ten cards face down at the side of each circle. The teacher asks a child to turn over any card. If, as above, the child was to turn a red 8 (see Figure 4.4), the teacher then explains that this card is presently in the yellow row and must be placed in the red row in the eighth position. The child might need to start at one and count each card to determine the eighth position. The child then picks up the card in the eighth position in the red row and replaces it with the red 8. This new card must then be placed in its correct position. The game ends when each card is in its correct position as shown in Figure 4.4.

Where do I go?

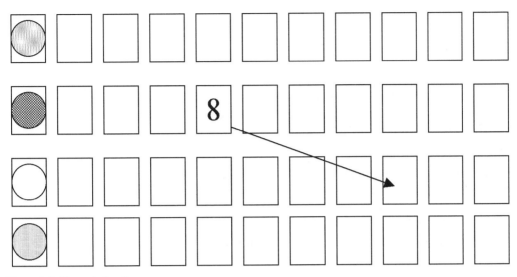

**Figure 4.4** Where do I go?

**Notes:**

▶ This activity is appropriate for children having difficulty coordinating number words and items or having difficulty with numeral identification.

▶ When children are familiar with this game they might observe that the numbers in a given column are the same. If they make a mistake in their perceptual counting the numbers are not the same and the error is apparent.

▶ This game helps those children who have difficulty with the identification and ordering of teen numbers.

▶ If the child turns over a card that is already in its correct position, any other card is turned over.

▶ Initially, two rows (two colors) rather than four could be used in order to reduce the complexity of the task.

▶ Children who count from one, often find more efficient ways of determining a card's placement. This is especially the case if cards in the 1 to 20 range are used. For example, there is an incentive to see that 19 is one less than 20 rather than count up to 19 from 1.

▶ This activity is suitable for individuals, pairs or small groups where children take turns in placing cards.

**Materials:** 40 cards (numbers 1 to 10 in four different colors), 4 colored circle cards.

## ACTIVITY IA4.6: Toy Box

**Intended learning:** To establish the number of items in (numerosity of) a collection.

**Description:** Place a collection of small objects in the center of the table. One child rolls a large die labeled 0 and 1. If the die displays 1, the child takes one object. If the die displays 0, the child does not take anything. Take turns with each child building individual collections. When one child has a few objects in their collection ask: *How many do you have?* Encourage the child to touch and count each object, saying each number in turn. Ask: *How many altogether?* Emphasize that the last number in the count corresponds to the number of objects in the collection. Continue to play until one child has five objects.

▶   Vary the size of the objects counted (larger objects, smaller objects).
▶   Vary the objects in the collections, sometimes all the same, sometimes different.
▶   Vary the way the children collect the objects, for example arranging in a row, a ring, or a container.
▶   Increase the number counted to a number in the range 6 to 10.
▶   Use a die numbered with 0,1, and 2.

**Notes:**

▶   Children might have difficulty keeping track of the number words as they are counting.
▶   Children might not know the number word sequence very well.
▶   Children might have difficulty coordinating a number word with each item.
▶   Suitable for small groups.

**Materials:** Collections of objects (toys), large die marked 0 and 1.

## ACTIVITY IA4.7: Teddy Bear Walk

**Intended learning:** To use counting-on and counting-back or more advanced strategies in addition and subtraction.

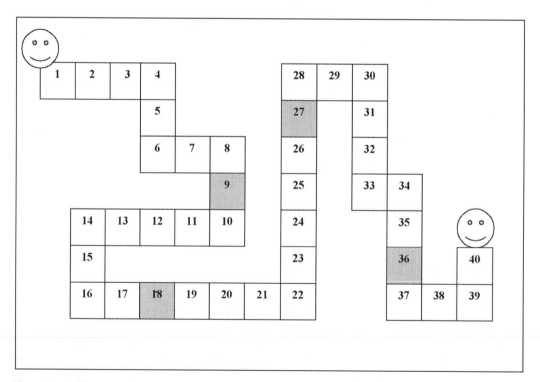

**Figure 4.5** Teddy Bear Walk

**Description:** Players take turns to: (a) roll a die; (b) predict which square their teddy bear will walk to by taking the number of steps indicated on the die; (c) move their teddy bear the number of steps and check whether or not their calculation was correct. The game ends when one teddy bear reaches the end of the walk.

**Notes:**

▶ Typically the die (or spinner) has the numerals 1, 2 and 3. When appropriate, a die with 1 and 2 only could be used.

▶ To include subtraction tasks, when a teddy bear lands on a shaded square the next roll will be a subtraction task and the teddy bear will need to retrace steps.

▶ If the teacher is present, observe the strategies used to solve the addition and subtraction tasks.

▶ The board can be altered to suit the children playing.

**Materials:** Teddy bear walk board, a teddy bear or counter for each player.

## ACTIVITY IA4.8: Chains

**Intended learning:** To establish the number of items in (numerosity of) a collection.

**Description:** Work in a large indoor or outdoor space. Provide 5 or 6 children with a colored band or braid. Children move as instructed by the teacher for example, slither like a snake, jump like a kangaroo. At the teacher's signal everyone must freeze (stand still). Children wearing bands touch as many children as they can without moving their feet! The children who have been touched form a human chain. Each chain must count how many and shout out their number. The game continues with each chain holding hands and moving together. When they freeze, each member of the chain can reach out to touch and collect new members. Continue until everyone (or almost everyone) joins a chain, and continue to count how many.

**Notes:**

▶ Chains should not be too long. Teachers need to be aware of the movement required by the chain.

▶ Define the area in which the children may move.

▶ Check the count! Fewer children with bands will give longer chains to count.

▶ Ask two chains to join together. *How many now?*

▶ Ask children to guess before counting. Ask: *Who has more than 3? Who has fewer than 4? Which chain is longest? Which is the shortest?*

▶ Join chains together and ask a child to count how many children. The class can join in the count.

▶ Suitable for class or large group.

**Materials:** Colored bands or braids.

## ACTIVITY IA4.9: Give me Five

**Intended learning:** To establish the number of items in (numerosity of) a collection.

**Description:** Group ten children into pairs. Place ping-pong balls numbered 1 to 10 in a bag or box. One pair of children pick out a ping-pong ball and say the number (with assistance if required). Each pair then goes to collect that number of named objects for example, pencils, books, beanbags. They bring the items back and place them in a hoop or container. Each pair checks the other children's collections to see if they have the correct number of objects. The group then counts each collection in turn using a child to act as pointer. Continue the activity with other numbers.

▶ Vary the activity by giving each pair a different number.
▶ Collect mixed items, for example, one pencil, one book, one beanbag.
▶ Place out containers with a differently numbered ping-pong ball in each. Children match the collections to the numbers.
▶ Use a wider range of numbers.
▶ Use bundles of straws or towers of cubes to extend to 2-digit numbers for example, ask children for 26 straws or cubes.
▶ Use a bead-string, number track or line to show how many are collected.

**Notes:**

▶ Children might have difficulty keeping track of the number words as they are counting.
▶ Children might not know the number word sequence very well.
▶ Children might have difficulty coordinating a number word with each item.
▶ Suitable for whole class, small groups or pairs.

**Materials:** Ping-pong balls numbered 1 to 10, bag or box, objects to collect, hoops or containers.

## ACTIVITY IA4.10: Pass It On

**Intended learning:** To establish the number of items in (numerosity of) a collection.

**Description:** Children sit in a circle. Each child has a collection of small objects, (for example, five objects). One child rolls a large die labeled 0, 1, 2. If the die lands on 0, they do not pass anything on. The next child rolls the die. If it lands on 1 or 2 they pass on that number of objects to the child sitting on their left. The game continues with each child taking a turn. When one child has a few in their collection, ask: *How many do you have?* Encourage children to touch and count each object, saying each number in turn. Ask: *How many altogether?* Emphasize that the last number in the count corresponds to the number of objects in the collection. The game continues until one child has run out of objects or one child reaches a specified number of items (for example, ten).

▶ Vary the objects in the collections – sometimes all the same, sometimes different.
▶ Vary the way the children collect the objects, for example, placing in a row, in a ring, in a container.
▶ Increase the number counted to a number in the range 11 to 15.
▶ Use a die numbered with 0, 1, 2, and 3.

**Notes:**

▶  Children might have difficulty keeping track of the number words as they are counting.
▶  Children might not know the number word sequence very well.
▶  Children might have difficulty coordinating a number word with each item.
▶  Suitable for large or small groups.

**Materials:** Collections of objects, large die marked with 0, 1, and 2.

# 5
# Structuring Numbers 1 to 10

## Summary

This chapter focusses on a new and important topic in early numeracy, that is, structuring numbers in the range 1 to 10. This topic relates to children's facility to combine and partition numbers without using counting-by-ones. Instead the child uses an emerging knowledge of doubles, and the five and ten structure of numbers, that is, using five and ten as reference points. Learning this topic provides an important basis for moving beyond a reliance on counting-by-ones.

## TOPIC OVERVIEW

### Combining and Partitioning Small Numbers

In Chapters 3 and 4, we explained several significant aspects of the developing number knowledge of children typical of 4–6-year-olds. These include numerosity, knowledge of number words and numerals (Chapter 3), and the development of early counting strategies (Chapter 4). Around the time that children have developed early counting strategies they also should learn to combine and partition small numbers without counting. This involves working with numbers, first in the range 1 to 10, and then in the range from 1 to 20.

> *Doubles to 10.* Typically the first combinations that children learn are the doubles of numbers in the range 1 to 5, that is, 1 and 1, 2 and 2, … 5 and 5.
> *Partitioning numbers 2 to 5.* Children can then learn the partitions of numbers in the range 2 to 5, that is, partitioning 2 into 1 + 1, 3 into 1 + 2, 2 + 1 and similarly for 4 and 5.
> *Partitioning numbers 6 to 10.* Children can then learn the partitions of numbers in the range 6 to 10. Six can be partitioned into 5 + 1, 4 + 2, 3 + 3, and so on, and similarly for 7 onward.
> *Doubles to 20.* Although instruction at this stage is mainly limited to the range 1 to 10, children can also begin to learn the doubles of the numbers from 6 to 10.

#### Approaches to Teaching Combining and Partitioning

Instructional strategies for combining and partitioning numbers in the range 1 to 10 typically involve using spatial patterns and finger patterns. Spatial patterns can be flashed on the overhead projector and children can be asked about combining and partitioning numbers represented in the spatial patterns. In the case of finger patterns, children can be asked to make finger patterns by placing their hands on top of their heads, in this way children are unable to observe their own patterns. Hands can be brought to the front for checking or correcting patterns. Spatial patterns and finger patterns are discussed in more detail below.

# Spatial Patterns

## Subitizing

**Subitizing** involves: (a) ascribing numerosity to a collection of items, typically a spatial arrangement of dots, but not necessarily so; (b) doing so immediately; and (c) doing so without counting the items. Writers and researchers in psychology and education have discussed and examined the phenomenon of subitizing since the 1940s. In psychological experiments, examining subitizing typically involves using a projection device to flash spatial arrangements of dots onto a screen, for a fraction of a second. When subitizing is examined in this way, adults typically can subitize collections of up to about five or six. Techniques involving **flashing** various collections of dots have been used extensively in research into infants' awareness of quantity.

For our purposes, activities with spatial arrangements, particularly regular patterns, can be important in young children's number learning. For many years, activities involving dot patterns have had an important place in early number instruction. Activities that are considered useful range from activities involving the use of materials such as dice, dominoes and cards, to instructional procedures where patterns are momentarily displayed (flashed).

As discussed above, an important instructional goal for early number instruction, is for children to be able to combine and partition small numbers without counting. Activities with spatial patterns can be one important avenue for developing children's knowledge with combining and partitioning. Teaching activities where the teacher briefly displays a spatial pattern, using an overhead projector, have been found to be beneficial for developing this knowledge. Initially, these activities can focus on developing children's familiarity with the standard dice patterns, for the numbers from one to six. Patterns where the dots appear in two horizontal rows, can also be used. In similar vein, instruction can involve flashing patterns on a five-frame or a ten-frame (using an overhead projector) and encouraging children to think numerically about what they have seen.

## Combining and Partitioning Using Spatial Patterns

Combining and partitioning can be introduced when children have developed familiarity with the patterns to six. Combining activities can involve using dots in two colors, for example, a 5-pattern consisting of two red dots forming a 2-pattern, and three green dots forming a 3-pattern. Children are asked to describe what they saw when the pattern was flashed. Similarly, partitioning can involve the teacher flashing a 4-pattern, and asking the children to describe two numbers that make up the 4-pattern. Partitioning activities of this kind can be extended to numbers in the range 6 to 10.

# Finger Patterns

The use of finger patterns in association with number activities such as counting, adding, subtracting, and so on is very widespread, being used in many cultures and by adults as well as children. For a long time, use of finger patterns typically was ignored or actively discouraged in classrooms, and for many children, using fingers was quite a prominent activity but it was carried out surreptitiously with fingers moving rapidly but hidden under the desk.

## Finger Patterns: Why and When?

The current view taken is that, in the early years, use of finger patterns should be encouraged because this can support the development of more sophisticated arithmetical strategies. In the middle and upper primary years, and beyond to adulthood, there are some instances where it makes sense to use finger patterns to support or augment arithmetical thinking. On the other hand, there are some ways that older children use fingers to support their mental arithmetic that are not regarded as being useful or productive. These typically involve children using long sequences based on counting-by-ones to work out additions and subtractions involving 2-digit numbers, or perhaps children counting-by-ones to solve multiplication or division problems. In cases such as these, children use a double count or a triple count that involves using their fingers to keep track.

## Numbers in the Range 1 to 5

Before doing combining and partitioning activities involving finger patterns, children need to be familiar with the basic patterns for numbers in the range 1 to 5 on each hand. Initially, some children will need to raise their fingers sequentially while looking at their fingers and counting to the required number. With practice most children can learn to raise fingers simultaneously and without looking at their hand, to make finger patterns on either hand, for numbers in the range 1 to 5.

## Numbers in the Range 6 to 10 using 5 as a Reference

Children's knowledge of finger patterns for numbers in the range 1 to 5 can be extended to numbers in the range 6 to 10. The patterns for these numbers should be made with five fingers on one hand. Thus seven is made as five on one hand and two on the other, and so on, and these patterns can be learned as combinations involving 5 and a number in the range 1 to 5. This supports the learning of five as a reference point (see below).

## Adding Two Numbers in the Range 1 to 5

Finger patterns involving one number on each hand, can also be learned for the doubles (1 + 1, 2 + 2, ... 5 + 5). This can be extended to all of the 25 combinations involving two numbers in the range 1 to 5, where one number is shown on each hand. Children should be encouraged to use finger patterns to work out the answers to these combinations, that is, without counting-from-one and without counting-by-ones. For example, in solving 4 + 3, raise the fifth finger on the 'four-hand' and lower one finger on the 'three-hand'. This results in the familiar pattern of 5 + 2 making 7.

## Five and Ten as Reference Points in the Range 1 to 10

As indicated in the earlier sections, children's beginning knowledge about adding and subtracting numbers develops in two main strands. One of these concerns the development of counting strategies which culminate in the advanced counting-by-one strategies, that is, counting-on-from, counting-on-to, counting-back-from and counting-back-to (Chapter 6). The second strand concerns children's developing abilities to combine and partition numbers without counting. An important part of the second strand is to use five and ten as reference points.

## Why Use Five and Ten as Reference Points?

Most adults and older children understand the tens and ones structure of numbers between 10 and 100. The natural thing is to think of a number such as 54 as comprising five tens and four ones. This structure is inherent in the numeration system because the system is a base-ten system. To use five as well as ten as a reference point is to think of numbers in terms of their tens and five structure. Thus 54 is 5 tens and one five less one; 17 is one ten, one five and two more; and 28 is three tens less two. In this way any number is no more than two from a reference point number (5, 10, 15, 20, and so on). Because of this, children who are fluent with five and ten as reference points are unlikely to rely on long sequences of counting-by-ones when adding or subtracting (so, too, with multiplication and division). This is the strong argument for teaching children from an early age to use five and ten as reference points. We can suppose that in countries and cultures where use of the abacus is prominent or use of the abacus has a strong historical tradition, using five and ten as reference points is virtually a natural occurrence.

## Five as a Reference Point

The notion of five as a reference point takes two main forms. First, for the numbers less than five, children know these numbers in terms of their five-complement, that is the number that goes with them to make five. Alternatively, we could say that the partitions of five are strongly emphasized in instruction, notwithstanding that children also need to know the partitions of all of the other numbers in the range 1 to 10. Second, for the numbers greater than five, children need to know these numbers in terms of their five-plus structure (five-plus-two for seven, five-plus-three for eight, and so on).

## Adding through Five

Adding through five can be used to work out the sum of two numbers with the answer in the range 6 to 10. As an example, a child might work out 4 and 3, by saying 4 and 1 make 5, and 2 more is 7. Three and six is calculated by saying 3 and 2 more is 5, and 5 and 4 is 9, or by changing 3 and 6 into 4 and 5. A key point about these calculations is that they do not involve counting-by-ones.

*Three steps.* Typically, these calculations involve three kinds of steps. First, the child partitions five, using the first addend: 5 is 4 + X. Thus in working out 4 and 3, the first step is to partition 5, knowing that 4 is the first number in the partition. Thus 5 is partitioned into 4 and 1. The second step is to partition the second addend 3, using the second number in the partition of five (1). Thus 3 is partitioned into 1 and 2. The final step is to add the second number in the partition of 3, that is 2, to 5. Thus 2 is added to 5 to make 7. Similarly, 3 and 6 could involve: (a) partitioning 5 into 2 and 3; (b) partitioning 6 into 2 and 4; and (c) adding 4 to 5 to obtain 9.

*Automatized knowledge.* In order to add through five the child needs to have automatized three segments of knowledge. Automatized knowledge is knowledge that is immediately available. First, the child needs to be able to partition 5. Second, the child needs to be able to partition any of the numbers 2 to 10. And third, the child needs to be able to add to 5, any number in the range 1 to 5.

## ASSESSMENT TASK GROUPS

### List of Assessment Task Groups

A5.1: Making finger patterns for numbers in the range 1 to 5
A5.2: Making finger patterns for numbers in the range 6 to 10
A5.3: Naming and visualizing domino patterns 1 to 6
A5.4: Naming and visualizing pair-wise patterns on a ten frame
A5.5: Naming and visualizing five-wise patterns on a ten frame
A5.6: Partitions of 5 and 10
A5.7: Addition and subtraction in the range 1 to 10

**TASK GROUP A5.1:** Making Finger Patterns for Numbers in the Range 1 to 5

**Materials:** None.
**What to do and say:** *Show me three on your fingers please.* Similarly, *2, 5, 1, 4. Now show me on your other hand: 3, 2, 5, 4, 1.*

Show me three on your fingers please.

**Notes:**

▶ Look for children who apparently need to look at their fingers. Also, look for children who raise fingers sequentially. Children who are facile with finger patterns will raise their fingers simultaneously and will not need to look at their fingers.

▶ Look for differences within one child, or across several children, in the ways they use their fingers on these tasks, for example, the particular fingers used to show one, two, and so on.

▶ Children's facility to make and read finger patterns is important when they use their fingers to keep track of counting. It is very common for children to use finger-based, counting strategies when doing addition, subtraction, multiplication or division calculations.

## TASK GROUP A5.2: Making Finger Patterns for Numbers in the Range 6 to 10

**Materials:** None.

**What to do and say:** *Can you show me 6 fingers please?* Similarly, 9, 7, 10, 8.

Show me eight.

**Notes:**

▶ The notes for Task Group A5.1 are also relevant to this task group.

▶ Many children are less facile with finger patterns in the range 6 to 10 compared with 1 to 5.

▶ Children might raise five fingers on one hand simultaneously, and then raise the additional fingers sequentially.

## TASK GROUP A5.3: Naming and Visualizing Domino Patterns 1 to 6

**Materials:** A card for each of the domino patterns from 1 to 6.

**What to do and say:** Flash cards in random order. *Tell me how many dots you see. What does the four pattern look like? Can you show me in the air?* Similarly with the other domino patterns.

**Notes:**

▶ Initially, children learn to name domino patterns in a pictorial sense (similar to the way they might learn to say 'dog' when shown a picture of a dog) rather than necessarily in a numerical sense.

▶ These kinds of spatial patterns can be an important basis for the development of number concepts. Children use visualized spatial patterns to keep track of counting when doing addition, subtraction, multiplication or division calculations.

▶ As well, facility with spatial patterns is an important basis for strategies that do not involve counting by ones.

Tell me how many dots you see

## TASK GROUP A5.4: Naming and Visualizing Pair-wise Patterns on a Ten Frame

**Materials:** A card showing a ten frame with the **pair-wise pattern** for each number from 1 to 10 (ten cards in all).

**What to do and say:** Flash cards in random order. *Tell me how many dots you see. What does four look like on the ten frame? Can you show me in the air?* Similarly with the other numbers.

**Notes:**

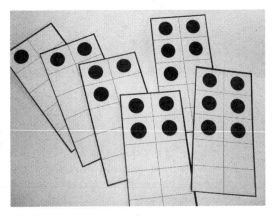

▶ The pair-wise patterns are made by progressively filling the columns of a 2 × 5 ten frame (2 rows and 5 columns).

▶ Children who take a few seconds to name a pattern, rather than answer immediately, might be visualizing the pattern and then counting the dots.

▶ Facility with these patterns is an important basis for strategies that do not involve counting by ones.

Pair-wise patterns on a ten-Frame

## TASK GROUP A5.5: Naming and Visualizing Five-Wise Patterns on a Ten Frame

**Materials:** A card showing a ten frame with the **five-wise (quinary) pattern** for each number from 1 to 10 (ten cards in all).

**What to do and say:** Flash cards in random order. *Tell me how many dots you see. What does six look like on the ten frame? Can you show me in the air?* Similarly with the other numbers.

**Notes:**

▶ The notes for Task Group A5.4 are also relevant to this task group.

▶ The five-wise patterns are made by progressively filling the rows of a 2 × 5 ten frame (2 rows and 5 columns).

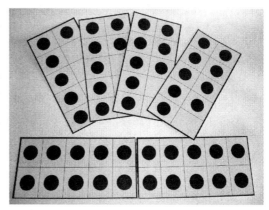

Five-wise patterns on a Ten-Frame

## TASK GROUP A5.6: Partitions of 5 and 10

**Materials:** None.

**What to do and say:** *I will say a number and you say the number that goes with it to make five: 3, 4, 2, 1.*

*I will say a number and you say the number that goes with it to make ten: 9, 5, 8, 3, and so on.*

**Notes:**

▶ Children usually have less difficulty when the unknown number is 1 or 2.

▶ After the child responds, they can be shown the number on a ten frame. In this way a correct response can be confirmed and an incorrect response can be reconsidered.

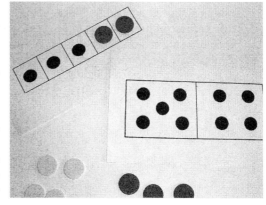

Partitions of 5 and 10

## TASK GROUP A5.7: Addition and Subtraction in the Range 1 to 10

**Materials:** Ten frames showing the pair-wise patterns (see Task Group A5.4) and the five-wise patterns (see Task Group A5.5).

**What to do and say:** Flash the pair-wise pattern for 6. *What number did you see? What is 6 and 2? Tell me how you worked that out?* Similarly, 4 + 3, 8 + 1, 5 + 3, and so on.

Flash the five-wise pattern for 7. *What number did you see? What is 7 and 2? Tell me how you worked that out?* Similarly, 4 + 2, 3 + 5, 6 + 3, and so on.

Flash the pair-wise pattern for 6. *What number did you see? What is 6 take away 2? Tell me how you worked that out?* Similarly, 9 – 6, 7 – 4, 8 – 2, 6 – 4, and so on.

Flash the five-wise pattern for 9. *What number did you see? What is 9 take away 3? Tell me how you worked that out?* Similarly, 6 – 4, 8 – 3, 7 – 5, and so on.

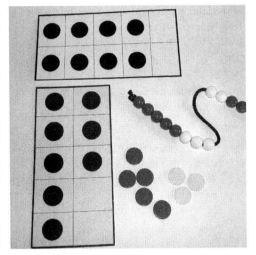

Addition and subtraction settings in the range 1–10

**Notes:**

▶ The general principle applied in these tasks is to flash the first stated number only. In the case of addition, the first addend is flashed. In the case of subtraction, the **minuend** is flashed.

▶ The purpose of these tasks is to gauge whether the children can use visualized patterns, rather than counting on and counting back, to solve addition and subtraction tasks.

▶ Children are likely to work flexibly with pair-wise, five-wise or other patterns.

▶ It is important to listen carefully to the child's explanation and to temper expectations that the child should use a particular strategy or pattern.

# INSTRUCTIONAL ACTIVITIES

## List of Instructional Activities

IA5.1: Bunny Ears
IA5.2: The Great Race
IA5.3: Quick Dots
IA5.4: Make Five Concentration
IA5.5 Five and Ten Frame Flashes
IA5.6: Memory Game
IA5.7: Domino Flashes
IA5.8: Domino Fish
IA5.9: Domino Snap
IA5.10: Make Ten Fish

## ACTIVITY IA5.1: Bunny Ears

**Intended learning:** To think figuratively about numbers in the range 1 to 10 and to partition numbers in the range 1 to 10. (For an explanation of figurative counting, see the Topic Overview for Chapter 4.)
**Description:** Children make two fists with their hands and then raise these to the top of their head to represent two bunny's ears. The teacher then says a number, for example, 6, and the child raises fingers on both hands to make the number. One child might raise 4 fingers on one hand and 2 on the other while another child might raise 5 fingers on one hand and 1 on the other. A third child might raise 3 fingers on each hand. The children must try to do this without looking at their hands, but some initially might find it difficult and have to check by looking. If it is decided to emphasize the five-plus combinations, children could be asked to make combinations six to ten with five on one hand, for example 7 would be 5 and 2, and 9 would be 5 and 4. A simpler task involves children holding one hand above their heads and the teacher asks them to show 1 to 5 fingers.

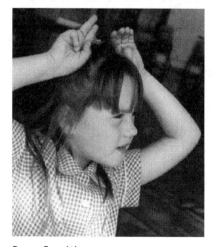

Bunny Ears (1)

Bunny Ears (2)

**Notes:**

▶ Young children might have problems in physically holding down fingers when they cannot look at them. If this is the case, allow them to check their finger pattern.

▶ This activity is suitable for pairs, small groups and whole class.

▶ Children should progress to keeping their hands above their heads, but still needing to count-on from 5, while raising each finger.

▶ Finally, children should be able to flash the finger patterns for 6 through 10 without counting.

▶ Vary the activity by showing children a ten frame card and asking children to show the Bunny Ears for that amount.

▶ Vary the activity by showing children a numeral card and asking children to show the Bunny Ears for that amount.

▶ Vary the activity with the teacher showing the Bunny Ears and children are asked to say the amount.

**Materials:** None.

## ACTIVITY IA5.2: The Great Race

**Intended learning:** To ascribe number to regular spatial patterns and match to a numeral in the range 1 to 6.

**Description:** A racer is placed in each starting position. A 1 to 6 dot die is rolled to indicate which racer advances. For example, if the five pattern is rolled, the racer in the lane with the numeral 5 advances one space. Continue rolling in succession until one of the racers reaches the finish (see Figure 5.1).

**Notes:**

▶ Initially children might need to count the spots on the die, but the goal is for children to recognize the pattern without counting.

▶ To promote visualization and subitizing, have one child roll the die and another child use a cup to cover the die after it is rolled.

▶ This game can be played individually or with partners taking turns rolling and advancing the indicated racer.

**Materials:** Great Race game board, 1 to 6 dot die, six game markers to represent the racers (such as plastic bears).

*Note*: It is recommended that all markers are identical so the focus is on the numeral rather than other attributes such as color or size.

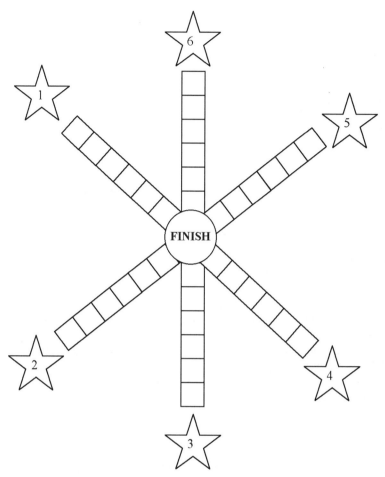

**Figure 5.1** Great Race game board

## ACTIVITY IA5.3: Quick Dots

**Intended learning:** To subitize (ascribe number instantaneously) in the context of regular spatial patterns to nine and irregular spatial patterns to five.

**Description:** Spatial pattern cards (see Figure 5.2), are flashed (displayed for approximately half a second). Students are asked how many dots they saw.

**Notes:**

▶ The ability to subitize helps children to develop structures for quantity. Subitizing can help advance the child's understanding of quantity to that of a composite unit, rather than as a numerical composite.

▶ Initially, children might visualize the pattern and then count the dots in the mental image. While this shows a strength in visualization, it is not subitizing.

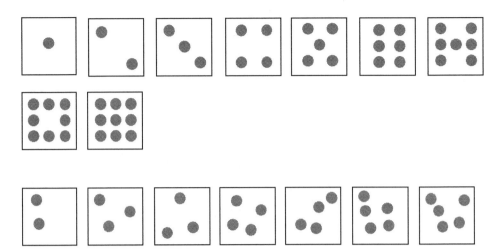

**Figure 5.2** Pattern cards

▶ It is important to realize that children might learn the number for regular patterns in a pictorial sense; that is, it might be attached to the shape of the pattern, rather than to a quantitative understanding.

▶ Along with stating the amount shown, children should be encouraged to describe the arrangement of the dots, especially for larger quantities.

▶ Students should be able to name and create the quantity. A related activity is to ask children to create the pattern using counters when prompted with a spoken number word or displayed numeral.

**Materials:** Spatial pattern cards.

## ACTIVITY IA5.4: Make Five Concentration

**Intended learning:** To develop facility with combinations to five.

**Description:** A set of twelve cards, two each of five frames for 0 to 5 (see Figure 5.3), are arranged in an array, face down on the table. Students try to collect pairs of cards that add to five (make five). The first player turns over one card from the array and announces the number represented. The player then turns a second card face up, announces the number represented and determines if the two cards total 5. For example, if a five frame showing 3 is turned up it would need to be matched with a five frame showing 2. If a match is made, the player keeps the cards. If a match is not made the cards are returned to their face-down position. Whether or not a match is made, play moves to the next player. Play continues until all cards have been matched. The winner is the child with the most cards.

**Notes:**

▶ The filled and empty cells in the five frame provide visual support, which can help children work out what quantity is needed to make 5.

▶ A more advanced version can be played using numerals 0 to 5 or a mix of five frames and numerals.

**Materials:** Five frame cards showing the quantities 0 to 5.

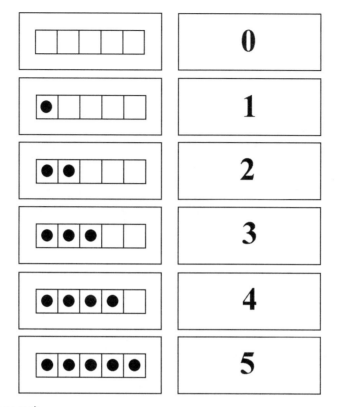

**Figure 5.3** Five frame cards

# ACTIVITY IA5.5: Five and Ten Frame Flashes

**Intended learning:** To develop facility with five and ten.

**Description:** A five frame is displayed on the overhead projector. The teacher asks: *How many squares are there?* Opaque counters are placed in some of the squares without initially showing the children (with the projector off or the light shielded with a sheet of cardboard). The five frame is then flashed (briefly displayed). The teacher asks: *How many dots? How many empty squares?* If preferred, a five-seat minibus and smiley faces on transparent counters (see Figure 5.4) can be used in place of the five frame.

The same procedure is followed using a ten frame or ten-seat minibus (see Figure 5.5). Doubles and five-plus patterns can be flashed.

**Notes:**

▶    A flash should be about half a second (not long enough for the items to be counted).
▶    These could be combined with finger patterns (bunny ears) described in Activity IA5.1.
▶    Children could also have their own five and ten frames and make combinations given by the teacher.
▶    This activity can be used with whole class, small groups, or individual children.

**Materials:** Five and ten frames, minibuses, counters.

Five  frame

**Figure 5.4** Five frame minibus

Ten frame

**Figure 5.5** Using ten frame and ten frame minibus

## ACTIVITY IA5.6: Memory Game

**Intended learning:** To increase children's figurative knowledge of numbers in the range 1 to 10.

**Description:** Use two or four sets of dot cards, either pair-wise or five-wise patterns for 1 to 10 (see Figures 5.6 and 5.7.) Mix up the cards and place them face down on table. The children take turns in turning over two cards. If they find a matching pair, they keep the pair. The winner is the child with the most cards at the end of the game.

**Materials:** Four sets of pair-wise dot cards and four sets of five-wise dot cards.

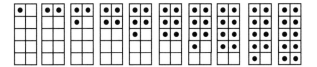

**Figure 5.6** Pair-wise dot cards

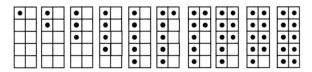

**Figure 5.7** Five-wise dot cards

**Notes:**

▶    This is a game for pairs or small groups.
▶    This game can be played with a set of playing cards with the picture cards removed.
▶    To make the game easier for less able children, the range might be limited to 1 to 5, for example.
▶    Ask children to say the number of dots on the card that is the double of the number.
▶    To make the game more challenging mix sets of pair-wise and five-wise dot cards so children need to match cards as shown in Figure 5.8.

**Figure 5.8** Five-wise and Pair-wise dot card for 6

## ACTIVITY IA5.7: Domino Flashes

**Intended learning:** To ascribe number to domino patterns.

**Description:** Using an overhead projector or large domino cards (Figure 5.9), the teacher briefly displays (flashes) the pattern and children either say the number of dots they see or make the number on their fingers and display their finger pattern.

**Notes:**

▶    This can be extended to other patterns such as the five-plus or doubles patterns.

**Materials:** Domino patterns (to display on the overhead projector) or large domino cards.

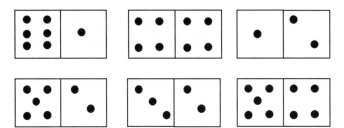

**Figure 5.9** Domino cards

## ACTIVITY IA5.8: Domino Fish

**Intended learning:** To extend knowledge of domino patterns

**Description:** The activity is played the same as Fish. Instead of traditional playing cards, the teacher makes up cards containing the domino patterns (see Figure 5.9) and the matching numerals. Five cards are dealt to each player. The remaining cards are placed in a stack in the centre of the players. Players try to make matching pairs of domino and numeral cards. Players take turns to ask another player for a particular card. If the player being asked does not have the required card they say: *Fish!* The player seeking the card takes the top card off the stack. The game continues until one player has no more cards. Players see how many pairs they have.

**Notes:**

▶ This game can be extended to other patterns such as the five-plus or doubles patterns.

**Materials:** Domino pattern cards, numeral cards.

## ACTIVITY IA5.9: Domino Snap

**Intended learning:** To extend knowledge of domino patterns.

**Description:** The activity is played the same as Snap. Instead of traditional playing cards, the teacher makes up cards containing the domino patterns (see Figure 5.9) and the matching numerals (as in Activity IA5.8). The cards are divided between two players and kept face down. Players take turns to put their top card on the stack. If this card matches the card on top of the stack, each player tries to put their hand on the stack saying 'Snap!', as they do it. The game proceeds until one player has all the cards.

**Notes:**

▶   This can be extended to other patterns such as the five plus or doubles patterns.

**Materials:** Domino pattern cards large enough for children to manipulate, numeral cards.

## ACTIVITY IA5.10: Make Ten Fish

**Intended learning:** To learn the partitions of ten.

**Description:** The activity is played the same as Fish. Instead of traditional playing cards, numeral cards 1 to 9 are used. These are clearer than playing cards. Five cards are dealt to each player. The remaining cards are placed in a stack in the centre of the players. Players try to make matching pairs of cards adding to 10. Players take turns to ask another player for a particular card. If the player being asked does not have the required card they say *Fish!*. The player seeking the card takes the top card off the stack. The game continues until one player has no more cards. Players see how many pairs they have.

**Notes:**

▶   The game provides examples of missing **subtrahend** tasks (for example: *I have six. How many more will make ten?*)

**Materials:** At least four sets of numeral cards from 1 to 10.

# 6

# Advanced Counting, Addition and Subtraction

## Summary

This chapter continues on from Chapter 4 with a focus on the development of more advanced counting-by-ones strategies and the use of these strategies to solve addition and subtraction tasks. These are the strategies of counting-on, which includes counting-up-from and counting-up-to, and counting-back which includes counting-back-from and counting-back to. The chapter explains clearly the place of theses strategies in the overall development of early numeracy.

## TOPIC OVERVIEW

### Advanced Counting-by-ones Strategies

In Chapter 4 we describe how the counting-on child would solve a task such as 8 + 5 presented with two screened collections. Children who can count-on in this way can develop (or perhaps already have developed) similar kinds of strategies for subtractive tasks. Collectively, these strategies for additive and **subtractive tasks** involving two screened collections, are referred to as the advanced counting-by-ones strategies and they have the following characteristics:

▶ They involve commencing the count from a number other than one, that is they do not involve counting-from-one (in contrast to figurative and perceptual counting).
▶ They involve counting forwards or backwards by ones (in contrast to a non-count-by-one strategy).
▶ They involve some means of keeping track of counting-by-ones, typically using fingers or implicit or explicit double counting. There are four of these strategies in all, and each is typically associated with a particular kind of task. They are **counting-up-from**, **counting-up-to**, counting-back-from, and counting-back-to. Each is explained below.

#### Counting-up-from

Counting-up-from is typically associated with children's solutions of additive tasks involving two screened collections, for example 8 + 5. The counting-on strategy is referred to specifically as counting-up-from.

#### Counting-up-to

Counting-up-to is typically associated with children's solutions of **missing addend** tasks (a kind of subtractive task) where, for example, the child is told there are 8 counters in the first collection and 13 counters in all, and has to figure out how many are in the second collection. The counting-on strategy is referred to specifically as counting-up-to. The child starts at 'eight' and counts up to 'thirteen', and keeps track of the number of counts after eight, that is, five counts. Missing addend tasks are described in the section on assessment tasks (see below).

## Counting-back-from

Counting-back-from is typically associated with children's solutions of a second kind of subtractive task, that is, the removed items task. In this case the child is told how many counters in a collection, and then how many are removed from the collection. For example, there are 13 counters under the screen, and then 5 are removed, how many are left under the screen? The child uses a counting-back strategy which is referred to specifically as counting-back-from, that is, the child starts at 13, and counts back 5 from 13, to obtain the answer 8. Removed items tasks are described in the section on assessment tasks (see below).

## Counting-back-to

Counting-back-to is typically associated with children's solutions of a third kind of subtractive task, that is, the missing subtrahend task. In this case the child is told how many counters in a collection and how many remain after some are removed. For example, there are 13 counters under the screen, and then some are removed and 8 remain, how many were removed? The child uses a counting-back strategy which is referred to specifically as counting-back-to, that is, the child starts at 13, and counts back to 8, and keeps track of the number of counts after 13, that is 5. Missing subtrahend tasks are described in the section on assessment tasks (see below).

# Counting-forward-from-one-three-times

A common approach to the initial teaching of addition and subtraction involves giving children word problems to solve and encouraging them to use materials such as counters to solve the problems. Often associated with this approach is the notion that it is important to let children use the materials to solve these problems for an extended sequence of lessons. In these situations children typically use a strategy that we refer to as counting-forward-from-one-three-times. This strategy is used for addition or subtraction problems.

> *Counting-forward-from-one-three-times for addition.* For an addition problem the child counts out the number of counters corresponding to the first addend, then does the same thing for the second addend, and finally counts all of the counters from one.
> *Counting-forward-from-one-three-times for subtraction.* In the case of a subtraction problem, the child counts out the number of counters corresponding to the minuend, then, using the collection just counted out, counts out and removes the number of counters corresponding to the subtrahend, and finally counts the remaining counters.
> *A critique.* We are critical of this approach to instruction because in our view, it tends to perpetuate the use of what we would regard as primitive counting strategies, that is strategies characterized by (a) always counting with perceptual (visible) items, (b) always counting from one, and (c) always counting forwards. An additional, common characteristic of this approach is to have little regard for the relative size of the numbers that the children work with. This, too, we regard as problematic and we expand on this point below.

## Screened Collections versus Word Problems

In the above sections we described four kinds of tasks, one additive and three subtractive, which can be presented using screened collections of counters. Although these tasks could alternatively be presented in word problem format rather than in a format involving screened collections, we would not advocate doing so. We believe that, at least in the initial period, the use of screened collections has benefits over the use of word problems. These benefits include that the children are provided with a consistent setting (collections of counters) which they can easily imagine (when the collections are screened). Also, the use of screened collections facilitates the development of the notion of verification, that is, children come to see that it is possible to check their answers when the collections have been unscreened.

## Choosing Numbers for Additive and Subtractive Tasks

We emphasize that, because the strategies associated with these tasks (the four advanced counting-by-ones strategies described above) involve counting forward or backward, the particular choice of numbers that the teacher uses in posing such tasks, is regarded as very important.

### Counting in the Range 2 to 5 Only

As a general rule, the number of counts the child makes using any particular strategy, should be in the range 2 to 5 only. In terms of advancing children's number knowledge, we think it is unproductive to have children counting long sequences of numbers, and keeping track of their counts, which is inherent to these strategies. Thus, if the instructional goal is to develop these counting strategies, then it would not be useful in our view to present a missing addend task such as $6 + X = 15$ (where it is understood that this is presented using screened collections or as a word problem). Similarly, a removed items task such as $22 - 13$ would not be useful. Nor would an addition task such as $8 + 13$ be useful if one's goal is to develop the counting-up-from strategy.

### Using Advanced Counting-by-ones Strategies in the Range 20 to 100

As explained in the previous paragraph, the tasks that children solve using advanced counting-by-ones strategies should involve counts in the range 2 to 5 only. As long as this principle is kept in mind, these strategies can be used by children in the range 20 to 100. Thus a child might be asked to solve tasks such as the following: (a) an addition task, 38 red counters and 4 green counters; (b) a removed items task, 37 counters are placed under a screen and 3 are removed; (c) a missing addend task, 88 red counters and some green counters make 93 in all; and (d) a missing subtrahend task, 57 counters under a screen, some are removed and 55 remain. Tasks such as those just described, could alternatively be presented as word problems. These kinds of tasks introduce children to addition and subtraction involving numbers throughout the range 20 to 100, and set the scene for addition and subtraction involving two 2-digit numbers (Chapters 8 and 9).

### Finger Patterns and Advanced Counting-by-ones Strategies

Children who have well-developed finger patterns for numbers in the range 1 to 5, will use their fingers to keep track, as part of the advanced counting-by-ones strategies.

*Using fingers to keep track on an additive task.* Thus a child might work out $8 + 5$ by counting-on from 'eight' and raising a finger for each number word from 'nine' onward in turn for the number words from 'nine' to 'thirteen'. The child stops at 'thirteen' because they have raised five fingers (they recognize the finger pattern for five). Thus when they raise the fifth finger, they know that they have made five counts, that is from nine to thirteen. In this case, it is not necessary for the child to separately count the fingers from 'one' to 'five'. Use of finger patterns in this way is relatively sophisticated. That the child raises the five fingers sequentially (versus simultaneously) does not indicate a lack of facility with finger patterns.

*Using fingers to keep track on a missing subtrahend task.* A second example of more facile use of finger patterns is: 11 counters are screened, and then some are removed and now there are only 7. How many counters were removed? The child counts back from 'eleven' and raises a finger for each number word in turn, from 'ten' to 'seven'. The child stops because they got to 'seven', and then looks at their finger pattern and says 'four', that is, the child can recognize the finger pattern for four, without having to count their fingers from one.

## Contrasting Two Solution Strategies Involving Finger Patterns

Two children are asked to solve the additive task 5 + 4 using two screened collections. Both children make use of their fingers to solve the task. The first child raises five fingers on one hand sequentially, then raises four fingers on the other hand sequentially, and then counts their raised fingers from one to nine. The second child counts-on from six to nine, and raises a finger in coordination with each of the number words from six to nine. The first child is using perceptual counting whereas the second is using counting-on. Although the first child has solved an additive task involving two screened collections, they have done so by building perceptual replacements. In the case of the first child, what remains to be seen is whether the child can solve an additive task when the first addend is greater than five, for example, 8 + 4. On such a task it is not feasible for the child to use their fingers to build simultaneously replacements for the two addends eight and four.

## ASSESSMENT TASK GROUPS

### List of Assessment Task Groups

A6.1:  Additive tasks involving two screened collections
A6.2:  Missing addend task involving two screened collections
A6.3:  Removed items task involving a screened collection
A6.4:  Missing subtrahend task involving a screened collection
A6.5:  Comparative subtraction involving two screened collections
A6.6:  Subtraction with bare numbers

## TASK GROUP A6.1: Additive Tasks Involving Two Screened Collections

**Materials:** A collection of counters of one color (red) and a collection of another color (green); two screens of cardboard or cloth.

**What to do and say:** Briefly display and then screen eight red counters. *Here are eight red counters.* Briefly display and then screen five green counters. *Here are five green counters. How many counters altogether?* Similarly with collections such as 9 red and 3 green, 15 red and 2 green, 11 red and 4 green, and so on.

**Notes:**

▶    These tasks are of the same kind as those in Task Group 4.6.
▶    The purpose of these tasks is to gauge the child's ability to use counting on. This strategy is referred to specifically as counting-up-from (for example, counting up three from eight). It is quite common for children to use their fingers to keep track of counting.
▶    Some children will use a strategy that involves little or no counting-by-ones.
▶    Some children might solve these tasks by counting from one. They are apparently unable to use counting-on to solve these kinds of tasks.
▶    In the case of children who are not able solve these tasks, the second collection (green counters) can be unscreened.
▶    The general approach with these tasks is to have the number of counters in the second collection (green counters) typically in the range 2 to 5, and the number in the first collection (red counters) larger than the number in the second collection (green counters). The number in the first collection can be in the range 4 to 20 or beyond 20.

## TASK GROUP A6.2: Missing Addend Task Involving Two Screened Collections

**Materials:** A collection of counters of one color (red) and a collection of another color (green); one screen of cardboard or cloth.

**What to do and say:** Briefly display and then screen four red counters. *Here are four red counters. I am going to add some green counters to those red counters.* Place two green counters with the red counters

Here are four red counters

I added some green counters and now there are six counters. How many green counters did I add?

without allowing the child to see them. *I added some green counters to the four red counters and now there are six counters altogether. How many green counters did I add?* Similarly as follows: 6 + X = 10, 9 + X = 12, 11 + X = 13, and so on.

**Notes:**

▸ The purpose of these tasks is to gauge the child's ability to use counting on. This strategy is referred to specifically as counting-up-to (for example, begin at four and count up to six). It is quite common for children to use their fingers to keep track of counting.

▸ Some children will use a strategy that involves little or no counting-by-ones.

▸ It is common for children initially to misinterpret a missing addend task as an addition task, for example, 4 + X = 6 is misinterpreted as 4 + 6. In such cases the interviewer can present the task again and rephrase the task.

▸ In similar vein to Task Group A6.1, the general approach with these missing addend tasks is to have the number of counters in the second collection (green counters) typically in the range 2 to 5, and the number in the first collection (red counters) larger than the number in the second collection (green counters). The number in the first collection can be in the range 4 to 20 or beyond 20.

## TASK GROUP A6.3: Removed Items Task Involving a Screened Collection

**Materials:** A collection of counters of one color (red); two screens of cardboard or cloth.

**What to do and say:** Briefly display and then screen seven red counters. *Here are seven red counters. I am going to take two counters away.* Remove two counters and screen them without allowing the child to see them. *I took away two of the red counters. How many counters are left?* Similarly as follows: 10 remove 3, 12 remove 4, 16 remove 2, and so on.

**Notes:**

▸ The purpose of these tasks is to gauge the child's ability to use counting-back. This strategy is referred to specifically as counting-back-from (for example, count back two from seven). It is quite common for children to use their fingers to keep track of counting.

▸ Some children will use a strategy that involves little or no counting-by-ones.

▸ In similar vein to Task Group A6.1, the general approach with these removed items tasks is to have the number of removed items in the range 2 to 5.

## TASK GROUP A6.4: Missing Subtrahend Task Involving a Screened Collection

**Materials:** A collection of counters of one color (red); two screens of cardboard or cloth.

**What to do and say:** Briefly display and then screen nine red counters. *Here are nine red counters. I am going to take some counters away.* Remove two counters and screen them without allowing the child to see them. *I had nine red counters, then I took away some of the counters and now there are only seven left. How many counters did I take away?* Similarly as follows: 11 – X = 8, 13 – X = 10, and so on.

**Notes:**

▶ The purpose of these tasks is to gauge the child's ability to use counting back. This strategy is referred to specifically as counting-back-to (for example, begin at nine and count back to seven). It is quite common for children to use their fingers to keep track of counting.

▶ Children who use counting-back-from to solve removed items tasks (Task Group A6.3) might not be able to use counting-back-to to solve missing subtrahend tasks.

▶ Some children will use a strategy that involves little or no counting-by-ones.

▶ In similar vein to Task Group A6.1, the general approach with these tasks is to have the missing subtrahend in the range 2 to 5.

## TASK GROUP A6.5: Comparative Subtraction Involving Two Screened Collections

**Materials:** A collection of counters of one color (red) and a collection of another color (green); two screens of cardboard or cloth.

**What to do and say:** Briefly display and then screen seven red counters. *Here are seven red counters.* Briefly display and then screen four green counters. *Here are four green counters. If I put a green counter on each of the red counters, how many red counters would not be covered with a green counter?* Similarly as follows: 11 red and 7 green, 13 red and 8 green, 16 red and 13 green, and so on.

**Notes:**

▶ Children might use counting-up-to or counting-back-to to solve these tasks. For example, 7 – 4 is solved by starting at 4 and counting-up-to 7 or starting at 7 and counting-back-to 4.

▶ Some children will use a strategy that involves little or no counting-by-ones.

▶ In similar vein to Task Group A6.1, the general approach with these tasks is to have the unknown difference in the range 2 to 5.

## TASK GROUP A6.6: Subtraction with Bare Numbers

**Materials:** Subtraction tasks written on a card in horizontal format. One card for each task.

**What to do and say:** Present the task 16 – 12. *Read this number task. Do you have a way to work this out? Try to work it out.* Similarly as follows: 14 – 10, 17 – 14, 27 – 22, and so on.

**Notes:**

▶ These tasks are typically more difficult than the subtractive tasks above (Task Groups A6.2 to A6.5).

▶ It can be informative to present these bare number tasks before presenting the subtractive tasks (Tasks Groups A6.2 to A6.5) in order to gauge if the child has relatively sophisticated strategies for subtraction, including strategies that involve little or no counting.

▶ In similar vein to Task Group A6.1, the general approach with these tasks is to have the unknown difference in the range 2 to 5.

# INSTRUCTIONAL ACTIVITIES

## List of Instructional Activities

IA6.1:  Calculator Counting
IA6.2:  Class Count-on and Count-back
IA6.3:  One Hundred Square Activities
IA6.4:  Activities on a Bead Bar or Bead String
IA6.5:  Bucket Count-on
IA6.6:  Bucket Count-back
IA6.7:  Number Line Count-on
IA6.8:  Numeral Track Activities
IA6.9:  Under the Cloth

## ACTIVITY IA6.1: Calculator Counting

**Intended learning:** To extend knowledge of forward number word sequences (FNWSs) and backward number word sequences (BNWSs) to 100 and beyond.

**Description:** Children use a calculator or choose the calculator in Accessories from the programme menu on their computer. The child says the FNWS and watches the numbers increment on the calculator display. Similarly, the child says the BNWS and watches the numbers decrement on the calculator display. A child is working on numbers to 20 could start at 1 by keying in 1 + + and then pressing the = key repeatedly. The numbers will increment by ones with each press of the = key. If the child is working with numbers beyond that range they could start with any larger number (for example 63). In this case the child would key in 1 + + 63 and then repeatedly press the = key. The numbers will increment by ones from 63. To count backwards, the child presses 1 – – 100 and then repeatedly presses the = key. In this case the numbers displayed will decrement by ones from 100.

**Notes:**

▶    There are differences among calculators in the sequences of keystrokes required to perform functions such as incrementing and decrementing by a constant.
▶    This is a powerful visual aid to help children extend their knowledge of FNWSs and BNWSs. The range of numbers is limited only by the number of digits that will fit on the display.
▶    Children could be given worksheets showing consecutive sequences with missing numbers that they can find by means of the counting calculator.
▶    Children can practice counting in tens or hundreds, for example + + 10 = = or + + 100 = =, and so on.
▶    Children can practice counting off the decade in 10s, for example, 5 + + 10 = = = and so on will give 15, 25, 35, and so on.
▶    This is also a useful way to help children learn multiplication facts. By keying in + + 6 and repeatedly pressing the = sign, the calculator will display the multiples of 6. Similarly for other numbers.
▶    Remind children that it is necessary to press the operation key twice.
▶    Instructions for children should be displayed clearly so that they can undertake this activity independently.

**Materials:** Calculator, instructions, missing number sequences.

## **ACTIVITY IA6.2:** Class Count-on and Count-back

**Intended learning:** To count on or back in the range 2 to 5, from a given number and consolidate forward and backward number word sequences.

**Description:** Explain to the children that they are going to count around the class or circle. The teacher turns her back and listens to the count. At an appropriate time the teacher shouts *Stop!* and turns around. The child who has said the last number is then given a card by the teacher with an instruction. For example: *Count back 3. Add 5. What is 4 more?* The child completes the instruction and the count continues around the class.

**Notes:**

▶   The teacher can limit the range of counting, for example, when the count reaches 20 children change to counting backwards.

**Materials:** Instruction cards.

## **ACTIVITY IA6.3:** One Hundred Square Activities

**Intended learning:** To count forwards and backwards in the range 1 to 100, identifying numerals in this range, and counting on and back from given numbers.

**Description:** The teacher has a pack of 10 cards with instructions such as: *Count on two; Count back five*. The instructions involve numbers in the range 2 to 5. Problems are posed using the hundred square as a visual aid. The teacher chooses a number and asks a child to find it on the hundred square. The teacher highlights the chosen number and asks the child to choose a card from the top of the pack. The child carries out the instructions on the card. The rest of the children are asked to carry out the operation, providing answers verbally or on whiteboards. The child at the front demonstrates how they obtained the answer. Continue using other numbers. Children can work individually or in pairs with mini hundred squares and a set of instruction cards. They can generate their own number, write it down and then turn over a card, record the instruction and write the answer.

**Notes:**

▶   The numbers chosen for this activity should reflect children's facility with forward and backward sequences and with the hundred square.
▶   The activity can be made easier by using a 1 to 20 grid or a 1 to 50 grid, or more difficult by using a 101 to 200 grid.
▶   This activity is suitable for whole class, small groups and individuals.
▶   Children could use individual hundred squares.
▶   This activity helps children to see the position of numbers on a hundred square. It also supports the development of place value because the numbers are arranged in tens.

**Materials:** Hundred square, sets of cards for teacher and children.

## ACTIVITY IA6.4: Activities on a Bead Bar or Bead String

**Intended learning:** To develop understanding of quantity and position of numbers in the 1 to 100 range, and count on and back in the range 2 to 5, from a given number.

**Description:** The teacher uses a bead bar or bead string to pose questions to children. A 20s bar or 100s bar could be used. The beads are arranged in groups of ten in two different colors as shown in Figure 6.1.

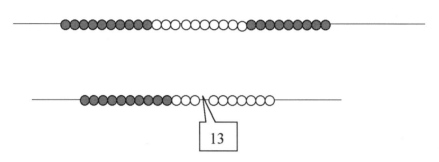

**Figure 6.1** Bead String

The teacher asks a child to place a peg on the bar (or string) to show a number of beads, for example, 13. The teacher attaches a card to the peg displaying the numeral 13, and asks the children to add or subtract a number in the range 2 to 5. Children could answer orally or write answers on an individual whiteboard. The teacher discusses the responses and chooses a child to demonstrate the answer using the beads.

**Notes:**

▶   The numbers chosen for this activity should reflect the children's facility with forward and back-ward number word sequences.
▶   This activity is suitable for whole class, small group or individuals.
▶   Children could use individual bead strings.
▶   This activity helps children to see the quantity value of numbers and the position of numbers on a number line. It also supports the development of place value because the beads are arranged in tens.

**Materials:** Bead bar or string.

## ACTIVITY IA6.5: Bucket Count-on

**Intended learning:** To count on from the larger number when adding numbers in the range 1 to 4.

**Description:** The teacher drops cubes into a bucket one by one, asking the children to count as each cube is dropped. After dropping, say, 7 cubes, the teacher asks the children how many cubes in all. Now the teacher places one to four cubes on her fingers and asks the children how many cubes there are altogether now. For example, the teacher might say: *There are seven cubes in the bucket and three on* *my fingers. How many is that altogether?* Encourage the children to say the numbers in their heads. Then check by having everyone count-on together. Continue with other numbers.

**Notes:**

▶   This is a multi-sensory activity in that the children see and hear the cubes going into the bucket one by one.

▶   The selection of the first number is dependent on the children's counting ability in a particular range. For example, if children are able to count no more than ten, the number of cubes dropped into the bucket should be no more than six. If children are able to count to 100, then much larger numbers can be used.

▶   When children are familiar with the activity, numbers larger than 20 can be imagined rather than counted into the bucket. For example, the teacher says: *I'm going to pretend that there are 24 cubes in the bucket now and 2 on my fingers*. The teacher places two cubes on fingers for children to see. *How many cubes are there altogether?*

▶   This activity is suitable for whole class, small group or individuals.

**Materials:** Opaque bucket, interlocking cubes.

## ACTIVITY IA6.6: Bucket Count-back

**Intended learning:** To count back to subtract numbers in the range 1 to 4.

**Description:** The teacher drops cubes into a bucket one by one, and asks the children to count as each cube is dropped. Now the teacher removes from 1 to 4 cubes, displays them on their fingers, and asks how many cubes are left. For example, the teacher says: *There were 11 cubes in the bucket and I've taken 3 out. How many will be left in the bucket?* Encourage the children to say the numbers in their heads initially and then check by getting everyone to count back together: *10, 9, 8*. Have children check the number left in the bucket. Continue with other numbers.

**Notes:**

▶   This activity involves two senses. Children see and hear the cubes going into the bucket one by one.

▶   The selection of the first number is dependent on the children's counting ability. Some children might be working in the range 1 to 10 and others in the range 1 to 100.

▶   When children are familiar with the activity, numbers larger than 20 can be imagined rather than put into the bucket. For example: *I'm going to pretend that there are 24 cubes in the bucket now and I'm taking 2 out (teacher places 2 cubes on fingers for children to see). How many cubes are left in the bucket?*

▶   The number of cubes removed should be in the range 1 to 4.

▶   This activity is suitable for whole class, small group or individuals.

▶   Alternative materials could be used.

**Materials:** Opaque bucket, interlocking cubes.

## ACTIVITY IA6.7: Number Line Count-on

**Intended learning:** To count on from the larger number when adding a small amount (1 to 4).

**Description:** The teacher has a pack of large-sized numeral cards, a die numbered 2, 2, 3, 3, 4, 4, and an empty number line drawn on the whiteboard. Children have individual whiteboards. The teacher turns over the first card in the pack and attaches it to the left-hand side of the empty number line (Figure 6.2).

**Figure 6.2** Number Line Count-on (1)

The teacher asks a child to come to the front and throw the die. The teacher asks, *We are starting at 14, and we count on 3, where do we finish?* Allow time for children to solve the task and record on their individual whiteboards. The teacher then demonstrates the three jumps on her whiteboard, counting *15, 16, 17* and marking only 17 on the empty number line (Figure 6.3).

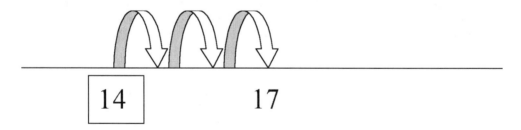

**Figure 6.3** Number Line Count-on (2)

Continue using other numbers. Then ask the children to draw a line on their boards and write down the next number from the pack on their number line. The teacher throws the die and children count on and record the final number on their boards.

**Notes:**

▶    The numbers chosen for this activity should reflect the children's facility with numeral identification and the forward number word sequence.
▶    This activity is suitable for whole class, small group or individuals.
▶    It is not necessary for children to draw their empty number lines as a straight line.
▶    Encourage children to solve the task mentally, and then record on the empty number line, rather than use the empty number line in their initial solution.

▶   Teachers could use an electronic version (for example the National Numeracy Strategy interactive teaching programme 'Number Line' in the UK) or a transparency of the number line on an overhead projector.

**Materials:** Pack of large-size numeral cards, blank die (for teacher to mark six faces as follows: 2, 2, 3, 3, 4, 4), small whiteboards, large whiteboard, dry wipe pens.

## ACTIVITY IA6.8: Numeral Track Activities

**Intended learning:** To extend knowledge of numerals to 100, forward number word sequences (FNWSs) and backward number word sequences (BNWSs) to 100, and facility in counting on or back from a given number in that range.

Numeral track activities

**Description:** The teacher uses a numeral track for these activities. A numeral track is a sequence of numerals with flaps over the numerals (Figure 6.4). Any set of numerals can be placed inside the track on a strip of card.

**Figure 6.4** Numeral Track Activities (1)

The teacher places a strip of 10 consecutive numerals inside the numeral track and lifts one of the lids. The teacher asks the children to say the number. The teacher then asks the children to say what the number would be, for example, 3 places further along the line. Children could answer orally or write their answer on individual whiteboards. The teacher then lifts the lid over the answer and asks children to check their answers. Continue with other numerals and jumps in the range 2 to 5. Tasks involving going backward by jumps in the range 1 to 5 can also be used (Figure 6.5).

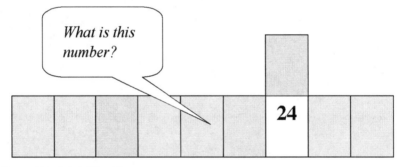

**Figure 6.5** Numeral Track Activities (2)

Numeral track: decade crossing

**Notes:**

▶ The numeral track is useful for developing facility with FNWSs and BNWSs to 100 and beyond, and with numeral identification.

▶ An alternative to the numeral track such as cards with numerals face down could be used.

▶ The numbers chosen for this activity should take account of children's facility with numeral identification, and counting forwards and backwards.

▶ This activity is suitable for whole class, small group or individuals.

**Materials:** Numeral track and inserts, or numbers on a card.

## ACTIVITY IA6.9: Under the Cloth

**Intended learning:** To use counting-back or counting-on to solve missing subtrahend tasks.

**Description:** The teacher counts out a group of cubes or other manipulatives (for example teddy bears) for the children to see. The teacher screens the cubes and asks the children to close their eyes. The teacher then removes a small number (in the range 1 to 5) and puts them out of sight. The children are asked to open their eyes and the teacher unscreens the cubes. Then the teacher says: *There were 12 cubes under the cloth. I have taken some away and now there are 8 cubes under the cloth. How many cubes did I take away?* Students are given time to work out their answers and then asked to explain their strategies. The cubes are unscreened and the activity is explained if necessary. Continue with other numbers.

**Notes:**

▶ Missing subtrahend tasks typically are more difficult than missing addend or removed item tasks involving similar numbers.

▶ Children can solve the above task by counting back from 12 to 8 or counting up from 8 to 12. Discussing different strategies will help children to understand that the task involves finding the **difference** between the two numbers.

▶ The minuend should be in the range where the children can count forwards and backwards.

▶ It is important to keep the missing subtrahend small (in the range 1 to 5) even when using minuends beyond 20.

▶ When using minuends beyond 20, interlocking cubes arranged in sets of 10 could be used.

▶ This activity is suitable for whole class, small group, pairs or individuals.

▶ An alternative is to use an upturned opaque container with 10 cubes on top. Some of the cubes are then hidden under the container and children try to guess how many are hidden.

▶ An alternative suited to the whole class is to use an overhead projector and translucent counters.

**Materials:** Cubes or other manipulatives, cloth large enough to screen the cubes.

# 7
# Structuring Numbers 1 to 20

**Summary**

This chapter extends the focus of Chapter 5 to the topic of structuring numbers in the range 1 to 20. This topic relates to the development and use of non-counting strategies in the range 1 to 20, and provides a crucial basis for the development of mental strategies for addition and subtraction involving 2-digit numbers. This chapter presents new approaches to teaching involving use of materials such as the arithmetic rack or the double ten frame.

## TOPIC OVERVIEW

In earlier chapters we describe how children's beginning knowledge about adding and subtracting numbers develops in two main strands. One of these concerns the development of counting strategies which culminate in the advanced counting-by-one strategies, that is, counting-on-from, counting-on-to, counting-back-from and counting-back-to (Chapters 4 and 6). The second strand concerns children's developing abilities to combine and partition numbers without counting, first in the range 1 to 10 (Chapter 5). Children who are fluent at combining and partitioning numbers in the range 1 to 10, are ready to extend this to the range 1 to 20. This is referred to as structuring numbers 1 to 20, and is the focus of this chapter.

## Using the Arithmetic Rack

The **arithmetic rack** (Figure 7.1) is a device for teaching children structuring numbers in the range 1 to 20. Ideally, each child has a rack and the teacher has a large rack for use with the whole class or group of children. Learning with the arithmetic rack involves the three main steps:

▶     making and reading numbers 1 to 20;
▶     adding two numbers;
▶     subtraction involving two numbers.

### Double Ten Frame

The double ten frame (Figure 7.2) is an alternative to the arithmetic rack. The activities described here for the arithmetic rack can be adapted for use with a double ten frame.

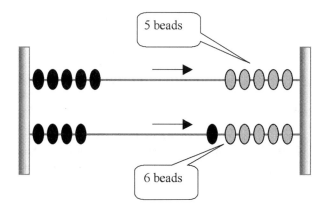

**Figure 7.1** Arithmetic Rack showing 11

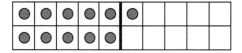

**Figure 7.2** Double Ten frame showing 11

# Making and Reading Numbers 1 to 20

Children learn to make the numbers in the following groups: 1 to 5; 6 to 10; 11 to 15; 16 to 20. The goal is for children to be able to make the numbers in one or two quick movements rather than moving beads one at a time. In general, numbers can be made in two main ways. One way relies on the five and ten structure of the rack and the other relies on the doubles structure.

### Numbers 1 to 5 on the Rack

The number 1 is made by moving one bead on the upper row to the left. The numbers 2, 3 ... 5 are made in two ways. One way involves moving two, three ... five beads on the upper row to the left. The other way shows each even number as a double and each odd number as a 'near double' (for example, 5 as 3 and 2). In this way two is shown as one bead on the upper row and one on the lower row, three is two beads on the upper row and one bead on the lower row, and so on.

### Numbers 6 to 10 on the Rack

Each of the numbers six, seven and eight is made in three main ways and it is important that children become fluent with these. Seven, for example, is made (a) with seven beads on the upper row (five red and two green); (b) with five beads on the upper row and two beads on the lower row; and (c) as a near double with four beads on the upper row and three on the lower row. Nine and 10 are made in two main ways only, that is, using the upper row only, or using five on the upper row and four or five respectively on the lower row.

### Numbers 11 to 14 on the Rack

In similar vein, the numbers from 11 to 14 are made in three main ways and children should also become fluent with these. Thirteen, for example, is made (a) with ten beads on the upper row and three on the lower row; (b) with eight beads on the upper row and five on the lower row; and (c) as a near double with seven beads on the upper row and six on the lower row.

### Numbers 15 to 20 on the Rack

Finally, the numbers from 15 to 18 are made in two main ways. Sixteen is made (a) with ten beads on the upper row and six on the lower row, and (b) with eight beads on each row. Nineteen and twenty are made with 10 beads on the upper row and 9 or 10 beads respectively, on the lower row.

### Interchanging the Rows

Children should also learn that, the number of beads on each row can be interchanged. Thus seven, for example, could be made as (a) seven beads on the lower row; (b) with two beads on the upper row and five beads on the lower row; and (c) as a near double with three beads on the upper row and four on the lower row. Similarly, thirteen, for example, could be made as (a) three beads on the upper row and ten on the lower row; (b) with five beads on the upper row and eight on the lower row; and (c) as a near double with six beads on the upper row and seven on the lower row.

### Reading Numbers on the Rack

The teacher screens the rack from the children and makes a number. The number is flashed (briefly displayed) and the children's task is to say the number displayed on the rack.

Adding two numbers on the arithmetic rack

# Adding two numbers

The rack is used to calculate addition of two numbers in the range 1 to 10. The first addend is made on the upper row and the second addend is made on the lower row. Instruction should allow for flexibility in the way children calculate rather than imposing a strict procedure to follow. Children learn that sometimes it is helpful to exchange beads on the upper row for an equal number of beads on the lower row. In other instances they can determine the sum without the need to move any beads. In many instances there are several ways the sum can be determined and children are encouraged to describe a variety of ways.

## Doubles: 1 + 1 to 5 +5

These should be straightforward because the children have already learned the doubles structure of the even numbers. In this case the children begin with the two addends (for example, 3 + 3), and have to realize that this can be regarded as the doubles structure for six.

## Five Plus a Number in the Range 1 to 5

For 5 + 3 for example, five beads are moved on the upper row and three on the lower row. Again, this can be regarded alternatively as 5 + 3 and also as 8.

## Two Addends in the Range 1 to 5

These additions should be straightforward because the children have already learned to combine and partition numbers in the range 1 to 10, and this familiar knowledge can be consolidated in the context of the arithmetic rack.

## Doubles: 6 + 6 to 10 + 10

These additions will be straightforward because the children have learned the doubles structure of the numbers 12, 14, and so on. Thus the children begin with the two addends, for example 7 + 7, and realize that this can be regarded as 7 + 7 and also as 14. Children can also learn to transform these into alternative structures through transformations such as the following:

6 + 6 becomes 10 + 2
7 + 7 becomes 10 + 4
8 + 8 becomes 10 + 6
9 + 9 becomes 10 + 8

## Ten Plus a Number in the Range 1 to 10

For 10 + 6 for example, ten beads are moved on the upper row and six on the lower row. The structure can be regarded alternatively as 10 + 6 and 16.

## Five Plus an Addend in the Range 6 to 9

For 5 + 8 for example, five beads are moved on the upper row and eight on the lower row. The structure can be regarded alternatively as 5 + 8 and also as 13. For 8 + 5, eight beads are moved on the upper row and five on the lower row. The structure can be regarded alternatively as 8 + 5 and 13.

### One Addend in the Range 6 to 9 and One Addend in the Range 1 to 4

Additions of this kind can be solved by transformations such as the following.

6 + 4 becomes 5 + 5 – swap one bead
8 + 3 becomes 10 + 1 – swap two beads
9 + 4 becomes 10 + 3 – swap one bead
7 + 4 becomes 5 + 5 + 1 or 6 + 5 – swap one bead
6 + 2 becomes 5 + 3 – swap one bead
8 + 1 becomes 9 – swap one bead
7 + 3 becomes 5 + 5 – swap two beads
9 + 2 becomes 10 + 1 – swap one bead
8 + 4 becomes 7 + 5 – swap one bead
7 + 2 becomes 5 + 4 – swap two beads and so on.

Sums which are the commutations (turnarounds) of these can be solved similarly. Thus 4 + 6 is solved similarly to 6 + 4, and so on.

### Two Different Addends in the range 6 to 9

Additions of this kind can involve transformations such as the following.

6 + 7 becomes 5 + 5 + 3 or 10 + 3 – swap one bead
8 +9  becomes 7 + 10– swap one bead
9 + 6 becomes 10 + 5 – swap one bead
7 + 8 becomes 5 + 5 + 5 or 10 + 5 – swap two beads
6 + 8 becomes 5 + 5 + 4 or 10 + 4 – swap one bead
7 + 9 becomes 6 + 10 – swap one bead

The other six sums of this kind are 7 + 6, 9 + 8, 6 + 9, 8 + 7, 8 + 6, and 9 + 7. Each of these is the commutation (turnaround) of one of those above. Thus 7 + 6 corresponds with 6 + 7, and so on.

### One Addend in the Range 11 to 19 and One Addend in the Range 1 to 10

In this case one of the addends is a teen and the sum is 20 or less. Some examples are 14 + 3, 12 + 7, 15 + 4. These are best calculated by linking to the corresponding sum involving two addends in the range 1 to 10. Thus 4 + 3 is used to solve 14 + 3, 2 + 7 is used to solve 12 + 7, and 5 + 4 is used to solve 15 + 4.

### Subtraction in the Range 1 to 20

Subtraction using the rack can take the forms of take away, difference or adding up. Also, the rack can first be used to consolidate subtraction in the range 1 to 10.

## Subtraction with the Minuend Less than or Equal to 10

Children have already learned to partition numbers in the range 1 to 10. The rack can be used to calculate or show partitions. Partitions in the range 1 to 10 can be calculated in two main ways, using both rows or using the upper row, and so on. Using both rows, partitions of eight can be calculated as follows: make eight using six on the upper row; make eight using three on the upper row, and so on. Using the upper row only, partitions of eight can be shown by moving eight beads to the left, and then partitioning those beads, for example, take two beads away. How many are left?

## Subtracting with Minuend in the Range 11 to 20

This includes subtractions such as 11 – 4, 17 – 8, 15 – 7, 12 – 9. In these cases the minuend is in the range 11 to 19 and both the known subtrahend and the unknown difference are less than 10. These subtractions can be thought of in three main ways: take away, finding the difference and adding up.

### Subtraction as Take Away

The example 11 – 4 can be calculated as follows: make 11 as 10 beads on the upper row and 1 bead on the lower row. Take away one bead on the lower row and three beads on the upper row. Thus 11 – 4 becomes 11 – 1 – 3 becomes 10 – 3 becomes 7. This is referred to as going through 10. Alternatively, children might use the near doubles structure for 11 of 6 on the upper row and 5 on the lower row, then subtract 4 from 5 leaving 1 to add to the six. Thus 11 – 4 becomes 6 + 5 – 4 becomes 6 + 1 becomes 7.

The example 16 – 7 can be calculated as follows: make 16 as 10 beads on the upper row and 6 beads on the lower row. Take away six beads on the lower row and one bead on the upper row. Thus 16 – 7 becomes 16 – 6 – 1 becomes 10 – 1 becomes 9. As above, this is called going through 10. Alternatively, children might use the doubles structure for 16. Thus 16 – 7 becomes 8 + 8 – 7 becomes 8 + 1 becomes 9.

### Subtraction as Finding the Difference

The example 12 – 9 is calculated as follows: make 12 as 10 beads on the upper row and 2 beads on the lower row. Take away two beads on the lower row and one bead on the upper row to leave 9. Thus 12 – 9 is thought of as 12 – X = 9, and this involves going through 10 (12 – 2 – 1 makes 9).

The example 13 – 8 is calculated as follows: make 13 as 10 beads on the upper row and 3 beads on the lower row. Take away three beads on the lower row and two beads on the upper row to leave 8. Thus 13 – 8 is thought of as 13 – X = 8. This also involves going through 10 (13 – 3 – 2 makes 8).

### Subtraction as Adding Up

The example 15 – 7 is calculated as follows: make 7 as 7 beads on the upper row. Calculate 7 + X = 15. This might be thought of as 7 + 3 + 5 makes 15, that is, going through 10. Alternatively a child might think of 7 + 7 + 1, that is, using the double structure of 14 rather than adding up through 10.

The example 11 – 8 is calculated as follows: make 8 as 8 beads on the upper row. Calculate 8 + x = 11, as 8 + 2 + 1, that is, going through 10.

# From Using the Rack to Mental Strategies

The above sections describe for addition and subtraction a progression from calculating involving smaller numbers and more familiar structures to that involving larger numbers and less familiar structures. Another important progression is from using the rack to mental strategies. This involves four main steps. For addition, these steps are:

▶   making both addends on the rack and exchanging beads as necessary;
▶   making the first addend only, and looking at the rack to determine the addition;
▶   making the first addend only, and then screening the rack;
▶   addition without making either addend on the rack and where the rack is removed from the children's view.

For subtraction, these steps are:

▶ making the minuend on the rack and exchanging beads as necessary to determine the subtraction;
▶ making the minuend only, and looking at the rack to determine the subtraction;
▶ making the minuend only, and then screening the rack;
▶ subtraction without making the minuend on the rack and where the rack is removed from the children's view.

## Working Flexibly with Doubles and Near Doubles, and Five and Ten

Children can work towards flexibly using doubles and near doubles, and five and ten for addition and subtraction in the range 1 to 20. Children can also develop awareness of the principle that the order of adding two numbers does not affect the sum of the two number (6 + 8 can be worked out by adding 6 to 8 or 8 to 6). This is known as the commutativity of addition. Alternatively, addition is **commutative**. This is sometimes referred to as 'turn arounds'.

As indicated earlier there are particular segments of knowledge that children should automatize, in order to develop good facility with addition and subtraction in the range 1 to 20. These are: (a) knowing the doubles from 1 + 1 to 5 + 5; (b) learning the partitions of the numbers from 2 to 5; (c) learning to partition 10 into 9 + 1 and 8 + 2; (d) learning the commutative property; (e) learning the partitions of the numbers from 6 to 10; and (f) learning the doubles from 6 + 6 to 10 + 10.

Instruction should focus on using these segments of knowledge as a basis for addition and subtraction in the range 1 to 20. For example, a child might work out 6 + 7 by partitioning 6 into 5 and 1, and 7 into 5 and 2, and then adding two 5s to 10, and 2 and 1 to 3, making 13 in all. The task of 8 + 9 might involve partitioning 8 and 9 into 5 and 3 and 5 and 4 respectively, and then adding two 5s to make 10, and adding 4 and 3 by adding through 5 to make 7, making 17 in all. The task of 13 minus 8 might involve adding 2 to 8 to make 10 and 3 to 10 to make 13, making 5 added in all.

## ASSESSMENT TASK GROUPS

### List of Assessment Task Groups

A7.1: Naming and visualizing pair-wise patterns for 1 to 10
A7.2: Naming and visualizing five-wise patterns for 1 to 10
A7.3: Naming and visualizing pair-wise patterns for 11 to 20
A7.4: Naming and visualizing five-wise and ten-wise patterns for 11 to 14
A7.5: Naming and visualizing ten-wise patterns for 15 to 20
A7.6: Addition using doubles, fives and tens – addends less than 11
A7.7: Subtraction using doubles, fives and tens – subtrahend and difference less than 11
A7.8: Addition using doubles, fives and tens – one addend greater than 10
A7.9: Subtraction using doubles, fives and tens – subtrahend or difference greater than 10

## TASK GROUP A7.1: Naming and Visualizing Pair-Wise Patterns for 1 to 10

**Materials:** Arithmetic rack, screen.

**What to do and say:** Make a pair-wise pattern for 7 and screen the pattern. *I am going to show you a number on the rack. Tell me what number you see?* Flash the pattern for seven. Similarly for the other numbers.
   *What does 5 look like on the arithmetic rack when I am building pairs? Can you tell me? What does 5 look like if I try to make it using pairs?* Similarly for the other numbers.

**Notes:**

▶ These tasks are of the same kind as those in Task Group 5.4.
▶ On the visualization task, if the child describes a five-wise pattern ask additional questions designed to support them to visualize a pair-wise pattern.
▶ A double ten frame structure can be used in place of an arithmetic rack. Using a double ten frame structure will require a separate ten-frame for each number.
▶ For 9, the pair-wise pattern and the five-wise pattern using two rows are identical. Similarly for 10.
▶ As a general rule, the arrangements of numbers on the upper and lower rows can be inter-changed. For example, a pair-wise pattern for 7 is made with 4 on the upper row and might also be made with 4 on the lower row. To avoid unnecessary complexity here, these are not regarded as distinct forms. At the same time children should experience both these forms.

## TASK GROUP A7.2: Naming and Visualizing Five-wise Patterns for 1 to 10

**Materials:** Arithmetic rack, screen.

**What to do and say:** Using two rows with five on the upper row, make a five-wise pattern for 6 and screen the pattern. *I am going to show you a number on the rack. Tell me what number you see?* Flash the pattern for 6. Similarly for other numbers in the range 1 to 10.

Using the upper row only, make a five-wise pattern for 7. *This time I will use the top row only. What number did you see?* Flash the pattern for 7.

*What does 8 look like on the arithmetic rack when I am building fives using two rows? Can you tell me? What does 8 look like if I try to make it using a five?* Similarly with the other numbers.

*What does 9 look like on the arithmetic rack when I use the upper row only?* Similarly with the other numbers.

**Notes:**

▶ These tasks are of the same kind as those in Task Group 5.5.

▶ On the visualization task, if the child describes a pair-wise pattern ask additional questions designed to support them to visualize a five-wise pattern.

▶ For the numbers from 1 to 5, the five-wise patterns can be made one way only, that is, using the upper row.

▶ For the numbers from 6 to 10, it is important that children learn the two forms of the five-wise patterns: (a) using the upper row only; and (b) using five on the upper row, and the remainder on the lower row.

▶ As a general rule, the arrangements of numbers on the upper and lower rows can be interchanged. For example, a five-wise pattern for 7 is made with 5 on the upper row and might also be made with 5 on the lower row. To avoid unnecessary complexity here, these are not regarded as distinct forms. At the same time children should experience both of these forms.

## TASK GROUP A7.3: Naming and Visualizing Pair-wise Patterns for 11 to 20

**Materials:** Arithmetic rack, screen.

**What to do and say:** Make a pair-wise pattern for 15 and screen the pattern. *I am going to show you a number on the rack. Tell me what number you see?* Flash the pattern for 15. Similarly for other numbers in the range 11 to 20.

Showing fourteen on the arithmetic rack

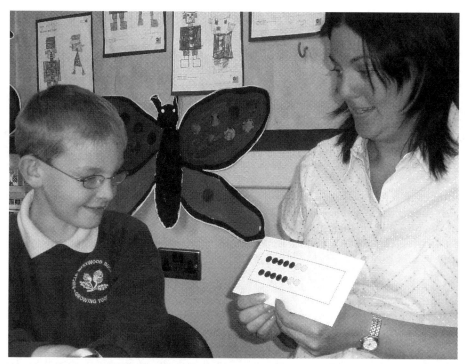

Naming and visualizing pair-wise image patterns for 11–20

*What does 12 look like on the arithmetic rack when I am building pairs? Can you tell me?* Similarly with the other numbers.

**Notes:**

▶ Refer to the notes for Task Group A7.1 above.
▶ For 19, the pair-wise pattern and the five-wise pattern are identical. Similarly for 20.

## TASK GROUP A7.4: Naming and Visualizing Five-wise and Ten-wise Patterns for 11 to 14

**Materials:** Arithmetic rack, screen.

**What to do and say:** Using two rows with 7 on the upper row and 5 on the lower row, make a five-wise pattern for 12 and screen the pattern. *I am going to show you a number on the rack. Tell me what number you see?* Flash the pattern for 12. Similarly for 11, 13 and 14.

Using two rows with 10 on the upper row and 3 on the lower row, make a ten-wise pattern for 13 and screen the pattern. *I am going to show you a number on the rack. Tell me what number you see?* Flash the pattern for 13. Similarly for 11, 12 and 14.

*What does 14 look like on the arithmetic rack when I am building fives using two rows? Can you tell me? What does 14 look like if I try to make it using fives?* Similarly for 11, 12 and 13.

*What does 11 look like on the arithmetic rack when I use 10 on the upper row?* Similarly for 12, 13 and 14.

**Notes:**

▶   Refer to the notes for Task Group A7.2 above.

▶   For the numbers from 11 to 14, it is important that children learn: (a) the five-wise patterns (five only on the lower row); and (b) the ten-wise patterns (ten on the upper row).

## TASK GROUP A7.5: Naming and Visualizing Ten-Wise Patterns for 15 to 20

**Materials:** Arithmetic rack, screen.

**What to do and say:** Using 10 on the upper row, make a ten-wise pattern for 18 and screen the pattern. *I am going to show you a number on the rack. Tell me what number you see?* Flash the pattern for 18. Similarly for the other numbers.

   *What does 16 look like on the arithmetic rack when I use 10 on the upper row?* Similarly for the other numbers.

**Notes:**

▶   For the numbers from 15 to 20, the five-wise patterns and the ten-wise patterns take the same form. Nevertheless, these patterns can be described both in terms of their ten structure: 16 has 10 and 6, and their five structure: 16 has three fives and one.

## TASK GROUP A7.6: Addition Using Doubles, Fives and Tens – Addends Less than 11

**Materials:** Arithmetic rack, screen, addition tasks written on a card in horizontal format (one card for each task).

**What to do and say:** Using the upper row, make a five-wise structure for 9. Flash the structure. *What number did you see?* Display the following task on a card: 9 + 3. *Use the rack to work this out. How did you do it?*

   Using the upper row, make a five-wise structure for 7. Flash the structure. *What number did you see?* Display the following task on a card: 7 + 5. *Use the rack to work this out. How did you do it?*

   Make a pair-wise structure for 8. Flash the structure. *What number did you see?* Display the following task on a card: 8 + 6. *Use the rack to work this out. How did you do it?*

   Similarly with additions such as: 9 + 2, 4 + 7, 10 + 3, 5 + 9, and so on.

**Notes:**

▶   Children are likely to work flexibly with pair-wise, five-wise and other patterns.

▶   It is important to listen carefully to the child's explanation and to temper expectations that the child should use a particular strategy or pattern.

## TASK GROUP A7.7: Subtraction Using Doubles, Fives and Tens – Subtrahend and Difference Less than 11

**Materials:** Arithmetic rack, screen, subtraction and missing addend tasks written on a card in horizontal format. One card for each task.

**What to do and say:** Make a ten-wise structure for 14. Flash the structure. *What number did you see?* Display the following task on a card: 14 – 5. *Use the rack to work this out. How did you do it?*

Make a five-wise structure for 12. Flash the structure. *What number did you see?* Display the following task on a card: 12 – 7. *Use the rack to work this out. How did you do it?*

Make a pair-wise structure for 17. Flash the structure. *What number did you see?* Display the following task on a card: 17 – 8. *Use the rack to work this out. How did you do it?*

Make a five-wise structure for 8. Flash the structure. *What number did you see?* Display the following task on a card: 8 + X = 11. *Use the rack to work this out. How did you do it?*

Make a five-wise structure for 6. Flash the structure. *What number did you see?* Display the following task on a card: 6 + X = 15. *Use the rack to work this out. How did you do it?*

Make a pair-wise structure for 8. Flash the structure. *What number did you see?* Display the following task on a card 8 + X = 12. *Use the rack to work this out. How did you do it?*

Similarly with other subtraction and missing addend tasks.

**Notes:**

▶ The notes for Task Group A7.6 are also relevant to this task group.
▶ In the case of subtraction and missing addend tasks, children are likely to use a relatively wide range of strategies.

## TASK GROUP A7.8: Addition Using Doubles, Fives and Tens – One Addend Greater than 10

**Materials:** Arithmetic rack, screen, addition tasks written on a card in horizontal format. One card for each task.

**What to do and say:** Make a ten-wise structure for 11. Flash the structure. *What number did you see?* Display the following task on a card: 11 + 3. *Use the rack to work this out. How did you do it?*

Make a five-wise structure for 14. Flash the structure. *What number did you see?* Display the following task on a card: 14 + 5. *Use the rack to work this out. How did you do it?*

Make a pair-wise structure for 12. Flash the structure. *What number did you see?* Display the following task on a card: 12 + 7. *Use the rack to work this out. How did you do it?*

Similarly with additions such as: 16 + 2, 13 + 4, 17 + 3, and so on.

**Notes:**

▶ The notes for Task Group A7.6 are also relevant to this task group.
▶ Children might use a known sum in the range 1 to 10. For example, 4 + 4 is used to work out 14 + 4.

## TASK GROUP A7.9: Subtraction Using Doubles, Fives and Tens – Subtrahend or Difference Greater than 10

**Materials:** Arithmetic rack, screen, subtraction and missing addend tasks written on a card in horizontal format. One card for each task.

**What to do and say:** Make a ten-wise structure for 19. Flash the structure. *What number did you see?* Display the following task on a card: 19 – 5. *Use the rack to work this out. How did you do it?*

Make a five-wise structure for 13. Flash the structure. *What number did you see?* Display the following task on a card: 13 – 2. *Use the rack to work this out. How did you do it?*

Make a pair-wise structure for 16. Flash the structure. *What number did you see?* Display the following task on a card: 16 – 3. *Use the rack to work this out. How did you do it?*

Make a ten-wise structure for 11. Flash the structure. *What number did you see?* Display the following task on a card: 11 + X = 16. *Use the rack to work this out. How did you do it?*

Make a five-wise structure for 12. Flash the structure. *What number did you see?* Display the following task on a card: 12 + X = 19. *Use the rack to work this out. How did you do it?*

Make a pair-wise structure for 14. Flash the structure. *What number did you see?* Display the following task on a card 14 + X = 18. *Use the rack to work this out. How did you do it?*

Similarly with other subtraction and missing addend tasks.

**Notes:**
▶    The notes for Task Groups A7.6 and A7.7 are also relevant to this task group.
▶    Children might use a known difference in the range 1 to 10. For example, 6 – 3 is used to work out 16 – 3.

# INSTRUCTIONAL ACTIVITIES

## List of Instructional Activities

IA7.1: Double Decker Bus Flashes
IA7.2: Getting On and Off the Bus
IA7.3: Bus Snap
IA7.4: Make Combinations to Twenty Fish
IA7.5: Using Ten-plus Combinations
IA7.6: Five and Ten Game
IA7.7: Chocolate Boxes
IA7.8: Double Ten Frame Facts
IA7.9: Bead Board

## ACTIVITY IA7.1: Double Decker Bus Flashes

**Intended learning:** To learn addition in the range 1 to 20.

**Description:** An empty bus is displayed on an overhead projector (see Figure 7.3). The class is asked what they observe. The purpose is for them to see that the upper and lower rows each have ten windows. There is a heavier line after the fifth window in both upper and lower rows. Examples of activities:

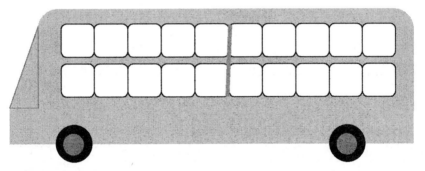

**Figure 7.3** Double Deck Bus Flashes

▶   Doubles combinations are flashed (for example, four on the upper row and four on the lower row).
▶   Ten-plus combinations are flashed (for example, ten on the lower row and three on upper row). Children are asked how many people are on the bus?
▶   Pairs of children are given a bus and 20 counters. They are asked to show numbers of people on the bus. After each task, the teacher asks each pair to explain how the people were arranged on their bus.
▶   How many ways can 12 people be arranged on the bus? Have the children list their results.

To emphasize the ten-plus combinations the teacher could indicate that the driver always likes the lower row filled before people are allowed upstairs to the upper row. Using this idea give these tasks:

▶   Ask each pair to show arrangements of between 10 and 20 people (for example, 16 would be 10 and 6).
▶   Ask each pair to seat between 10 and 20 people on the bus. Discuss these arrangements. Now have each pair change the counters to show a ten-plus combination (that is, fill the lower row first).

**Notes:**

▶   It is important to discuss the combinations made by the children.
▶   The ten-plus combinations help to build knowledge of the ten and ones aspect of teen numbers.

**Materials:** Double ten bus transparency for the overhead projector, student double ten buses, counters (each set of 20 should be of one color).

## ACTIVITY IA7.2: Getting On and Off the Bus

**Intended learning:** To learn addition and subtraction in the range 1 to 20.

**Description:** On the overhead projector, demonstrate people getting on the bus. For example, there are 9 people on the bus. If another four get on, how many will there be altogether? Discuss the different ways of working this out. When the children are familiar with these tasks, modify the task by briefly displaying and then screening the projection – the bus has gone behind a building (Figure 7.4). Similarly with people getting off the bus.

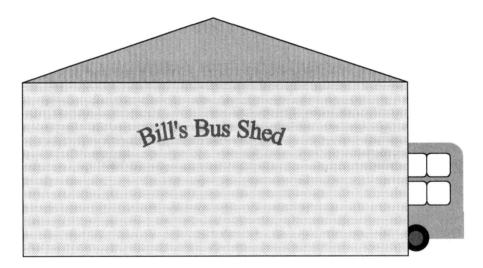

**Figure 7.4** Getting on and off the bus (screened)

**Notes:**

▶    This is an excellent setting to emphasize adding and subtracting through ten. For example 8 + 5. Two more are needed to make up 10 (the lower row is filled) leaving three more to go upstairs, (10 and 3) making a total of 13.

**Materials:** Double ten bus transparency for the overhead projector, student double ten buses, counters (each set of 20 should be one color).

## ACTIVITY IA7.3: Bus Snap

**Intended learning:** To learn addition in the range 1 to 20.

**Description:** This is played the same as traditional Snap. Double ten bus cards are used instead of playing cards or numeral cards. A mixture of bus and numeral cards could be used (Figure 7.5). A stack of cards is shuffled and divided between two players who take turns to place their top card face up in the middle. If this card matches the card already showing on the growing center stack, the players try to be the first to put their hand on the stack and call *Snap!* The player who does this, gets all the cards in the stack. The game proceeds until one player has all of the cards.

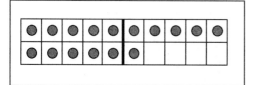 

**Figure 7.5** Double ten cards and numeral cards

**Notes:**

▶    This is an excellent game for building knowledge of the addition combinations to 20.
▶    Provide children with a set of cards and encourage them to play this game at home.

**Materials:** Double ten bus cards, numeral cards 10 to 20.

## ACTIVITY IA7.4: Make Combinations to Twenty Fish

**Intended learning:** To visualize pairs-wise and ten-plus patterns in the range 10 to 20.

**Description:** The activity is played the same as Fish. Instead of traditional playing cards, dot pattern cards for numbers in the range 10 to 20 are used. Five cards are dealt to each player. The remaining cards are placed in a stack in the center of the players. Players try to make matching pairs of cards, for example a double 8 with a 10 + 6 as displayed in Figure 7.6.

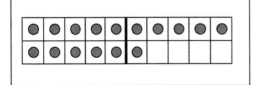
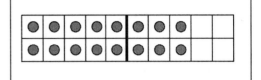

**Figure 7.6** Making combinations to Twenty Fish (1)

Players take turns to ask another player for a particular card. If the player being asked does not have the required card they say *Fish!* The player seeking the card takes the top card off the stack. The game continues until one player has no more cards. Players count to see how many pairs they have.

**Notes:**

▶    Numeral cards could also be used and matched with the dot pattern cards.
▶    Cards displaying combinations like 9 dots and 6 dots (see Figure 7.7) also could be used.
▶    As a variation, players could form sets of three cards instead of pairs.

**Materials:** At least two sets of pair-wise and ten-plus pattern cards 10 to 20, other pattern cards as required.

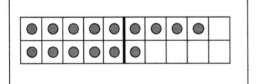
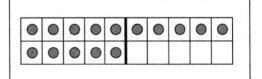

**Figure 7.7** Making combinations to Twenty Fish (2)

## ACTIVITY IA7.5: Using Ten-plus Combinations

**Intended learning:** To use ten-plus combinations to solve other additions.

**Description:** The teacher displays a nine-plus combination using a double ten bus on the overhead projector for example, 9 on the lower row and 6 on the upper row (see Figure 7.8). *How many are on the bus? What happens if one person comes down from the upper row to fill the vacant seat on the lower row? How many are on the bus now?*

Other upper and lower bus combinations are used. The children note these on a sheet (Figure 7.9) and change them to ten-plus combinations.

**Figure 7.8** How many on the bus?

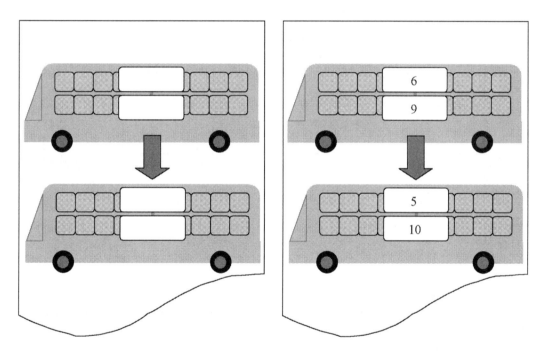

**Figure 7.9** Ten-plus combinations

**Note:**

▶ As children become familiar with this task, try giving the combinations verbally without using the bus.

**Materials:** Bus and counters for the overhead projector, student bus sheets (as shown above in Figures 7.8 and 7.9).

## ACTIVITY IA7.6: Five and Ten Game

**Intended learning:** To solve addition problems involving five and ten.

**Description:** Players take turns to: (a) roll the five and ten die (for example, a 10 is face up) and write the number rolled on the game sheet; (b) roll the one to six die (for example, a 4 is face up) and write this number on the game sheet; and (c) add these two numbers and put the answer on the game sheet (Figure 7.10). The game progresses until the game sheet is full.

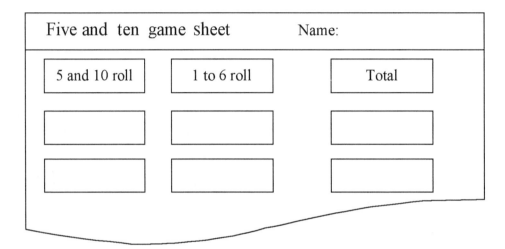

**Figure 7.10** Five and Ten Game Sheet

**Notes:**

▶ This activity is suitable for pairs or individuals.
▶ The die can have five and ten dot patterns and numerals as children become more proficient.
▶ This activity can be extended to any decade number or hundred number.

**Materials:** A five and ten die and a one to six (traditional) die, game sheet.

## ACTIVITY IA7.7: Chocolate Boxes

**Intended learning:** Using ten to solve additions involving eight and nine.

**Description:** Initially the teacher displays a double ten chocolate box on the overhead projector (see Figure 7.11).

**Figure 7.11** Chocolate box

Children are asked: *How many squares?* The dark line showing the five can be indicated. Some chocolates (counters) can be put in the box in a variety of arrangements and the children are asked to tell how many chocolates and how many empty spaces, and so on.

Cards like those illustrated in Figure 7.12 are made up and used to play this game. Players take turns to: (a) select a card from the blue stack (8 and 9 combinations); (b) select a card from the green stack showing 1 to 6 dots (or roll a one to six die); (c) add the two numbers by making a ten in the chocolate box. The other player can check the answer using a chocolate box and counters if required. If correct, the player keeps these cards. If incorrect, the cards are placed at the bottom of their stacks. When the activity is finished, the players count to see how many cards they have.

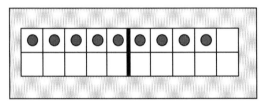

Blue cards

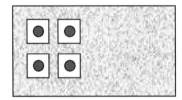

Green cards

**Figure 7.12** Chocolate box cards

**Notes:**

▶ This activity is suitable for pairs.
▶ It can be used as a whole-class activity by arranging students into pairs, with each pair playing the game.
▶ After the game is finished, see if children can solve these additions without using the cards: *What is nine and four? What is eight and six?*

**Materials:** Green and blue chocolate box cards (seen in Figure 7.12), die (if required).

## ACTIVITY IA7.8: Double Ten Frame Facts

**Intended learning:** To use spatial arrangements involving fives, tens and doubles to work out addition facts to 20.

**Description:** Double ten frame cards with dots in some of the cells (Figure 7.13) are flashed to the class. The teacher asks: *How many dots in the upper row? How many dots in the lower row? How many dots altogether? How many more dots to make 20?*

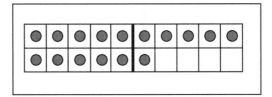

**Figure 7.13** Double ten frame patterns

**Notes:**

▶    Double ten frame cards can be used in the same ways as traditional flash cards.
▶    This activity is suitable for whole class or small groups. Children can work in pairs on this activity.
▶    Ten frame cards with a full ten are easier for students.
▶    A good idea is to work with particular subsets of ten frame cards, for example, cards with doubles, cards with nine on the upper row, cards with eight on the upper row.
▶    The correct responses to the four questions can be written on the back of each card so that children can monitor the responses of others.

**Materials:** Double ten frame cards.

## ACTIVITY IA7.9: Bead Board

**Intended learning:** To use 5 and 10 as reference points in arithmetical situations.

**Description:** The bead board (Figure 7.14) is a small, inexpensive version of the arithmetic rack described earlier in this chapter. This setting provides a structure for numbers to 20 with an emphasis on references to 5 and 10. The bead board can be used for a variety of activities. Students can be asked to name numbers displayed on the bead board or, conversely, children can be asked to display numbers on the bead board. Students can use the bead board to solve additive and subtractive tasks. Students can use the bead board to explore number relationships, such as commutativity and the inverse relationship between addition and subtraction.

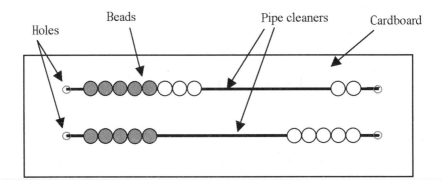

**Figure 7.14** Ten bead board

**Notes:**

▶   Bead boards can be provided to children for specific tasks.
▶   Bead boards could be accessible for children, as needed.
▶   To make a bead board, string beads in two colors onto pipe cleaners, slip pipe cleaners into slits in a rectangle of matte board and twist together in the back.

**Materials:** Ten bead board.

# 8
# 2-digit Addition and Subtraction: Jump Strategies

## Summary

This chapter focusses on the development of a range of strategies which are referred to as jump strategies – in the case of addition, the student begins from one addend goes forward in jumps of tens and ones accordingly to the second addend. The chapter includes detailed descriptions of approaches to the development of these strategies for addition and subtraction.

## TOPIC OVERVIEW

Chapter 7 focusses on the development in children of a range of flexible strategies for addition and subtraction in the range 1 to 20. We refer to these as non-count-by-ones strategies. The emphasis is on procedures that do not involve counting by ones. Included among these are strategies in which 5 or 10 is used as a reference point, strategies involving doubles, and strategies involving various ways of partitioning numbers. Chapter 6 refers to extending the use of advanced counting-by-ones strategies in the range of 20 to 100, keeping in mind that this should involve counting in the range 2 to 5 only. Children who have developed facile non-count-by-ones strategies for adding and subtracting in the range 1 to 20, and who can use the advanced counting-by-ones strategies in the range 1 to 100 are ready to develop mental strategies for addition and subtraction involving two 2-digit numbers.

In Chapter 2 we describe two different kinds of mental strategies used by children when adding or subtracting two 2-digit numbers. These kinds of strategies are referred to as jump and split. In the rest of this chapter we provide an overview of an approach that fosters the development of jump strategies. Chapter 9 focusses on an approach that fosters the development of split strategies. We take the view that instruction can focus on one or both of these approaches, and that the focus on jump strategies can precede the focus on split strategies or vice versa.

## Fostering the Development of Jump Strategies

As described in Chapter 2, in the case of addition, jump strategies involve working from one of the numbers and partitioning the second in order to make several jumps forward. In the case of subtraction, jump strategies involve making several jumps backward or alternatively, jumping forward from the smaller number to the larger, and keeping track to work out the total jump. Jump strategies have the advantage that they are not significantly more difficult to use when the addition of the numbers in the ones exceeds nine. For example, working out 26 + 38 in not necessarily much more difficult than working out 26 + 32. Being facile with addition and subtraction in the range 1 to 20 is a prerequisite for learning jump strategies. Thus, children learning to use jump strategies should not be limited to strategies involving counting-by-ones and should not incorporate counting-by-ones into their developing jump strategies.

The reader is invited to work out the following examples using a jump strategy:

| | | | |
|---|---|---|---|
| 33 + 21 | 56 + 23 | 46 + 38 | 37 + 43 |
| 47 – 11 | 86 – 24 | 92 – 83 | 63 – 37 |

## The Role of the Empty Number Line

The empty number line (ENL) is an instructional device that is regarded as particularly suited to fostering the development of jump strategies. Children use the ENL to make a written record that serves to summarize their particular strategy. In this way children make a record for themselves, for future reference, about how they solved particular tasks. Also, children can use an ENL in this way to communicate their method to their colleagues and the teacher. Examples of the use of the ENL to record jump strategies are provided in Figure 8.1.

## ENL as a Recording Device versus ENL as a Means of Solving a Task

The view taken in this book is that the most productive way for children to use the ENL is as a means of recording a mental strategy. Therefore, children should be strongly encouraged to solve tasks mentally, write their answers, and finally to use the ENL to record their method. This contrasts with the use of the ENL in a procedural way to solve the task. This approach is problematic, we believe, because children will develop a reliance on using the ENL to solve addition and subtraction tasks. The important goal for children is the development of flexible mental strategies. The goal is not to develop an alternative written method for solving addition and subtraction tasks.

## Alternative Means of Recording for Split Strategies

Although this chapter focuses on jump strategies and the use of the ENL for recording jump strategies, teachers should be particularly mindful that, in spite of instruction aimed at fostering jump strategies, children might sometimes use a split strategy and a few children might have a continuing, strong preference for split strategies. As a general rule, it is not productive to use an ENL to record a split strategy. The alternative is to use horizontal number sentences or branching notation to record the child's strategy. Recording split strategies in this way is described in Chapter 9.

## Jump versus Split

Becoming facile with jump strategies is particularly useful because jump strategies tend to be more versatile and flexible than split strategies. This relates in part to the point made above, that is, that some children will find split strategies difficult in cases where the combination (addition or subtraction) in the ones, is beyond the range 1 to 10, that is, calculations that, in terms of the traditional algorithm, involve carrying in the case of addition, or borrowing (regrouping, renaming) in the case of subtraction. It is quite common for children who mainly develop and use split strategies to have particular difficulty when they first encounter subtraction with regrouping. What typically happens in the case of these children is that they do the following: 62 – 25: 60 – 20 = 40; 5 – 2 = 3; answer 43.

53 + 36

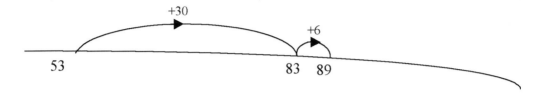

38 + 24

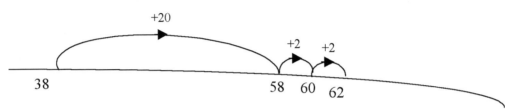

87 - 22

64 - 27

**Figure 8.1** Using the ENL to record jump strategies

## Some Children's Initial Preference for Split Strategies

Children who have difficulty with mental strategies will tend to find the initial split strategy easier to use than the corresponding jump strategy. Thus a child having general difficulty with this topic, when working out 43 + 35, for example, will probably find it easier to use a split strategy than a jump strategy. One reason for this is that using a jump strategy involves incrementing (for addition) or decrementing (for subtraction) off the decade. Thus a child might have difficulty using a jump strategy to work out 47 + 32 because they have difficulty with saying, for example, 47, 57, 67, 77, and simultaneously keeping track of the increments. In order to stop at 77, it is necessary to monitor the increments of ten, and to realize that three increments have been made (corresponding to adding 30 to 47). Instruction focussing on incrementing and decrementing 2-digit numbers on and off the decade is described below. This topic, and the topic of learning to add and subtract through decade numbers, constitute important building blocks for the development of jump strategies.

## Learning to Add and Subtract through Decade Numbers

Children who are facile at adding and subtracting in the range 1 to 20 are ready to extend this to the range 1 to 100. Learning to add and subtract through decade numbers is an important initial step for addition and subtraction involving two 2-digit numbers. The following are two groups of tasks related to this topic, which are important because they can constitute one or more steps of the jump strategy.

### Adding and Subtracting Involving a Decade Number and a Number from 1 to 9

This includes cases such as:

(a) 60 + 5, 40 + 6. For example, 60 + 5 might arise as the final step when using a jump strategy to work out 38 + 27.
(b) 52 − X = 50, 74 − X = 70. For example, 74 − X =7 0 might arise as an interim step when using a jump strategy to work out 94 − 26.
(c) 27 + X = 30, 58 + X = 60. For example, 58 + X = 60 might arise as an interim step when using a jump strategy to work out 38 + 27.
(d) 80 − 6, 50 − 5. For example, 50 − 5 might arise as the final step when using a jump strategy to work out 72 − 27.

### Adding and Subtracting Involving a Non-decade Number and a Number from 1 to 9

This includes cases such as:

(e) 62 + 5, 43 + 6. For example, 62 + 5 might arise the final step when using a jump strategy to work out 32 + 35.
(f) 56 − 3, 48 − 5. For example, 48 − 5 might arise as the final step when using a jump strategy to work out 98 − 55.
(g) 67 + 8, 88 + 4. For example, 88 + 4 might arise as the final step when using a jump strategy to work out 68 + 24.
(h) 53 − 6, 41 − 5. For example, 41 − 5 might arise as the final step when using a jump strategy to work out 71 − 35.

## Learning to Increment and Decrement 2-digit Numbers

Learning to increment and decrement 2-digit numbers by 10 is an important first step in developing strategies for addition and subtraction involving 2-digit numbers. This topic consists of two main steps. These are, incrementing and decrementing on the decade and incrementing and decrementing off the decade. The decade numbers are the numbers 10, 20, ... 100.

### Incrementing and Decrementing on the Decade

Incrementing by 10 on the decade involves being able to say immediately, the number that is 10 more than a given decade number. This corresponds with being able to say the next highest decade number after a given decade number. Similarly, decrementing by 10 on the decade corresponds to saying the next lowest decade number.

### Incrementing and Decrementing off the Decade

Incrementing by 10 off the decade refers to incrementing a non-decade number by 10, that is, saying immediately the number that is 10 more than a given non-decade number; for example, saying immediately the number that is 10 more than 72 (82). Similarly, an example of decrementing off the decade is to say immediately, the number that is 10 less than 47 (37).

### Incrementing and Decrementing versus Counting-by-ones

While the tasks of incrementing and decrementing on and off the decade seem rather trivial and easily learned, significant numbers of children in the middle and upper elementary years and beyond seem unable to do these, at least in the context of trying to solve 2-digit addition and subtraction tasks, and to solve these mentally rather than use a standard written method, that is, a standard algorithm. Children who might be expected to increment or decrement by 10, and cannot do so, typically will use counting-on or counting-back by ones to solve the task in question. For example, to work out what is ten more than 72, they will count-on from 72 and keep track of their counts, and stop when they have made 10 counts, that is, they will stop at 82.

### Incrementing and Decrementing by Several 10s

Children who can increment or decrement by 10, can easily extend this to incrementing or decrementing by several tens; that is, they can learn to work out, for example, 54 and three more 10s or 54 and 30 more. Instructional strategies for children to learn to increment and decrement by 10 and by several 10s are based on the use of one or more of the materials commonly used as a basis for learning about 2-digit numbers, such as ten-strips or bundling sticks.

### Incrementing and Decrementing Flexibly by 10s and Ones

Children should also learn to increment and decrement flexibly by 10s and ones. As an example of incrementing, the child might start from 14 and add 10, then add 15 to the answer, add 32 to that answer and so on. As an example of decrementing, the child might start from 96 and take 10, then take 13 from the answer, then take 25 from the answer and so on. Tasks of this kind can be presented initially using ten-strips. This can progress to tasks presented verbally or in written form without the use of materials such as ten-strips.

## Fostering the Development of a Range of Strategies

Over a series of lessons where children are encouraged to use jump and split strategies (see Chapter 9), the children can develop to the point where they can flexibly use either strategy according to their own particular preference. This can also involve development and use of a range of mental strategies. The following are some of the other strategies children frequently use. Many of these are quite similar to jump strategies. Also, except for the strategies involving transforming (see below), these can also be recorded on an ENL.

## Split-jump for Addition

The first step of this strategy involves splitting and working with the tens part of each number, the second step involves adding on the ones part of one number and finally adding on the ones part of the other number.

37 + 45:  30 + 40 is → 70, 70 + 7 → 77, 77 + 3 → 80, 80 + 2 → 82.

## Split-jump for Subtraction

Again, the first step of this strategy involves splitting and working with the tens part of each number, the second step involves adding on the ones part of the minuend. Finally, the ones part of one subtrahend is subtracted.

75 – 26:  70 – 20 → 50, 50 + 5 → 55, 55 – 5 → 50, 50 – 1 → 49

## Subtraction by Adding Up

This involves starting from the subtrahend, adding numbers until the minend is reached, and keeping track of the numbers added.

63 – 48:  48 + 10 → 58, 58 + 2 → 60, 60 + 3 → 63, making 15 in all.

## Addition by Jumping To 10

38 + 47:  38 + 2 → 40, 40 + 40 → 80, 80 + 5 → 85

## Subtraction by Jumping To 10

64 – 49:   64 – 4 → 60,  60 – 40 → 20,  20 – 5 → 15

## Addition by Transforming

48 + 27:   transform to 50 + 25

## Subtraction by Transforming

96 – 39:   transform to 97 – 40

## Addition by Compensation

24 + 49:  24 + 49 → 24 + 50 – 1, that is, 74 – 1 → 73

## Subtraction by Compensation

73 – 48:  73 – 48 → 73 – 50 + 2 → 23 + 2 → 25

# ASSESSMENT TASK GROUPS

## List of Assessment Task Groups

A8.1: Forward and backward number word sequences by 10s, on and off the decade
A8.2: Adding from a decade and subtracting to a decade
A8.3: Adding to a decade and subtracting from a decade
A8.4: Incrementing and decrementing by 10s on and off the decade
A8.5: Incrementing flexibly by10s and ones
A8.6: Adding 10s to a 2-digit number and subtracting 10s from a 2-digit number
A8.7: Adding two 2-digit numbers without and with regrouping
A8.8: Subtraction involving two 2-digit numbers without and with regrouping
A8.9: Addition and subtraction using transforming, compensating and other strategies

## TASK GROUP A8.1: Forward and Backward Number Word Sequences by 10s, on and off the Decade

**Materials:** None.

**What to do and say:** On the decade: *Can you count by tens? Okay, can you start from 90 and go backwards?*

Off the decade: *Can you start from 24 and count by tens? Okay, can you start from 97 and go backwards by tens?*

**Notes:**

▷ If the child has difficulty, say the first two or three number words. For example: *Can you count by tens – 10, 20 –? Can you start from 24? From 34?*
▷ In the case of saying the forward sequence off the decade, the first three words (four, fourteen, twenty-four) can be difficult for children because there is not a simple verbal pattern compared with twenty-four, thirty-four, forty-four.
▷ These tasks differ from those in Task Group A8.4 because in Task Group A8.4 the children are incrementing and decrementing in the context of base-ten materials.
▷ Developing facility with these tasks is important for the development of jump strategies for addition and subtraction involving two 2-digit numbers.

## TASK GROUP A8.2: Adding from a Decade and Subtracting to a Decade

**Materials:** Writing book and pens/pencils.

**What to do and say:** Adding from a decade. Use tasks such as the following: 40 + 7, 20 + 5, 90 + 3, and so on. Draw an (empty number line ENL) and mark 40 on the line (use a vertical stroke and write '40' under the stroke). Write the task 40 + 7 below the ENL. *What is 40 plus 7? Use this ENL to show that.* Similarly for 20 + 5, 90 + 3, and so on.

Subtracting to a decade. Use tasks such as the following: 63 – X = 60, 86 – X = 80, 39 – X = 30, and so on. Draw an ENL and mark 63 (as in Task Group A8.1). *What is the next decade number below 63?* Write the task 63 – X = 60 below the ENL. *What taken from 63 leaves 60? Use this ENL to show that.* Similarly for 86 – X= 80, 39 – X = 30, and so on.

**Notes:**

▶ In order to solve these tasks children should have knowledge of the use of the ENL to record addition and subtraction.

▶ Adding from a decade and subtracting to a decade are important building blocks for the development of mental strategies for addition and subtraction involving two 2-digit numbers.

▶ Observe closely to see if the child uses counting by ones to keep track.

## TASK GROUP A8.3: Adding to a Decade and Subtracting from a Decade

**Materials:** Writing book and pens/pencils.

**What to do and say:** Adding to a decade (1 to 5). Use tasks such as the following: 38 + X = 40, 75 + X = 80, 26 + X = 30, and so on. Draw an ENL and mark 38 (as in Task Group A8.1). Write the task 38 + X = 40 below the ENL. *What is the next decade number after 38? What number added to 38 makes 40? Use this ENL to show that.* Similarly for 75 + X = 80, 26 + X = 30, and so on.

Subtracting from a decade (1 to 5). Use tasks such as the following: 30 – 4, 60 – 2, 90 – 5 etc. Draw an ENL and mark 30. Write the task 30 – 4 below the ENL. *What is 30 – 4? Use this ENL to show that.* Similarly for 60 – 2, 90 – 5, and so on.

Adding to a decade (6 to 9). Use tasks such as the following: 54 + X = 60, 21 + X = 30, 83 + X = 90, and so on. Draw an ENL and mark 54. *What is the next decade number after 54?* Write the task 54 + X = 60 below the ENL. *What number added to 54 makes 60? Use this ENL to show that.* Similarly for 75 + X = 80, 26 + X =30, and so on.

Subtracting from a decade (6 to 9). Use tasks such as the following: 60 – 7, 40 – 9, 60 – 6, and so on. Draw an ENL and mark 60. Write the task 60 – 7 below the ENL. *What is 30 – 4? Use this ENL to show that.* Similarly for 40 – 9, 60 – 6, and so on.

**Notes:**

▶ In order to solve these tasks children should have knowledge of the use of the ENL to record addition and subtraction.

▶ Adding to a decade and subtracting from a decade are important building blocks for the development of mental strategies for addition and subtraction involving two 2-digit numbers.

▶ Observe closely to see if the child uses counting-by-ones to keep track.

## TASK GROUP A8.4: Incrementing and Decrementing by 10s on and off the Decade

**Materials:** Ten-strips (strips of cardboard of length 10 cm containing 10 dots), four-strips, and so on (like a ten-strip but with only 4 dots), a screen of cardboard or cloth.

**What to do and say:** Incrementing on the decade. Place out three ten-strips. *How many dots are there? How many tens are there?* Screen the 3 tens. Place another ten-strip under the screen. *How many dots are there now? How many tens are there?* Continue up to 100, adding one or two ten-strips at a time.

Incrementing by Tens

Decrementing on the decade. Place out nine ten-strips. *How many dots are there? How many tens are there?* Screen the nine ten-strips. Take one ten from under the screen. *How many dots are there now? How many tens are there?* Continue down to zero, taking one or two ten-strips at a time.

Incrementing off the decade. Place out two ten-strips and a four-strip. *How many dots are there?* Screen the 24 dots. Place another ten-strip under the screen. *How many dots are there now?* Continue up to 104, adding one or two ten-strips at a time.

Decrementing off the decade. Place out nine ten-strips and a six-strip. *How many dots are there?* Screen the 96 dots. Take one ten-strip from under the screen. *How many dots are there now?* Continue down to 6, taking one or two ten-strips at a time.

**Notes:**

▶ Observe closely to see if the child uses counting-by-ones. For example, 30 and ten more *(31, 32, 33, ... 40)* and, 96 take away ten *(95, 94, 93, ... 86)*.

▶ Children who use counting by ones are likely to use their fingers to keep track of ten counts.

## TASK GROUP A8.5: Incrementing Flexibly by 10s and Ones

**Materials:** Piece of cardboard about 40 cm long containing the following sets: a ten-strip; a six-strip; two ten-strips; a ten-strip and a two-strip; two ten-strips and a four-strip aligned on the piece of cardboard as follows: 10; 6; 10 and 10; 10 and 2; 10 and 10 and 4. Two screens about 30 cm in length as seen in Figure 8.2.

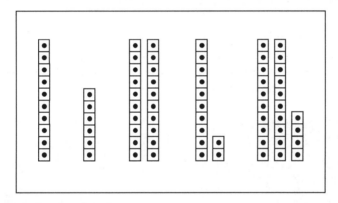

**Figure 8.2** Incrementing by Tens and Ones

**What to do and say:** Screen all of the number strips. Move the screen to the right, thereby unscreening the first ten-strip. *How many dots are there (10)?* Uncover the six-strip. *How many dots altogether now (16)?* Uncover the next two ten-strips. *How many altogether now (36)?* Use the second strip to screen the first 36 dots, and then unscreen the next ten-strip and the two-strip. *How many altogether now (48)?* Now unscreen the remaining two ten-strips and the four-strip. *How many altogether now (72)? How many more would I need to make 100?*

**Notes:**

▶ This task has six parts. Children might use counting-by-ones during any of these parts.

▶ Some children might increment by tens on the first two or three parts of the task, and then count by ones for the latter parts.

Uncovering Tasks (1)

Uncovering Tasks (2)

## TASK GROUP A8.6: Adding 10s to a 2-digit Number and Subtracting 10s from a 2-digit Number

**Materials:** Writing book and pens and pencils.

**What to do and say:** Adding 10 to a 2-digit number. Use tasks such as the following: 42 + 10, 67 + 10, 24 + 10, and so on. Draw an ENL and mark 42. Write the task 42 + 10 below the ENL. *What is 42 plus 10? Use this ENL to show that.* Similarly for 67 + 10, 24 + 10 etc.

Subtracting 10 from a two-digit number

Subtracting 10 from a 2-digit number. Use tasks such as the following: 73 – 10, 58 – 10, 95 – 10, and so on. Draw an ENL and mark 73. Write the task 73 – 10 below the ENL. *What is 73 take away 10? Use this ENL to show that.* Similarly for 58 – 10, 95 – 10, and so on.

Adding larger decades to a 2-digit number. Use tasks such as the following: 64 + 20, 23 + 50, 62 + 30, and so on. Draw an ENL and mark 64. Write the task 64 + 20 below the ENL. *What is 64 plus 20? Use this ENL to show that.* Similarly for 23 + 50, 62 + 30, and so on.

Subtracting larger decades from a 2-digit number. Use tasks such as the following: 72 – 20, 91 – 70, 45 – 30, and so on. Draw an ENL and mark 72. Write the task 72 – 20 below the ENL. *What is 72 take away 20? Use this ENL to show that.* Similarly for 91 – 70, 45 – 30, and so on.

**Notes:**

▶ These are also important building blocks for the development of mental strategies for addition and subtraction involving two 2-digit numbers.

▶ For tasks involving larger decades (20, 30, and so on, rather than 10) gauge to what extent the child increments or decrements one 10 at a time (versus work with the larger decade number).

▶ Children who increment or decrement one 10 at a time, might use counting- by-ones to keep track of the number of 10s, particularly in the case of larger decade numbers (40, 50, 60, and so on).

## TASK GROUP A8.7: Adding Two 2-digit Numbers without and with Regrouping

**Materials:** Writing book and pens/pencils.

**What to do and say:** Addition without regrouping. Use tasks such as the following: 52 + 24, 65 + 33, 37 + 42 etc. Draw an ENL and mark 52. Write the task 52 + 24 below the ENL. *What is 52 plus 24? Use this ENL to show that.* Similarly for 65 + 33, 37 + 42, and so on.

Addition with regrouping. Use tasks such as the following: 59 + 34, 38 + 25, 64 + 28, and so on. Draw an ENL and mark 59. Write the task 59 + 34 below the ENL. *What is 59 plus 34? Use this ENL to show that.* Similarly for 38 + 25, 64 + 28, and so on.

**Notes:**

▶ Children are likely to work left to right, although some might work right to left (working with the ones first then the 10s). Working right to left is much more likely if the child has received formal or informal instruction in the standard written algorithm.

▶ It is important to gauge whether the child's tendency is to use a jump strategy, a split strategy or some other strategy, or whether the child uses a range of strategy types (jump, split, split-jump, and so on).

▶ The ENL is particularly suited to recording jump strategies and similar strategies, (for example, jumping to ten – see earlier in this chapter).

▶ In the case of addition with regrouping, some children might use a jumping to ten strategy (59 + 34: 60 + 33: 93)

▶ If the child has a strong tendency to use split strategies, the interviewer should indicate to the child an alternative means of recording involving a sequence of number sentences (52 + 24: 50 + 20 = 70, 2 + 4 = 6, 70 + 6 = 76) rather than the ENL.

▶ Observe closely to see if, when using a jump strategy, the child uses counting-by-ones to keep track of the 10s or the ones (52, 62, 72, then 73, 74, 75, 76!). Using counting-by-ones might also be indicated in the child's recording on the ENL.

▶ Rather than use an advanced strategy (jump, split, split-jump, and so on) some children will use counting-by-ones (52, 53, 54, 55 ... 76). This involves a triple count: keeping track of the ones in each 10, the number of tens counted (2), and the overall total. Children who use counting-by-ones are likely to use their 10 fingers to keep track of the ones in each 10.

## TASK GROUP A8.8: Subtraction Involving Two 2-digit Numbers without and with Regrouping

**Materials:** Writing book and pens/pencils.

**What to do and say:** Subtraction without regrouping. Use tasks such as the following: 87 – 32, 45 – 24, 99 – 65, and so on. Draw an ENL and mark 87. Write the task 87 – 32 below the ENL. *What is 87 take away 32? Use this ENL to show that.* Similarly for 45 – 24, 99 – 65, and so on.

Subtraction with regrouping. Use tasks such as the following: 62 – 28, 81 – 29, 73 – 34, and so on. Draw an ENL and mark 62. Write the task 62 – 28 below the ENL. *What is 62 take away 28? Use this ENL to show that.* Similarly for 81 – 29, 73 – 34, and so on.

**Notes:**

▶ Many of the notes for Task Group A8.7 apply to this task group as well.
▶ As with addition (Task Group A8.7), the ENL is particularly suited to recording jump strategies and similar strategies.
▶ Examples of strategies similar to jump strategies which can be recorded on the ENL include: jumping to ten in the case of regrouping (62 – 28: 60, 40, 34); adding up (99 – 65: 65, 95, 99 → 34); and compensating (82 – 39: 42, 43).
▶ Children who have a strong tendency to use split strategies might have significant difficulties with subtraction with regrouping.
▶ A very common difficulty is the following: 62 – 28: 60 – 20 = 40; 8 – 2 = 6; 40 + 6 = 46. Also 60 – 20 = 40; 12 – 8 = 4; 40 + 4 = 44.

## TASK GROUP A8.9: Addition and Subtraction using Transforming, Compensating and Other Strategies

**Materials:** Writing book and pens/pencils.

**What to do and say:** Addition. Use tasks such as the following: 32 + 34, 48 + 29, 17 + 58, 28 + 29, and so on. Draw an ENL and mark 32. Write the task 32 + 34 below the ENL. *What is 32 plus 34? Use this ENL or write number sentences to show how you work it out.* Similarly for 48 + 29, 17 + 58, and so on.

**Subtraction:** Use tasks such as the following: 72 – 68, 51 – 25, 77 – 29, and so on. Draw an ENL and mark 72. Write the task 72 – 68 below the ENL. *What is 72 minus 68? Use this ENL or write number sentences to show how you work it out.* Similarly for 51 – 25, 77 – 29, and so on.

**Notes:**

▶    Close observation of children's solutions is an excellent way to learn about the diverse range of strategies used by children.

▶    Examples of transforming: 32 + 34 is the same as 33 + 33 → 66! 77 – 29 is the same as 78 – 30 → 48.

▶    Examples of compensating: 17 + 58, I will add on 60 and take off 2 → 77 → 75! 77 – 29, I will take off 30 and add on one → 47 → 48.

▶    Examples of using a known sum: 28 + 29, I know 30 + 30 = 60, so 28 + 29 is 60 –3 → 57; 51-25, I know 25 + 25 = 50, so 51 – 25 is 26.

▶    Example of subtraction by adding up: 72 – 68, 68 + 2 is 70, 70 + 2 is 72 → 4.

# INSTRUCTIONAL ACTIVITIES

## List of Instructional Activities

IA8.1: Leap Frog
IA8.2: Bead String with Ten Catcher
IA8.3: Add or Subtract 11
IA8.4: Add to or Subtract from 49
IA8.5: Calculator Challenge
IA8.6: Jump to 100
IA8.7: Jump from 100
IA8.8: Target Number
IA8.9: Walk-about Sequences
IA8.10: Non-standard Measurement Plan

## ACTIVITY IA8.1: Leap Frog

**Intended learning:** To develop knowledge of 2-digit addition and subtraction with and without regrouping.

**Description:** A Leap Frog game board and special spinners are used (see Figures 8.3 and 8.4 to generate mixed addition and subtraction problems. Playing rules:

| 90 | 23 | 51 | 38 | 22 |
|----|----|----|----|-----|
| 28 | 48 | 92 | 63 | 92 |
| 33 | 63 | 42 | 37 | 104 |
| 52 | 75 | 22 | 62 | 28 |
| 78 | 13 | 37 | 90 | 75 |

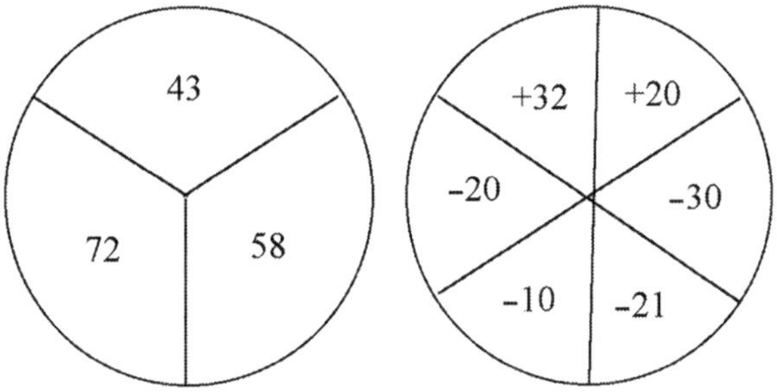

Leap Frog A Spinners

(Spinner 1: 43, 72, 58)
(Spinner 2: +32, +20, −30, −21, −10, −20)

**Figure 8.3** Leap Frog A

▶ Player 1 spins to create an addition or subtraction problem.

▶ The player states the number sentence and places the counter on the answer. The player may use an empty number line or number chart to solve the problem.

▶ The next player then has a turn.

▶ Players take turns until one player has three counters in a row (horizontally, vertically or diagonally).

| 78 | 40 | 18 | 113 | 89 |
|----|----|----|-----|----|
| 100 | 29 | 91 | 7 | 18 |
| 18 | 81 | 64 | 89 | 70 |
| 86 | 7 | 102 | 81 | 29 |
| 75 | 91 | 40 | 64 | 92 |

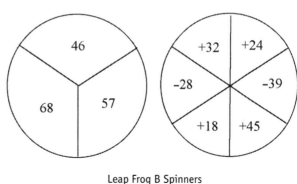

Leap Frog B Spinners

**Figure 8.4** Leap Frog B

Notes:

▶    None of the possible problems from Leap Frog A involve regrouping.
▶    Some of the problems possible from Leap Frog B involve regrouping.
▶    The empty number line or a number chart may be used to provide additional learner support.
▶    Spinners are created by holding a pencil point through a paper clip to the centre of the spinner as seen in Figure 8.5. Flick the paper clip to spin.
▶    The spinners can be varied to suit the needs of the children.
▶    This activity is suitable for small group, pairs and individuals.

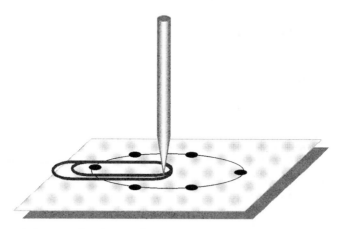

**Figure 8.5** Spinner made from pencil and paper clip

**Materials:** Leap Frog game board and spinners, two different kinds of counters or markers, paper clips (for spinners), pencil, scrap paper for empty number line (optional).

## ACTIVITY IA8.2: Bead String with Ten Catcher

**Intended Learning:** To add ten and tens to any number.

**Description:** Use a bead string with alternating colors for each set of 10 beads. Briefly show the first collection and then cover with a tube or piece of cloth (a). Use a ten catcher to slide a second collection beside the first as illustrated (b). Leave the second collection uncovered. Ask: *How many in all? How did you know?*

**Variation:** both collections may be screened.

**Notes:**

▶   This activity is suitable for whole class, small group or individuals.
▶   Choose the progression of problems carefully to support learning.

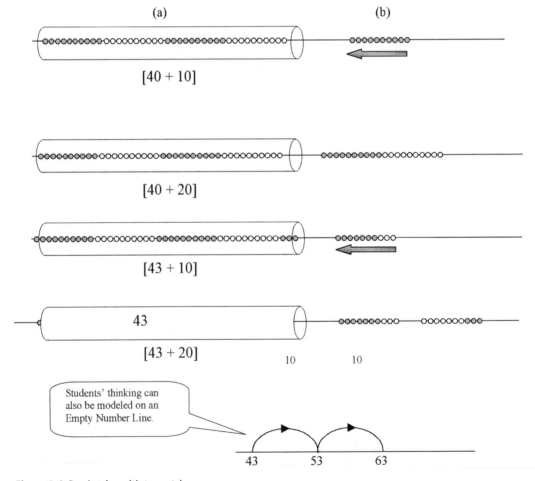

**Figure 8.6** Bead string with ten catcher

**Materials**: String of 100 beads in alternating colors of lots of ten, tube or cloth for cover, chalk or white board for recording thinking.

## ACTIVITY IA8.3: Add or Subtract 11

**Intended Learning:** To add or subtract 11 from any 2-digit number.

**Description:** Use the Add or Subtract 11 game board to generate problems with addends and subtrahends of 11. A hundred chart could be used to support learning.

The object is to cover three squares in a row with counters. Player A spins to create an addition or subtraction problem. This player states the number sentence and places the counter on the answer. An empty number line can be used to solve the problem. Player B repeats this process. Players take turns until one player has three counters in a row horizontally, vertically or diagonally.

| 43 | 21 | 14 | 35 | 21 |
|----|----|----|----|----|
| 39 | 15 | 43 | 21 | 43 |
| 21 | 35 | 39 | 14 | 15 |
| 14 | 21 | 35 | 15 | 39 |
| 40 | 43 | 15 | 35 | 14 |

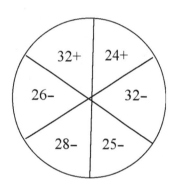

**Figure 8.7** Add or Subtract 11

**Notes:**

▶ This activity is suitable for whole class, small group, pairs or individuals.
▶ As a variation, have children create their own game board and spinner. The games could be named after the creator and added to a collection of maths activities for use by the class.

**Materials**: Add or Subtract 11 game board and spinner, two different types of counters or markers, paper clip and pencil (for spinner).

## ACTIVITY IA8.4: Add to, or Subtract from, 49

**Intended learning:** To solve 2-digit addition and subtraction problems with addends and subtrahends that are multiples of ten.

**Description:** Use the Add or Subtract from 49 game board to generate addition and subtraction problems that involve making jumps that are multiples of ten. The object is to cover three squares in a row with counters. Player A spins to determine the amount to add or subtract to 49. This player states the number sentence and places the counter on the answer. Player B repeats this process. Players take turns until one player has three counters in a row horizontally, vertically or diagonally.

| 29 | 19 | 9 | 79 | 89 |
|----|----|----|----|----|
| 69 | 59 | 29 | 19 | 79 |
| 9 | 69 | 89 | 9 | 39 |
| 39 | 29 | 9 | 79 | 89 |
| 39 | 59 | 69 | 19 | 9 |

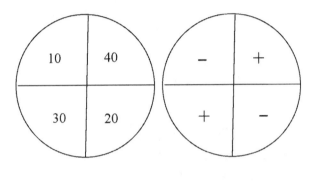

**Figure 8.8** Add to, or subtract from, 49

**Notes:**

▶   This activity is suitable for whole class, small group, pairs or individuals.
▶   A hundred chart and empty number line may be used to support learning.
▶   As a variation use the Add or Subtract from 89 game board to bridge 100.

**Materials:** Add or Subtract from 49 game board and spinners, two kinds of counters or markers, paper clips and pencils for spinners, hundred chart (optional). (See Figure 8.8)

## ACTIVITY IA8.5: Calculator Challenge

**Intended learning:** To solve problems involving 2-digit addition and subtraction with missing addends and subtrahends.

**Description:** The teacher instructs the children to enter a number into their calculator, (for example, 54). Then tells them a new target number, (for example, 34). Their challenge is to change the display screen so that the new target number appears in the screen without entering that number. They may use the +, – and = keys, but not the C (clear key).

**Figure 8.9** Calculator challenge

The individual or team who can reach the new target number by pushing the least number of keys, wins the challenge.

Variation: the children might be given the restriction that they can only add or subtract 10 or 1.
Variation: the beginning numbers and target numbers could be on a worksheet and children would record the keys pressed to reach the target numbers.

Notes:

▶   This activity is suitable for whole class, small group, pairs, one on one and individuals.
▶   At first, sets of numbers should be achievable by making jumps of ten only.
▶   For a challenge, the target number might be achieved by adding a multiple of ten and subtracting one or adding two.

**Materials:** Calculator for each individual or team, paper and pencil (optional).

## ACTIVITY IA8.6: Jump to 100

**Intended learning:** To add two 2-digit numbers using the jump method and using the empty number line to record the strategy.

**Description:** Use the hundred square and spinners to generate 2-digit addition problems. Record each problem that is generated as a separate horizontal number sentence. Pairs may be substituted for individual players. Player A places a marker on 1. Each spinner is spun to make the number that is to be added. The number Player A is on and the number spun are recorded. Use the jump method to move the marker to find the sum. The sum of the two numbers is recorded. Player B repeats these steps. Players alternate turns until both players have reached at least 100. For example: Player A is on 23 and spins 30 and 4. Record 23 + 34. Player A works out the sum mentally and uses an empty number line to record their strategy.

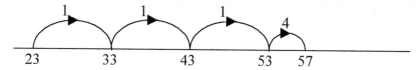

**Figure 8.10** Using the ENL to record the solution to 23 + 34

Record 23 + 34 = 57.

Notes:

▶   Spinners are created by holding a pencil point through a paper clip to the centre of the spinner. Flick the paper clip to spin, (see Figure 8.5).

▶    This activity is suitable for small groups or pairs.
▶    The game can be extended beyond 100.

**Materials:** Hundred square, two paper clips (for spinners), different tokens or markers such as dried beans for each player or team, pencil and paper.

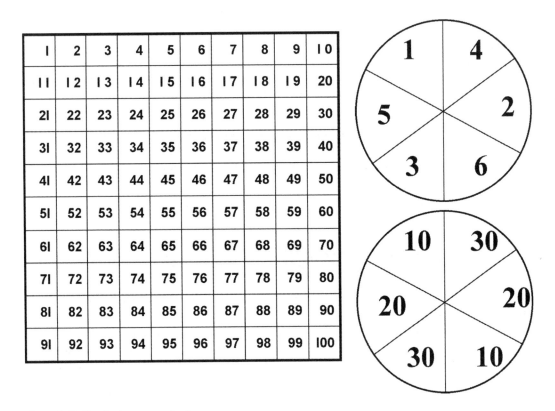

**Figure 8.11** Hundred square and spinners

## ACTIVITY IA8.7: Jump from 100

**Intended learning:** To subtract a 2-digit numbers using the jump method with the support of the number chart.

**Description:** Use the hundred square (see Activity 8.6) and spinners to generate 2-digit subtraction problems. Record each problem that is generated as a separate horizontal number sentence. Pairs may be substituted for individual players. Player A places a marker on 100. Each spinner is spun to make the number that is to be subtracted. The number Player A is on and the number spun are recorded. Use the jump method to move the marker to find the solution. The difference of the two numbers is recorded. Player B repeats these steps. Players alternate turns until both players have reached at least 1. For example: Player A is on 58 and spins 30 and 4. Record 58 – 34. Start at 58 and jump up 3 rows and left 4 columns. Record 58 – 34 = 24.

Notes:

▶   As an alternative, use an empty number line as in Activity IA8.6.

**Materials:** Hundred square and spinners shown above in Activity IA8.6, two paper clips (for spinners), different tokens or markers such as dried beans for each player or team, pencil and paper.

## ACTIVITY IA8.8: Target Number

**Intended learning:** To jump by tens on a hundred square.

**Description:** A hundred square is placed on an overhead projector. The teacher selects a target number (53, for example) and places a translucent counter on this square. The teacher underlines a starting number (for example, 89) with a water based pen and also puts a translucent counter on this square. Students are selected individually to come to the front and show how the starting counter can be moved to get to the target number. The different strategies are discussed with students deciding how many were added or subtracted on each move. The whole class could then participate in this activity. Individuals or pairs of students could have their own hundred square to try to find the quickest way to get the target number.

Notes:

▶   When the strategies are being discussed, note those students who count by ones and those who count by tens.

▶   A similar activity can be found at the site: www.oswego.org/ocsd-web/games/SplatSquares/splatre100.html

**Materials:** Hundred square transparency, student hundred squares and counters.

## ACTIVITY IA8.9: Walk-about Sequences

**Intended learning:** To practice the forward and backward number word sequences by ten on and off the decade numbers.

**Description:** The teacher begins the activity by roaming about the room while saying the number word sequence aloud. At some point, she touches a child. That child will then pick up the sequencing and wandering. When the teacher says *Stop!* the sequencer touches the nearest child. That child then continues the walk-about sequencing. The activity can be done with any number word sequence. Repeat from various starting points.

Notes:

▶   A number chart may be used for additional learning support.
▶   This activity is suitable for whole-class warm-up or an indoor recess activity.
▶   The child could choose when to tap the next person.
▶   For a challenge, extend the sequence beyond 100.

**Materials:** None.

## ACTIVITY IA8.10: Non-standard Measurement Plan

**Intended learning:** To use non-standard measurements to facilitate the development of the linear concept of number and use of the empty number line.

**Description:** Determine a reasonable scenario for the children that involves measuring items in the classroom. For example, students might be measuring to create a floor plan so that the teacher can decide how to arrange the furniture. Have students use Unifix cubes (or another brand of connecting cubes) to measure. Give them various objects to measure. Have them record their measurements for later use. Some of the objects should be quite long to encourage the children to develop a means of keeping track of tens. After sufficient time has been given for measurement, hold a discussion in which individuals share their findings. String together 100 Unifix cubes, alternating two colors in lots of five or ten. Record their findings on a strip of adding machine tape affixed below the cubes. Have the children use the cubes to confirm the placement of the measurement on the tape. Encourage the use of already recorded measurements in locating other measurements. Begin with the smallest objects and work toward the larger ones. On subsequent days, add new measurements to the plan. Ask children to determine the length if two items are combined. As they explain their thinking, record operations with a series of arcs drawn above the tape. In future discussions, refer back to the adding machine tape as the empty number line emerges as a tool for communicating mathematical thinking.

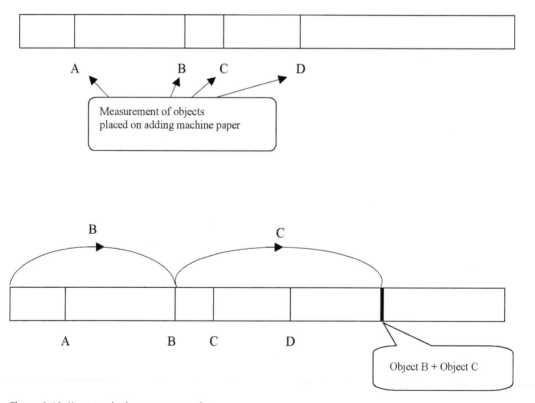

**Figure 8.12** Non-standard measurement plan

**Notes:**

▶    Put special emphasis on benchmark numbers such as decade numbers.
▶    This activity may involve whole class, small group, pairs or individuals.

**Materials:** Connecting cubes, string (for cubes attached to board), adding machine tape, various items to measure.

This activity is based on the research of Stephan et al. (2003) and modified from the video study of Cameron et al. (2004).

# 9
# 2-digit Addition and Subtraction: Split Strategies

***Summary***

This chapter focusses on the development of a range of strategies which are referred to as split strategies – in the case of addition, the student splits each of the two addends into tens and ones and then separately combines, tens with tens and ones with ones. The chapter includes detailed descriptions of approaches to the development of these strategies for addition and subtraction.

## TOPIC OVERVIEW

Chapter 8 focussed on the development of jump strategies and related kinds of strategies for adding and subtracting two 2-digit numbers. This chapter focusses on the development of split strategies. As indicated in Chapter 8, base-ten materials are considered important for the development of split strategies, and this chapter includes a focus on the use of base-ten materials. This chapter also includes the topic of higher decade addition and subtraction, a forerunner to 2-digit addition and subtraction. Also included is a focus on extending strategies for adding and subtracting 2-digit numbers, to working with two 3-digit numbers.

## Higher Decade Addition and Subtraction

Higher decade addition and subtraction involves a 2-digit number and a number in the range 1 to 10. This is because each addition or subtraction of this kind, can be linked to a corresponding addition or subtraction respectively, in the range 1 to 10 or 1 to 20. For example, 43 + 5 can be linked to 3 + 5, 75 – 2 can be linked to 5 – 2, 76 + 9, can be linked to 6 + 9, and 52 – 7 can be linked to 12 – 7. Thus solving a higher decade addition or subtraction task can involve using the corresponding addition or subtraction respectively. For example, 3 + 4 is used to work out 53 + 4, 7 + 8 is used to work out 37 + 8, 7 – 2 is used to work out 87 – 2 and 14 – 9 is used to work out 44 – 9. Second, by starting with addition (or subtraction) in the range 1 to 10 or 1 to 20, a sequence of additions (or subtractions) can be determined. For example, 3 + 4, 13 + 4, 23 + 4, and so on; 7 + 8, 17 + 8, 27 + 8, and so on; 7 – 2, 17 – 2, 27 – 2, and so on.; 14 – 9, 24 – 9, 34 – 9, and so on. Children can come to see the simple pattern in these kinds of sequences involving addition or subtraction.

### Within the Decade – Addition

This involves cases such as 47 + 2, 83 + 5, 64 + 4, and so on. Children should be able to solve these tasks using the corresponding addition in the range 1 to 10, for example, using 7 + 2 to work out

47 + 2. Tasks of this kind can be an important building block for adding two 2-digit numbers. For example, when a child works out 27 + 22 by first adding 27 and 20, the next step involves adding 47 and 2.

## Within the Decade – Subtraction

This involves cases such as 49 – 2, 88 – 5, 68 – 4, and so on. Children should be able to solve these tasks using the corresponding subtraction in the range 1 to 10, for example, using 9 – 2 to work out 49 – 2. Tasks of this kind can be an important building block for subtracting two 2-digit numbers. For example, when a child works out 69 – 22 by first working out 69 – 20, the next step involves working out 49 – 2.

## Beyond the Decade – Addition

This involves cases such as 46 + 7, 77 + 5, 29 + 6, and so on. Two ways that children might work out this problem are: (a) using the corresponding addition in the range 1 to 20, for example, using 6 + 7 to work out 46 + 7; and (b) working the addition out directly without using 6 + 7, for example, first solving 46 + X = 50, then partitioning 7 into 4 and 3, and finally adding 50 and 3. Tasks of this kind can be an important building block for adding two 2-digit numbers. For example, when a child works out 26 + 27 by first adding 26 and 20, the next step involves adding 46 and 7.

## Beyond the Decade – Subtraction

This involves cases such as 53 – 7, 82 – 5, 35 – 6, and so on. Two ways that children might work out this problem are: (a) using the corresponding subtraction in the range 1 to 20, for example, using 13 – 7 to work out 53 – 7; and (b) first solving 53 – X = 50, and then partitioning 7 into 3 and 4, and finally solving 50 – 4. Tasks of this kind can be an important building block for subtracting two 2-digit numbers. For example, when a child works out 73 – 27 by first working out 73 – 20, the next step involves working out 53 – 7.

## Sequences in Higher Decade Addition and Subtraction

Children can work with and record sequences such as the following:

5 + 2 = 7; 15 + 2 = 17; 25 + 2 = 27; 35 + 2 = 37; and so on.
8 – 3 = 5; 18 – 3 = 15; 28 – 3 = 25; 38 – 3 = 35; and so on.
8 + 4 = 12; 18 + 4 = 22; 28 + 4 = 32; 38 + 4 = 42; and so on.
11 – 6 = 5; 21 – 6 = 15; 31 – 6 = 25; 41 – 6 = 35; and so on.

Working with these sequences can help children make connections from a higher decade addition or subtraction to a corresponding addition or subtraction in the range 1 to 10 or 1 to 20.

# Fostering the Development of Split Strategies

As described in Chapter 2, split strategies involve calculating separately with tens and ones. First, the child calculates with the tens, then with the ones, and finally the resultant tens and ones are combined. The split strategy is easier to use when the calculation in the ones does not involve numbers larger than 9. Here are some examples in the case of addition: 42 + 25; 36 + 21; 36 + 53, and in the case of subtraction: 86 – 32; 44 – 23; 97 – 55.

## Prior knowledge for the Split Strategy

An important point to keep in mind is that when children are working these examples, they should be facile with adding and subtracting in the range 1 to 10. When a child works out 36 + 53, they should be able to calculate each of 30 + 50 (using 3 + 5), and 6 + 3 almost instantaneously, and similarly calculate 80 + 9 almost instantaneously. The child who is using strategies involving counting-by-ones to calculate 3 + 5 and 6 + 3 is not ready to learn 2-digit addition to 100. This applies similarly in the case of subtraction. In using a split strategy to work out 86 – 32, the child should be able to calculate each of 80 – 30 and 6 – 2 almost instantaneously.

## Base-ten Blocks and Bundling Sticks

Settings such as bundling sticks or base-ten blocks are very useful for fostering the development of split strategies. These can be used by the teacher working with a group or whole class, for example, on an overhead projector. Also, the teacher can gradually develop situations in which the materials are screened (hidden from view) to encourage visualization on the part of the children. An important point is that simply giving base-ten materials to each child with instructions to work examples such as those above is unlikely to foster split strategies. In this situation our instructional goal is to foster mental strategies. When children are given the materials they are likely to use several strategies that are not conducive to developing more facile strategies. Strategies that tend to be counterproductive at this point include: counting a collection of blocks from one; counting-by-ones; and counting blocks that can be seen. Children who have developed split strategies for adding and subtracting two 2-digit numbers are ready to extend use of these strategies to working with 3-digit numbers.

# Extending to 3-digit Addition, Subtraction and Place Value

Children who have developed facile and flexible jump (Chapter 8) and split strategies for adding and subtracting two 2-digit numbers are ready to extend these strategies to working with 3-digit numbers. In order to do so, children need: (a) to be facile with number word sequences and numerals in the range 100 to 1,000, and (b) to be able to increment and decrement 3-digit numbers, by 10 and by 100. These two topics are now described.

## Number Words and Numerals to 1,000

This refers to learning to name and write 3-digit numerals and learning to say number word sequences forward and backward in the range 100 to 1,000. The latter topic refers to saying the sequence forward or backward from a given 3-digit number, or knowing what comes after or before a given 3-digit number. Some examples are: (a) being able to count-on or-back from 810, 701, 297, and so on; (b) knowing what comes after 246, 310, 700, 899, and so on; and (c) knowing what comes before 416, 800, 920, and so on. Developing children's knowledge of number word sequences and numerals in the range 100 to 1,000, should be developed in parallel with the development of jump and split strategies in the range 1 to 100.

## Incrementing and Decrementing by Tens

Extending to 3-digit addition and subtraction involves several steps: First, the strategies of incrementing and decrementing by tens on and off the decade in the range 1 to 100 can be extended beyond 100: For example, (a) going forward by tens from 350, from 287, and from 790; (b) going backward by tens from 650, from 289, and from 800.

## Incrementing and Decrementing by Hundreds

Second, children can learn to increment and decrement by hundreds both on and off the decade and on and off the hundred. For example, (a) going forwards by hundreds from 100, from 260, from 407, from 165; (b) going backwards by hundreds from 1,000, from 920, from 608, and from 482. Becoming facile with number word sequences in this way provides a basis for using strategies akin to jump and split strategies to do addition or subtraction involving two 3-digit numbers. For example, children might solve tasks such as the following using (a) a split strategy and (b) a jump strategy:

| | | | |
|---|---|---|---|
| 634 + 211 | 459 + 203 | 175 + 282 | 367 + 255 |
| 889 – 236 | 372 – 106 | 416 – 121 | 723 – 235 |

## Developing Strategies for 3-digit Addition and Subtraction

In similar vein to the case of 2–digit addition and subtraction, children's development of flexible jump and split strategies involving 3-digit addition and subtraction will support a corresponding development of an understanding of place value to 1,000. Thus, as in the case of 2-digit numbers, place value knowledge is developed in conjunction with, rather than prior to, the development of flexible strategies for adding and subtracting. Also as before, base-ten materials (hundreds, tens and ones) are particularly suited to the development of split strategies. Further, situations which invoke low-level counting strategies should generally be avoided. As before, this can be done by displaying and then covering base-ten materials to encourage visualization or imaging on the part of the children. Again, as described in Chapter 8, the empty number line (ENL) can be used to support the development of jump strategies. The ENL enables children to record, discuss, explain, and reflect on their strategies.

## ASSESSMENT TASK GROUPS

### List of Assessment Task Groups

A9.1: Higher decade addition and subtraction without and with bridging the decade
A9.2: Partitioning and combining involving 2-digit numbers
A9.3: Combining and partitioning involving **non-canonical** forms
A9.4: Addition involving two 2-digit numbers without and with regrouping
A9.5: Subtraction involving two 2-digit numbers without and with regrouping

**TASK GROUP A9.1:** Higher Decade Addition and Subtraction without and with Bridging the Decade

**Materials:** Base-ten materials, a screen.

**What to do and say:** Addition without bridging. Place out 6 tens and 2 ones. *How many sticks altogether?* Screen the 62 sticks. Add 2 sticks. *How many sticks are there now?* Continue with tasks such as the following: 35 + 4, 82 + 6, 53 + 4, and so on. Continue to use base-ten materials to present the tasks.

Subtraction without bridging: Place out 5 tens and 7 ones. *How many sticks altogether?* Screen the 57 sticks. Remove 3 sticks. *How many sticks are there now?* Continue with tasks such as the following: 88 – 4, 23 – 2, 96 – 3, and so on, using base-ten materials to present the tasks.

Addition with bridging. Place out 4 tens and 9 ones. *How many sticks altogether?* Screen the 49 sticks. Add 6 sticks. *How many sticks are there now?* Continue with tasks such as the following: 86 + 6, 35 + 8, 67 + 4, and so on, using base-ten materials.

Subtraction with bridging. Place out 8 tens and 4 ones. *How many sticks altogether?* Screen the 84 sticks. Remove 6 sticks. *How many sticks are there now?* Continue with tasks such as the following: 63 – 9, 25 – 8, 72 – 5, and so on, using base-ten materials.

**Notes:**

▷ For more advanced children an alternative is to present these tasks in the form of number sentences in horizontal format.

▷ In the cases of addition and subtraction without bridging, children might use a known fact in the range 1 to 10. For example, 62 + 2: 2 and 2 are 4 so 62 and 2 are 64. And, 96 – 3: 6 take 3 is 3 so 96 take 3 is 93.

▷ In the cases of addition and subtraction with bridging, children might use a strategy involving going through ten. For example, 49 + 5: 1 more is 50, and 4 more makes 54. And 72 – 5: 72 take 2 is 70, and 70 take 3 is 67.

▷ In the cases of addition and subtraction with bridging, some children might use a known fact in the range 1 to 20. For example, 49 + 5: 9 + 5 is 14, so 49 + 5 is 54. And 72 – 5: 12 take 5 is 7, so 72 take 5 is 67.

▷ In the case of addition with bridging a preliminary step such as the following could be used: 49 + 5, 49 and one more is 50.

▷ Some children might use counting-by-ones on these tasks. For example, 82 + 6: 83, 84, 85, 86, 87, 88. And 72 – 5: 71, 70, 69, 68, 67.

▷ Children who use counting-by-ones are likely to use their fingers to keep track of their counts.

## TASK GROUP A9.2: Partitioning and Combining Involving 2-digit Numbers

**Materials:** Base-ten materials, screen.

**What to do and say:** Partitioning. Ask the child to look away. Place 4 tens and 3 ones under the screen. *Under here there are 43 sticks. How many tens are there? How many ones are there?* Remove the screen. *Check to see if you are correct.* Similarly with 2 tens and 4 ones, 5 tens and 1 one, and so on.

Combining. Ask the child to look away. Place 3 tens and 2 ones under the screen. *Under here there are 3 tens. How many sticks would that be? There are also 2 ones, how many sticks altogether?* Similarly with 6 tens and 2 ones, 4 tens and 8 ones, and so on.

**Notes:**

▶ This task group is important because these kinds of tasks can arise in children's mental computation involving adding or subtracting two 2-digit numbers. Tasks like these can also arise in multiplication and division.

▶ These tasks are particularly important in cases where children tend to use split strategies for adding or subtracting two 2-digit numbers. Split strategies involve working separately with the tens and ones.

▶ On the combining task, observe closely to see if the child uses counting-by-ones. For example, 40 and 8: 40, 41, 42, ... 48.

## TASK GROUP A49.3: Combining and Partitioning Involving Non-canonical Forms

**Materials:** Base-ten materials of one color (red), base-ten materials of another color (green), two screens.

**What to do and say:** Combining. Using red, place out 4 tens. *How many tens are there?* How many red sticks are there? Screen the 40 red sticks. Using green, place out 1 ten and 6 ones. *How many green sticks are there?* Screen the 16 green sticks. *I have 40 red under here and 16 green under here. How many altogether?* Similarly with combinations such as: 50 red and 12 green, 30 red and 18 green, and so on.

Partitioning. Ask the child to look away. Place 5 red tens, 1 green ten and 3 green ones under a screen. *Under this screen I have 63 sticks. Thirteen are green and the remainder are red. How many red sticks are there?* Similarly with combinations such as 20 red and 15 green, 70 red and 11 green, and so on.

Place 7 red tens, 1 green ten and 7 green ones under a screen. *Under this screen I have 87 sticks. Seventy are red and the remainder are green. How many green sticks are there?* Similarly with combinations such as: 40 red and 16 green, 40 red and 13 green, and so on.

**Notes:**

▶ Partitioning for example, 64 into 60 and 4 can be regarded as a standard partition for 64. Partitioning 64 into 50 and 14 is referred to as a non-canonical (non-standard) partition of 64.

▶ Children should be facile with, not only working with the standard partition for any 2-digit number, but also working with the non-canonical partitions of 2-digit numbers.

▶ Combining non-canonical forms arises in the case of addition with two 2-digit numbers involving regrouping (carrying). For example, combining 70 and 13 might arise when 35 + 48 is solved using a split strategy.

▶ Partitioning non-canonical forms arises in the case of subtraction with two 2-digit numbers involving regrouping (borrowing). For example, partitioning 72 into 60 and 12 might arise when 72 – 35 is solved by a split stategy.

▶ These tasks are particularly important in cases where children tend to use split strategies for adding or subtracting two 2-digit numbers. Split strategies involve working separately with the tens and ones.

▶ Observe closely to see if the child uses counting by ones. For example, 40 + 16 → 41, 42, 43, ... 56. And, 63 – 13 → 62, 61, 60, 59, ... 50.

## TASK GROUP A9.4: Addition Involving Two 2-digit Numbers Without and With Regrouping

**Materials:** Base-ten materials of one color (red), base-ten materials of another color (green), two screens.

**What to do and say:** Without regrouping. Using red place 45 under one screen. Using green place 22 under another screen. *I have 45 red under here and 22 green under here. How many altogether?* Similarly for 54 + 35, 63 + 22, 31 + 57, and so on.

  With regrouping. Using red place 28 under one screen. Using green place 37 under another screen. *I have 28 red under here and 37 green under here. How many altogether?* Similarly for 67 + 24, 35 + 28, 49 + 35, and so on.

**Notes:**

▶ Observe closely to see if the child uses: (a) a jump strategy: 45 + 22: 65, 67! (b) a split strategy: 45 + 22: 40 + 20 is 60, 5 + 2 is 7, 67 or (c) counting-by-ones: 45 + 22: 46, 47, 48, ... 67.

▶ Use of base-ten materials (as used in these tasks) can tend to elicit split strategies rather than jump strategies.

## TASK GROUP A9.5: Subtraction Involving Two 2-digit Numbers Without and With Regrouping

**Materials:** Base-ten materials, a screen.

**What to do and say:** Without regrouping. Place 68 under the screen. *I have 68 under here. Look away.* Take away 21. *I took away 21. How many are left?* Similarly for 96 – 34, 87 – 36, 46 – 23, and so on.

  With regrouping. Place 52 under the screen. *I have 52 under here. If I took away 29, how many would be left?* Similarly for 85 – 37, 62 – 46, 91 – 66, and so on.

**Notes:**

▶ Observe closely to see if the child uses: (a) a jump strategy: 68 – 21: 48, 47! (b) a split strategy: 68 – 21: 60 – 20 is 40, 8 – 1 is 7, 47 or (c) counting-by-ones: 68 – 21: 67, 66, 65, ... 47.

▶ Use of base-ten materials (as used in these tasks) can tend to elicit split strategies rather than jump strategies.

▶ Children using split strategies might be successful in the case of subtraction without regrouping but not in the case of subtraction with regrouping.

▶ A very common error in the case of subtraction with regrouping using a split strategy is as follows: 52 – 29: 50 – 20 is 30, 9 – 2 is 7, 37: instead of 23. Another error is: 52 – 29: 50 – 20 is 30, 12 – 9 is 3, 33: instead of 23.

# INSTRUCTIONAL ACTIVITIES

## List of Instructional Activities

IA9.1:  Follow the Pattern
IA9.2:  Ten More or Ten Less
IA9.3:  Counting by Tens
IA9.4:  Add or Subtract Tens
IA9.5:  Adding Tens and Ones Using Money
IA9.6:  Screened Subtraction Task
IA9.7:  Split the Subtrahend (Multiples of 10)

## ACTIVITY IA9.1: Follow the Pattern

**Intended learning:** To use known facts in higher decade addition.

**Description:** Children continue patterns provided by the teacher. Example: 3 + 4 = 7, 13 + 4 = 17, 23 + 4 = 27. Children are given the first three number sentences but must then try to see the pattern and continue it. The number sentences could also be subtraction number sentences. Example: 6 – 4 = 2, 16 – 4 = 12, 26 – 4 = 22. Some children might need their own hundred square to help them initially. Examples should also include bridging the decade in addition: 7 + 8 = 15, 17 + 8 = 25, 27 + 8 = 35; and in subtraction: 11 – 3 = 8, 21 – 3 = 18, 31 – 3 = 28.

**Notes:**

▶ This activity is only suitable for children who are able to sequence and identify numbers in the range 1 – 100.
▶ More able children can work with patterns using 3- or 4-digit numbers, for example: 296 – 8 = 288, 286 – 8 = 278, 276 – 8 = 268, including patterns that bridge a hundreds number (for example, 721 – 3 = 718, 711 – 3 = 708, 701 – 3 = 698).
▶ This activity will also support the development of place value knowledge.

**Materials:** Worksheets with number patterns for the children to continue.

## ACTIVITY IA9.2: Ten More or Ten Less

**Intended learning:** To add 10 to a number or subtract 10 from a number.

**Description:** Use base-ten material (bundling sticks, Unifix cubes, base-ten blocks, and so on.) to add a 10. Place several 10s on the overhead or carpet and screen them. Add one more 10. You may need to leave this 10 unscreened at first. Ask: *How many in all?* Begin with multiples of 10 (40, 50, 60) and progress to numbers with 10s and 1s, such as 48 + 10 and 89 – 10. Variation: use a whiteboard as the screen for the 10s and 1s. Record the starting number on the board. The addition or subtraction number sentence can also be recorded.

**Notes:**

▶   This activity is suitable for whole class, small group, or one to one teaching.

▶   Add 10s to 3-digit numbers to extend the 10s pattern beyond 100.

**Materials:** Base-ten materials and a screen large enough for materials, whiteboard for recording.

## ACTIVITY IA9.3: Counting-by-Tens

**Intended learning:** To link counting forward by 10s to addition of 10s, and counting backward by 10s to subtraction of 10s.

**Description:** Use a base-ten material (bundling sticks, Unifix cubes, base-ten blocks, and so on.) to count forward or backward by 10s. Begin with one 10 on the overhead projector or carpet and the class says, 'ten'. Add another 10, class says, 'twenty'. Continue adding 10s as class counts by 10 with you. Once you get to 100 (or whatever number is your goal), take a 10 away and have the class count backward by 10s as you take the 10s away. Begin this activity counting by 10s on the decade and progress to counting by 10s off the decade. For example, place four 1s on the overhead projector or carpet. Add 10, class says, 'fourteen'. Continue to count by 10s until the target number is reached. Then remove the 10s to count backward. This activity should also be done with the 10s screened.

**Notes:**

▶   This activity is effective in small groups or one to one. Give each child a few 10s. Students take turns putting in or taking out the 10s as they count. These can also be screened.

▶   Do not always stop at 100. Students need practice counting by 10s past 100. Counting off the decade past 100 (for example, 104, 114, 124). Numbers in the teen range can be difficult.

**Materials:** Base-ten materials and a screen large enough for materials.

## ACTIVITY IA9.4: Add or Subtract Tens

**Intended learning:** To add 10s to a number and subtract 10s from a number.

Description: Use a base-ten material (bundling sticks, Unifix cubes, base-ten blocks, and so on) to add 10s. Place several 10s on the overhead or carpet and screen them. Add a few more 10s. You may need to leave these 10s unscreened at first. Ask: *How many in all?* Begin with multiples of 10 (40, 50, 60) and progress to numbers with 10s and 1s, such as 64 + 30 and 59 − 20. Variation: use a whiteboard as the screen for the 10s and 1s. Record the beginning number on the board. You could also record the addition or subtraction number sentence and the child's thinking.

**Notes:**

▶   This activity is suitable for whole class, small group, or one to one.

▶   Add 10s to numbers in the hundreds to extend the 10s pattern past 100.

▶   Students can chose to jump or split to solve these tasks.

**Materials:** Base-ten materials and a screen large enough for materials, whiteboard for recording.

## ACTIVITY IA9.5: Adding Tens and Ones Using Money

**Intended learning:** To add 2-digit numbers with and without regrouping using money as the base-ten material.

**Description:** Use imitation currency ($10 and $1 bills, £10 and £1 notes) to add the cost of two items. Advertisements can be cut out of newspapers. Have children cut out or bring in items, or create pictures with the cost next to them. Students select two items to buy and take the number of 10s and 1s indicated in the cost. They then count the total number of 10s and total number of 1s to find the total cost of two items.

**Notes:**

▶    This activity is suitable for whole class, small group, or one to one.
▶    Students can add 3-digit numbers by using $100 bills (£100 notes).
▶    Students can also select more than two items to buy.
▶    Using $5 bills (£5 notes) as well would encourage adding using five as a reference point.
▶    As a variation, coins such as cents and dimes (pennies) could also be used.

**Materials:** Bills (notes) or coins, advertisements or pictures of items with their cost.

## ACTIVITY IA9.6: Screened Subtraction Task

**Intended learning:** To subtract 10s and 1s without regrouping.

**Description:** Using base-ten material, place several 2-digit numbers on the overhead or carpet and screen them. Take away a few 10s. Have children record their answer as you record the number sentence (for example, 74 – 20 = 54) on the board for all to see. You could also record children's strategies on the board. Replace the 74 and screen them. Take away two 10s and a one. Children record their answer as you record the number sentence (74 – 21 = 53). The next problem could be 74 – 22 using screened base-ten materials. Do several problems such as these, taking away an additional one each time. Look for patterns and discuss how tasks were solved. Once children learn how to subtract the 10s and then the 1s, give varied problems such as 58 – 22, 85 – 33, 96 – 41.

**Notes:**

▶    This activity is suitable for whole class, small group, or one to one.
▶    Some children might use the jump method to solve these tasks. Encourage the jump strategy, as it is a more effective strategy for subtracting with regrouping.
▶    Do not include subtraction with regrouping in the screened tasks unless they are done as a part of the subtraction patterns of subtracting one more.

**Materials:** Base-ten materials and a screen large enough for materials, board and paper for recording.

## ACTIVITY IA9.7: Split the Subtrahend (Multiples of 10)

**Intended learning:** To subtract 10s and 1s with or without regrouping.

**Description:** Place several 10s (for example, 80) on the overhead projector or carpet. Be sure to use 10s material that can be taken apart (for example, bundling sticks). Ask: *What would happen if you took 20 away?* (60). Then ask: *What if one is taken away?* (59). Record the problem as 80 – 20 – 1 = 59 and as 80 – 21. Continue with other decade numbers. Gradually increase the number of 1s being taken away. When students gain competence introduce screening of the materials.

**Notes:**

▶    This activity is suitable for whole class, small group, or one to one.
▶    Students should also be able to solve problems with subtrahends that are multiples of 5.
▶    Some children may use the jump method to solve these tasks. Encourage the jump strategy, as it is a more effective strategy for subtracting with regrouping.
▶    Progress to tasks such as 63 take 20 and then take another one (63 – 20 – 1 = 42).

**Materials:** Base-ten materials and a screen large enough for materials, board and paper for recording.

# 10
# Early Multiplication and Division

**Summary**

This chapter focusses on the development of early multiplication and division knowledge. This includes the emergent notions of repeated equal groups and sharing, the development of skip counting and the use of arrays in teaching multiplication and division. Also explained are the ideas of numerical composite and abstract composite unit – important milestones in the development of numerical thinking, the idea of commutitivity, and the inverse relationship between multiplication and division.

## TOPIC OVERVIEW

This chapter focusses on the development of children's knowledge of the arithmetic operations of multiplication and division. This begins with very simple notions of equal groups and sharing and learning number word sequences of multiples (for example, three, six, nine … ), and extends to developing facile strategies to work out multiplication and division tasks in the range 1 to 100. In the following section, this development is described in detail.

## Repeated Equal Groups and Sharing

In Chapter 4 we saw that children's initial ideas of addition arise from the idea of combining two groups of items. In similar vein, children's initial ideas of multiplication are linked to combining a number of groups, each of which contain an equal number of items, for example, combining six groups each of which contains three items. This situation is referred to as repeated equal groups (see Figure 10.1). Finally, children's initial ideas of division are linked to sharing a collection of items into equal groups (see Figure 10.2).

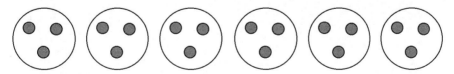

**Figure 10.1** Multiplication as repeated equal groups

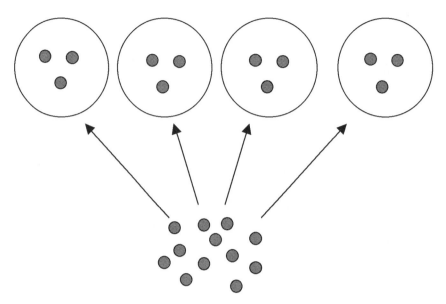

**Figure 10.2** Sharing into equal groups

Children should be provided with experiences that involve the activity of making repeated equal groups where the number in each group and the number of groups is specified; for example: *Make 6 groups of 3, 5 groups of 4, 8 groups of 2.* Children should also be provided with experiences that involve the activity of sharing a given number of items into a specified number of equal groups; for example: *Share 8 items into 4 equal groups, 10 items into 2 equal groups, 15 items into 3 equal groups.* Activities can also involve everyday materials and situations in which repeated equal groups or sharing arise naturally; for example: *How many legs on four chairs? How many fingers on six hands?* For all the above activities, it is important to foster in children, the development of the appropriate mathematical language; for example: *Three groups of four. 18 shared into six equal groups.*

Making equal groups

## Number Word Sequences of Multiples – Skip Counting

Number word sequences of multiples are sequences such as 'two, four, six, eight, …' – the sequence of multiples of two; and 'five, ten, fifteen, twenty, …' – the sequence of multiples of five. The activity of saying such sequences is typically referred to as counting-by-twos, counting-by-fives, and so on. This is also referred to as skip counting. It is important to keep in mind the distinction between, on the one hand, merely saying the sequence of multiples and, on the other hand, using the sequence of multiples to count the items in repeated equal groups, for example, six groups of two. Learning the common sequences of multiples is important as a basis for multiplication and division. Typically, children's learning of these sequences proceeds in the following order: by twos, by fives, by tens and by threes. Of course, children begin to learn each new sequence before the previous sequence is known completely. The sequences by other numbers in the range 1 to 10, that is, by fours, sixes, sevens, eights and nines generally are not learned to the same extent as those stated earlier. Nevertheless, knowledge of these sequences will constitute an important basis for automatizing the basic facts of multiplication. Activities such as number rhymes can be useful for learning the common sequences (by twos, fives, tens and threes).

Counting-by-twos (skip counting)

## Counting Repeated Equal Groups

When children are learning the common sequences of multiples (twos, fives, and so on), they should also be given experiences in using these sequences in situations involving materials, that is, situations involving repeated equal groups of items. In these situations, teachers can demonstrate for children, counting by twos, by fives, and so on. For example, counting a collection of 20 red counters by twos involves moving a pair of counters together, in coordination with saying each word in the sequence – two, four, six, eight, and so on. It is tempting to regard activities such as counting by twos, by fives, and so on, as simple and straightforward activities that children can easily learn through imitation of the teacher. However, there is a tendency on the part of the teacher to imagine that the child, as well as imitating the teacher's actions also imitates the teacher's thinking. On the other hand, close observation of children counting by twos and so on can reveal interesting limitations on their thinking. For example, a child who had been shown how to count by twos was asked to count a collection of counters by twos. The collection contained nine counters. The child counted by twos – two, four, six, eight, in coordination with moving a pair of counters for each number word. After saying 'eight' he moved the final counter and said 'ten'. That there was one counter rather than two remaining did not seem to be problematic for the child. To emphasize the point being made: as obvious as it might seem to an adult that, when counting a collection of counters by twos, each number word refers to two counters, this is not necessarily obvious to children! As another example, children might regard the number of items in a collection as being dependent on how it is counted (by ones, by twos, by threes, and so on).

## Division as Sharing or Measuring

In an earlier section, division was explained as arising from situations involving sharing into equal groups. In this context there are essentially two different kinds of situations that give rise to division and, as a teacher, it is important to take account of these. Try the following situation for yourself. You will need two sets of 12 counters, for example, blue and red. Use the red counters to solve the following task: arrange 12 counters into 3 equal groups. Use the blue counters to solve the following task: arrange 12 counters into groups of 3. Draw a diagram corresponding to your solution of each of the two tasks. Each of these corresponds to 12 ÷ 3. Alternatively, one could say there are two different ways that the problem 12 ÷ 3 can be demonstrated using a collection of 12 counters and using the number 3. These are called (a) sharing or partitive division and (b) measuring or quotitive division. To interpret 12 ÷ 3 in the sense of sharing, is to regard the divisor (3) as indicating the number of equal groups. To interpret 12 ÷ 3 in the sense of measuring is to regard the divisor (3) as indicating the number in each of the equal groups. From the children's perspective, a division situation leads to a division expression 12 ÷ 3, rather than an expression leading to a situation. That is to say, it is usual for teachers to present children with a division situation before presenting the written expression.

12 ÷ 3 interpreted as
sharing or partition

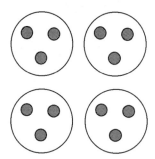

12 ÷ 3 interpreted as
measuring or quotition

**Figure 10.3** Division as sharing or measuring

Figure 10.3 shows examples of division in the sharing and measuring senses. The typical approach in teaching is to begin by working wholly or mainly with one only of the situations, typically the sharing situation. The thinking underlying this is that sharing into a given number of equal groups is typically a very common experience for young children. Ultimately children should be familiar with each of these two division situations. Given a number story relating to either situation, children should be able to generate the corresponding division expression. Try for yourself to write five number stories involving simple division in the sharing sense and similarly write five number stories involving simple division in the measuring sense. For each story, write the appropriate division expression.

## Abstract Composite Unit

As children become more facile at working with repeated equal groups and sharing, and thinking in terms of multiples, they are able to think more abstractly about the numbers involved in multiplication and division situations. A major advancement is the ability to regard as a unit a number larger than one when it is appropriate to do so. Prior to this advancement, children who can think abstractly about numbers are able to think of numbers as composites but not as units. Steffe and Cobb (1988) referred to these two levels of thinking as a numerical composite and an abstract composite unit. These are explained in Figure 10.4. Developing the idea of an abstract composite unit is fundamental for learning multiplication and division. For example, with the idea of an abstract composite unit, a child who is asked how many threes in 18, can think abstractly in terms of repeated threes. Because the child can regard three as a unit (as well as a composite), they can think in terms of counting the units, that is, how many units of three make 18?

| | |
|---|---|
| *3 more*     *3 more* | *one 3*     *another 3*     *another 3* |
| Numerical composite | Abstract composite unit |

**Figure 10.4** Numerical composite and abstract composite unit

## Using Arrays

As described above, experience with counters and so on organized into repeated equal groups can provide an important basis for the early development of multiplication and division ideas. As children's knowledge of multiplication and division develops, arrays (see Figure 10.5) can be very useful. Arrays in this sense consist of rectangular arrangements of dots in rows and columns.

Initially, children can explore the idea that there are the same number of dots in each row (similarly in each column). It is important to move children beyond the activity of counting the dots by ones. In teaching situations, arrays can be used on a chart-board or overhead projector in ways so that some or all of the rows are each covered by a strip. In this situation children are encouraged to count by multiples corresponding to the number in each row. This can be extended by covering the whole array, and encouraging children to visualize the array in order to count the dots in multiples. The array can then be uncovered so that each row is covered by a strip, and children can again count the dots in the array in multiples.

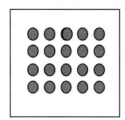

A 4 × 5 array has 4 rows
and 5 columns

A 7 × 3 array has 7 rows
and 3 columns

**Figure 10.5** Using arrays in multiplication

## Commutativity and Inverse Operations

As children's knowledge of multiplication and division develops, two important ideas arise – commutativity and inverse. The idea of commutativity was discussed in Chapter 7, in the context of addition. Commutativity also applies to multiplication (but not subtraction and division). In the case of multiplication, commutativity refers to the principle that when any two numbers are multiplied they can be multiplied in either order without affecting the answer, for example, 6 × 4 = 24 and 4 × 6 = 24. This is sometimes expressed as follows: for any two numbers a and b, a × b = b × a. Figure 10.6 shows demonstrations of the idea of commutativity using sets and arrays. Arrays are ideal for demonstrating the idea of commutativity. As seen in Figure 10.6, the array for 4 × 6 can be turned through 90 degrees to show 6 × 4.

Multiplication and division are inverse operations, that is, division is the inverse of multiplication and multiplication is the inverse of division. The preceding statement refers to the principle that if a given number is multiplied by any number and the answer is then divided by the same number, then the answer is equal to the original number. This is demonstrated in Figure 10.7.

Children should develop sound knowledge of the principles of commutativity and inverse operations. This includes not only being implicitly aware of these principles but being able to use them flexibly. Examples of using commutativity are: (a) using the known fact of 2 sevens make 14 (2 × 7 = 14), to work out 7 twos; and (b) working out 9 fives in order to work out 5 nines. Examples of using the inverse operations principle are: (a) using the known fact of 4 fives make 20 (4 × 5=20) to work out 20 ÷ 4; and (b) using the known fact 7 sixes make 42 (7 × 6 = 42) to try to work out 42 ÷ 7.

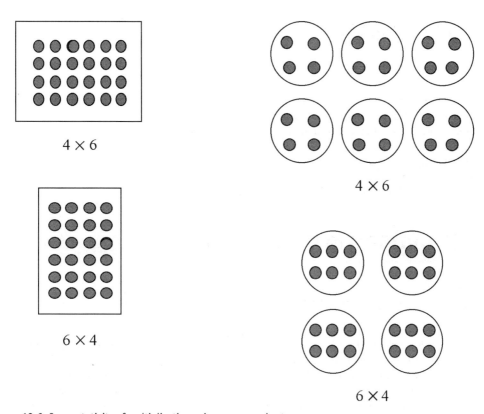

$4 \times 6$

$4 \times 6$

$6 \times 4$

$6 \times 4$

**Figure 10.6** Commutativity of multiplication using arrays and sets

$$6 \times 11 = 66$$
$$100 \div 4 = 25$$
$$66 \div 11 = 6$$
$$25 \times 4 = 100$$

**Figure 10.7** Multiplication and division are inverse operations

## Extending Multiplication and Division Knowledge

Children's work in multiplication and division extends from the ideas of equal groups and sharing, to the development of abstract composite unit. These ideas are further extended to include the principles of commutativity and inverse operations. During this time most of the work in multiplication and division is in the range 1 to 100. Within this range, children will begin to habituate some of the simplest basic facts of multiplication such as doubles (2 × 4) and squares (6 × 6). As well, children can use doubling of known facts to work out other facts, for example, 4 sixes is double 2 sixes, 8 fives is double 4 fives. When children have developed a range of facile multiplication and division strategies in the range 1 to 100, they are ready to work on habituating basic fact knowledge and extending multiplication and division to include 2-digit factors, for example, 2 × 30, 3 × 23.

## ASSESSMENT TASK GROUPS

## List of Assessment Task Groups

A10.1: Counting by 2s, 5s, 10s and 3s
A10.2: Repeated equal groups – visible
A10.3: Repeated equal groups – items screened and groups visible
A10.4: Repeated equal groups – groups screened and items screened
A10.5: Multiplication and division using arrays
A10.6: Word problems
A10.7: Relational thinking using bare number problems

## TASK GROUP A10.1: Counting by 2s, 5s, 10s and 3s

**Materials:** None.

**What to do and say:** *Can you count by 2s? Go on.* Similarly by 5s, 10s, and 3s.

**Notes:**

▶ Try to determine in each case (2s, 3s, and so on), the limit of the child's fluent skip counting.

▶ In the case of counting by 3s, for example, children might use counting-by-ones to figure out the next multiple of three: 3, 6, 9, 12, – 13, 14, 15. Counting-by-ones in this way involves a double count, that is, the child has to keep track of the number of counts after 12 (three counts).

▶ The more facile children can also be asked to count by 4s and 6s, for example. When counting by 4s or 6s, children sometimes use a non-counting addition strategy to determine the next multiple. For example, when counting by 6s, the child uses adding through 10, to determine that 24 is the next count after 18.

▶ The task of counting by 10s also occurs in Task Group A8.1.

## TASK GROUP A10.2: Repeated Equal Groups – Visible

**Materials:** Cards containing repeated equal groups as follows: 6 circles of 3 dots, 3 circles of 5 dots, 8 circles of 2 dots.

**What to do and say:** Display the card showing 6 groups of 3. *What do you see? How many groups are there? What do you notice about each group? How many dots are in each group? How many dots altogether?* Similarly with 3 groups of 5, 8 groups of 2, and so on.

**Notes:**

▶ Try to gauge the extent to which the child is aware that the groups contain the same number of dots.

▶ Children might use counting-by-ones, skip counting, or more advanced strategies; for example, knowing automatically that six 3s are 18, or using the known facts of five 2s and three 2s to work out eight 2s.

▶ Children might use counting-by-ones out of convenience. Using counting-by-ones to solve this task does not necessarily indicate that the child cannot use a more advanced strategy when the items are screened for example.

## TASK GROUP A10.3: Repeated Equal Groups – Items Screened and Groups Visible

**Materials:** Cards containing repeated equal groups as follows: 5 circles of 2 dots, 7 circles of 5 dots, 5 circles of 4 dots. On each card use small cardboard lids to screen each group separately. For example, the first card has 5 small lids with each lid concealing a circle of 2 dots.

**What to do and say:** Place out the card with 5 groups of 2, with the lids closed. *How many lids are there? Each of those lids has 2 dots under it. How many dots altogether?* If the child is not able to solve the task, lift each of the five lids. *How many dots are there in each group? How many dots altogether?* Similarly with 7 groups of 5, 5 groups of 4, and so on.

Repeated equal groups – items screened groups visible

**Notes:**

▶   Try to gauge the extent to which the child correctly construes the task, that is, the extent to which the child understands that there are repeated equal groups.

▶   Children might solve these tasks by counting-by-ones. For example, the child solves the first task by counting from one to 10, making two counts for each lid: 1, 2 … 3, 4 … 5, 6 … 7, 8 … 9, 10. Alternatively, children might count by twos, making one count for each lid: 2, 4, 6, 8, 10.

▶   Children who use counting-by-ones, might use fingers to keep track of the dots in each circle. For example, on the task involving 7 circles of 5 dots, this would involve raising five fingers sequentially, seven times. Alternatively, the child might count on from five, and raise five fingers sequentially, six times.

## TASK GROUP A10.4: Repeated Equal Groups – Groups Screened and Items Screened

**Materials:** Cards containing repeated equal groups as follows: 3 circles of 4 dots, 4 circles of 5 dots, 5 circles of 3 dots. On each card use small cardboard lids to screen each group separately and a large lid to screen all of the groups. For example, the first card has 3 small lids and one large lid to conceal the 3 small lids.

**What to do and say:** Place out the card with 3 groups of 4. Have the small lids screening the items in each group and the large lid screening the three small lids. *This card has three groups of 4. How many dots altogether?* If the child is not able to solve this task, lift the large lid. *How many lids are there? Each of those lids has 4 dots under it. How many dots altogether?* If the child is again not able to solve the task, lift each of the three small lids. *How many dots are there in each group? How many dots altogether?* Similarly with 4 groups of 5, 5 groups of 3, and so on.

**Notes:**

▶   Try to gauge the extent to which the child correctly construes the task, that is, does the child seem to understand that there are repeated equal groups?

▶    Using skip counting to solve the task in its initial form (items screened and groups screened) requires a double count, that is, the child needs to keep track of the number of skips: 4(1), 8(2), 12(3) → 12, as well as the number of items.

▶    Using counting-by-ones to solve the task in its initial form (items screened and groups screened), requires a triple count, that is, the child needs to keep track of the number of items in each group, as well as the number of groups and the number of items altogether.

▶    As in Task Groups A10.2 and A10.3, children might use counting-by-ones, skip counting or more advanced strategies.

▶    It is common for children to use fingers to keep track when using counting-by-ones or skip counting.

▶    Some children who use counting-by-ones involving a triple count use their fingers to keep track in two different ways. For example, one hand is used to keep track of the items in each group and the other is used to keep track of the number of groups. At the same time, they are mentally keeping track of the number of items altogether.

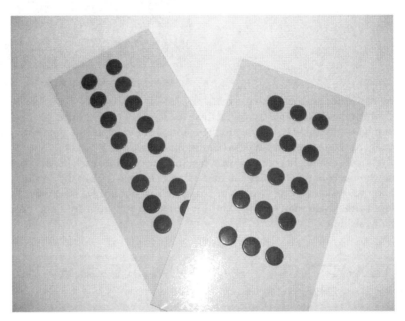

Using arrays

## TASK GROUP A10.5: Multiplication and Division using Arrays

**Materials:** A 6 × 5 array (oriented as 6 rows and five columns) and 7 × 2 array. Screen.

**What to do and say:** Place out the 6 × 5 array and, in doing so, screen all but the first row (5dots). *What do you see? How many dots in the row? The array has 6 rows of 5 dots. How many dots altogether?*

  Place out the 7 × 2 array and, in doing so, screen all but the first row (2 dots). *What do you see? How many dots in the row? The array has 14 dots altogether. How many rows does the array have?*

Notes:

▶ Try to gauge the child's sense of an array. This includes familiarity with the notions of rows and columns, and knowing that each row is equal in number and similarly for each column.

▶ Try to determine if the child uses counting-by-ones, skip counting or more advanced strategies.

▶ The notes in Task Group A10.3 about strategies involving skip counting and counting-by-ones apply here as well.

Using a partially screened array for multiplication (1)

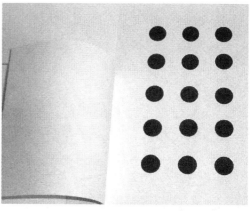

Using a partially screened array for multiplication (2)

## TASK GROUP A10.6: Word Problems

**Materials:** Word problems written on a card.

**What to do and say:** Multiplication. *There are 6 boxes and each box has 4 bottles. How many bottles altogether?*

Partitive division. *Thirty stickers are shared equally among 5 children. How many does each child get?*
Quotitive division. *I have 27 pencils and I give 3 pencils to each child. How many children are there?*

**Notes:**

▶ Try to gauge if the child properly construes the task.

▶ Try to determine whether the child's strategy involves counting-by-ones, skip counting or using a known fact.

## TASK GROUP A10.7: Relational Thinking Using Bare Number Problems

**Materials:** Cards on which tasks are written: $7 \times 3$, $3 \times 7$; $8 \times 4$, $9 \times 4$; $9 \times 5$, $45 \div 9$; $8 \times 5$, $5 \times 5$, $13 \times 5$.

**What to do and say:** Commutativity. Display the following: $7 \times 3$ (read as 7 threes). *Can you work this out?* If the child is correct, display the following immediately beneath the previous card: $3 \times 7$ (read as 3 sevens). *Can you use this ($7 \times 3$) to work out this ($3 \times 7$)?*

Relational thinking

Extending a known fact. Display the following: 8 × 4 (read as 8 fours). *Can you work this out?* If the child is correct, display the following immediately beneath the previous card: 9 × 4 (read as 9 fours). *Can you use this (8 × 4) to work out this (9 × 4)?*

Multiplication and division as inverses. Display the following: 9 × 5 (read as 9 fives). *Can you work this out?* If the child is correct, display the following immediately beneath the previous card: 45 ÷ 9 (read as 45 divided by 9). *Can you use this (9 × 5) to work out this (45 ÷ 9)?*

Distributive principle. Display the following: 8 × 5 (read as 8 fives). *Can you work this out?* If the child is correct, display the following immediately beneath the previous card: 5 × 5 (read as 5 fives). *Can you work this out?* If the child is correct, display the following immediately below the previous two cards: 13 × 5. *Can you use this (8 × 5) and this (5 × 5) to work out this (13 × 5)?*

**Notes:**

▶    Knowledge of these kinds of relations is important for the development of mental computation.
▶    The notion of commutativity (see first task) can also be tested in the context of an array being turned through 90 degrees. For example, using a 7 × 4 array (how many dots?). Turn the array so it becomes a 4 × 7 array (how many dots now?).
▶    Additional examples for extending a known fact (second task): use 10 × 6 = 60 to work out 9 × 6; use 4 × 8 = 32 to work out 8 × 8; use 7 × 3 = 21 to work out 7 × 6.

# INSTRUCTIONAL ACTIVITIES

## List of Instructional Activities

IA10.1:  Count Around – Multiples
IA10.2:  Trios for Multiples
IA10.3:  Quick Draw Multiples
IA10.4:  Rolling Groups
IA10.5:  Lemonade Stand
IA10.6:  Array Flip
IA10.7:  Dueling Arrays
IA10.8:  Mini Multo
IA10.9:  Four's a Winner
IA10.10: I Have … Who Has …

## ACTIVITY IA10.1: Count Around – Multiples

**Intended learning:** To develop facility with number word sequences in multiples.

**Description:** Children form a circle and count in turn. The progression of counting sequences in this activity supports children in moving from counting-by-ones to counting using a sequence of multiples. The first rounds involve a verbal count by ones with emphasis being placed on the multiples of a selected number, initially focussing on the first ten multiples. For example, for multiples of three, the count would be *1, 2, 3, 4, 5, 6, 7, 8, 9* … with the children who have a count that is a multiple of three calling it out loudly while raising their arms in the air. In subsequent rounds, the counts for the numbers not in the multiple sequence are de-emphasized. This might include going from a normal vocal count to a whisper count to an action, such as a clap or snap, to represent the count. This brings the multiple sequence to more prominence. Finally, Count Around can be played with only the multiples being said in sequence.

**Notes:**

▶ Knowledge of number word sequences in multiples is separate from knowledge of the group structure. That is, children who can recite skip counting sequences might not understand that when counting in multiples, what they are counting is an abstract composite unit.

▶ Sequences for multiples should also include starting not only at the beginning of the sequence, but also at different places within the sequence.

▶ Sequences for multiples should also include counting backwards by multiples. For example, starting at 30 and counting backwards by threes.

**Materials:** None.

## ACTIVITY IA10.2: Trios for Multiples

**Intended learning:** To identify sequences of numerals representing three consecutive multiples.

**Description:** Two or three players are each dealt five cards from a deck of numeral cards containing multiples of a given number. The remaining cards are placed face down, forming a draw pile, and the top card is turned over and placed beside the stack, forming a discard pile. The goal is to collect a series, or trio, of three consecutive multiples (for threes, an example is 9, 12, 15). At their turn, a player may take either the top card from the draw pile or the top card from the discard pile. If the player's hand contains a trio the cards are displayed on the table and saved by that player. Whether or not a trio is formed, the player's turn ends by selecting a card from their hand and placing it in the discard pile. If the draw pile is depleted, the discard pile is shuffled to form a new draw pile. The game ends when one player is out of cards.

**Notes:**

▶ The number of cards held in each player's hand can be increased to add to the potential trios that can be formed.
▶ To increase the level of difficulty, combine the decks for several sets of multiples. Children then must decide what sequence they are working on for a given number and which other numbers fit into that sequence.

**Materials:** Numeral card deck containing four each of the first ten multiples of a given number (for example, for multiples of three, the deck would contain four each of the numbers 3, 6, 9, 12, 15, 18, 21, 24, 27, 30).

## ACTIVITY IA10.3: Quick Draw Multiples

**Intended learning:** To generate sequences of multiples with numerals, both forwards and backwards.

**Description:** Two players are each dealt 15 cards from a deck of numeral cards containing multiples of a given number. These cards are placed in a stack face down in front of the player. The remaining ten cards are divided into two stacks of five and placed face down between the players with space enough between the stacks to turn up and display cards to start the play action. The larger stack in front of the player is the draw pile for that player. Each player draws three cards from their own draw pile. Next, both players simultaneously turn over a card from the middle stacks. A play is made from a player's hand by placing the next multiple, either forwards or backwards, on top of one of the turned up cards. Both players play at the same time and may make a series of plays, so long as the plays are made one card at a time. For example in a game using multiples of five, if a 25 is turned up a player may play either a 20 or a 30. An example of a sequence of cards is 30, 35, 40, 35, 30, 25, 20 (remember the next card can be the multiple of five before or after the previous card). As cards are played during the game, the player replenishes their hand from their draw pile. A player cannot have more than three cards at any one time. When neither player can play a card, new starter cards are turned up. If the starter cards are all used, the cards in the centre are shuffled and placed face down for new starter cards. The first player to play all cards from their draw pile is the winner.

**Note:**

▶ Children should have prior experience reciting multiple sequences, forwards and backwards, starting at different places within the sequence.

**Materials:** Numeral card deck containing four each of the first ten multiples of a given number (for example, for multiples of three, the deck would contain four each of the numbers 3, 6, 9, 12, 15, 18, 21, 24, 27, 30).

## ACTIVITY IA10.4: Rolling Groups

**Intended learning:** To develop strategies for multiplication using a repeated unit.
To develop facility with counting in multiples.

**Description:** Students roll one die to generate the number of groups and another die to generate the number in each group. Using the numbers generated by rolling the dice the child places on the table, the number of strips of the specified size. Students count to get the total number. Students may work individually, in pairs, or in small groups.

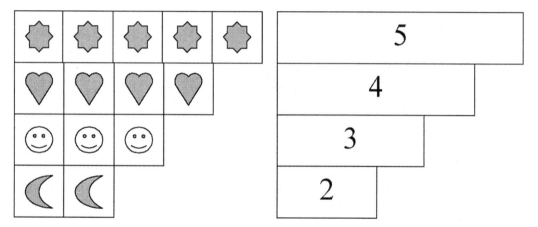

**Figure 10.8** Strips for rolling groups

**Notes:**

▶  Encourage the children to count in multiples.
▶  Students might demonstrate differing abilities in counting to find the total, for example: (a) using a multiple count (skip counting), such as **3, 6, 9, 12**; (b) using a stress count, such as 1, 2, **3**, 4, 5, **6**, 7, 8, **9**; (c) using a combination of stress and multiple counts, such as **3, 6, 9**, 10, 11, **12**, 13, 14, **15**.
▶  Each strip provides the child with a reference for both the group and the number of items in each group (that is, the strip is a container that holds the given number of items).
▶  Observe how the children arrange the strips. Do they arrange them in a row or column structure or do they place them in a line?
▶  Asking children how they got their total or asking them if they could arrange the strips another way can provide insight into the child's knowledge and skills.
▶  As needed, change the numbers on the die representing the number in each group to give children practice with the multiple sequences they do not already know.

▶ To move children away from using visible items to count, replace the strips having individual items with strips that only contain a numeral to represent the quantity in each strip.

▶ To modify this task so that it is based on an area model (Figure 10.9), children could color rows or columns on grid paper.

▶ To modify this task so that it is based on a linear model (Figure 10.10), children could show hops on a number line.

▶ Students could record the resulting equation on a piece of paper.

▶ Products could be verified using a calculator.

▶ Other dice and sets of strips could be created for work on other multiples.

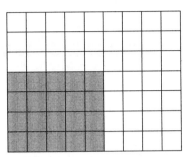

**Figure 10.9** Using an area model to illustrate 4 groups of 5

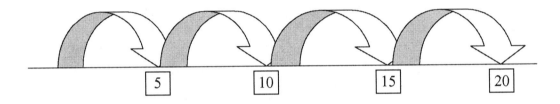

| 5 | | 10 | | 15 | | 20 |

**Figure 10.10** Using a linear model to illustrate 4 groups of 5

**Materials:** One die with the numbers 2, 3, 3, 4, 4, 5 (to generate the number in each group), one deca-die with numbers 0–9 (to generate the number of groups), nine strips of each of the following: 2 items, 3 items, 4 items, 5 items (see Figure 10.8).

## ACTIVITY IA10.5: Lemonade Stand

**Intended learning:** To develop strategies for multiplication. To form equal groups of a specified size and determine the total with individual items concealed.

**Description:** Pairs of children take turns preparing cups with ice-cubes for lemonade orders. Player A rolls both dice. The numeral die indicates how many cups and the dot die indicates how many ice-cubes are to be placed in each cup. This player sets out the appropriate number of cups, puts the indicated number of cubes into each cup, and places lids on the cups. The player must then work out how many ice-cubes were used for the entire order. The number of cups, number of ice-cubes per cup, and the total number of ice-cubes are recorded on the Lemonade Stand record sheet. Player B then rolls the dice and completes the task as above. The winner of the round is the player who used the most ice-cubes. More rounds are completed in the same way.

| LEMONADE STAND | | | | | |
|---|---|---|---|---|---|
| **ROUND 1** | | | | | |
| **PLAYER 1** | | | **PLAYER 2** | | |
| Number of Cups | Number of Ice-cubes | TOTAL Number of Ice-cubes | Number of Cups | Number of Ice-cubes | TOTAL Number of Ice-cubes |
| | | | | | |
| **ROUND 2** | | | | | |

**Figure 10.11** Lemonade stand record sheet

Notes:

▶ The lids are used intentionally to conceal the individual items within the groups, while the cup is available as a marker to indicate the group.
▶ Encourage the children to count in multiples.
▶ Students might demonstrate differing abilities in counting to find the total, for example: (a) using a multiple count (skip counting), such as **3, 6, 9, 12**; (b) using a stress count, such as 1, 2, **3**, 4, 5, **6**, 7, 8, **9**; (c) using a combination of stress and multiple counts, such as **3, 6, 9**, 10, 11, **12**, 13, 14, **15**.
▶ The dice can be customized to set the number of groups and the number within each group for different ability levels.

**Materials:** Ten-sided die with numerals 1 to 10, regular die with dots 1 to 6, 10 opaque cups, lids for the cups or cardboard covers, 60 small cubes, Lemonade Stand record sheet.

## ACTIVITY IA10.6: Array Flip

**Intended learning:** To develop strategies for multiplication and division. To use array structures to support the use of repeated groups.

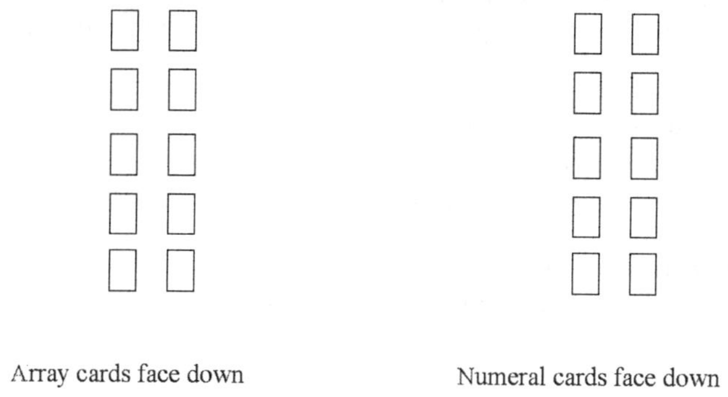

Array cards face down                    Numeral cards face down

**Figure 10.12** Layout of array and numeral cards

**Description:** Pairs of children place array cards face down in a 2 × 5 arrangement (see Figure 10.12). The numeral cards are also placed face down in a 2 × 5 arrangement. Students take turns turning over one array card and one numeral card trying to match the array to its product (see Figure 10.13). The game continues until all cards have been matched.

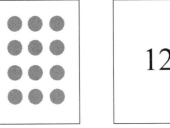

**Notes:**

▶ Students will need experiences forming equal groups and forming arrays, before undertaking this activity.

▶ Arrays with covers that leave one row and one column visible and that could be lifted, could be supportive (see Figure 10.14).

**Figure 10.13** Array and numeral cards

▶ Cards showing the groups as collections can be substituted for the array cards.

▶ Cards with multiplication expressions can be substituted for the numeral cards, for example, 4 × 5 instead of 20.

▶ Pay close attention to the strategies children use to determine the matching product or array; for example: (a) Are they counting each group by ones? (b) Are they using skip counting, or a combination of counting-by-ones and skip counting? (c) Do they use their fingers to keep track of the items in each group, the number of groups, or both? (d) Do they use multiplication facts if so, for which products?

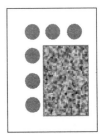

▶ The activity could be changed to a Go Fish format by making four sets of the numeral and array cards. Having five cards in their hand, children ask for the product or describe the array needed to make a match. For example, the child asks, 'Do you have 4 rows of 5'?

**Figure 10.14** Partially screened array card

**Materials:** Numeral and array cards for the first 10 multiples of a given number, partially covered array cards for the first 10 multiples of a given number.

## ACTIVITY IA10.7: Dueling Arrays

**Intended learning:** To develop strategies for multiplication and division. To determine the number of rows or the total for a partially covered array structure with all but one row hidden.

**Description:** The class forms a double circle with one child standing behind a child who is sitting. The teacher shows a dueling array card to a pair of children (see Figure 10.15). The first of the two children who answers correctly holds the standing position. The turn moves to the next pair of children.

**Notes:**

▶ Prior to using this activity, children should be able to find the total for array structures with all dots visible.

▶ Children should have at least partial knowledge of the accompanying skip-counting sequences prior to using this activity.

▶ Students of similar abilities can be paired for this activity.

▶ Differentiate for pairs by selecting cards of appropriate difficulty.

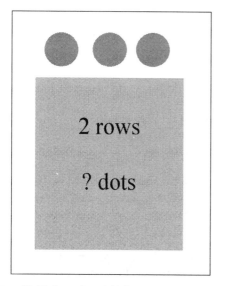 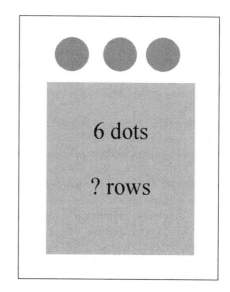

**Figure 10.15** Examples of dueling array cards

▶ Give children time to work out the answer, carefully watching for the child's strategy.
▶ For some children it might be necessary to make complete dot arrays with removable covers.

**Materials:** Dueling array cards.

## ACTIVITY IA10.8: Mini Multo

**Intended learning:** To develop automaticity with multiplication facts.

**Description:** Players begin by filling in a table on the Mini Multo game board with nine different multiples, chosen from the first ten multiples, of a selected number for the round (see Figure 10.16). These can be placed in any arrangement. The teacher, acting as the caller, shuffles the deck of numeral factor cards, 1 to 10, and places the stack face down. The teacher selects the top card and announces the factor to the players. The players then independently determine the product of the called factor

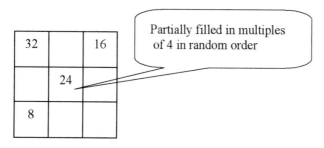

**Figure 10.16** Mini Multo game board

and the selected number for the round. If the product appears in the filled-in table, that box is crossed out. The winner is the first player(s) who has three boxes in a row marked off vertically, horizontally, or diagonally. The products can be verified against the factor cards that were called.

**Notes:**

▶ Students should have previously developed strategies for finding products that are to be used in this activity.

▶ Introduction of this activity might include explaining how the play will take place, but with little help given as to what numbers the children should place on their game board.

▶ Mini Multo can be differentiated to meet the needs of individual children. Within the same round, all children could be using multiples of the same number or children could select, or be assigned, different numbers to generate sets of multiples. The results can still be verified for any set of multiples based on the factor cards that are called during the game.

▶ This activity is appropriate for whole class or small groups.

▶ A child could take the role of the caller and could use a calculator to verify the products for the called numbers.

▶ This activity can be extended by using the sum of two dice to determine the called factor instead of the cards. This allows for the possibility of using a multiple more than one time on the board, as some multiples would be more likely than others. Although this will probably not be immediately apparent to the children, over time strategies for filling in the table of multiples will emerge. A larger table of multiples might also be used in this case. A record-keeping system should be used to keep track of what factors were called.

**Materials:** Mini Multo game board.

## ACTIVITY IA10.9: Four's a Winner

**Intended learning:** To use multiplication and division in determining products and factors.

**Description:** Pairs of children take turns forming factor pairs and covering the product on the game board with a game marker. To begin the game, place factor markers on the 1s in each factor strip. Player 1 moves a factor marker anywhere on either of the factor strips and places one of their colored markers on the product of the two indicated factors. Player 2 now moves one of the factor markers on either of the factor strips and covers the resulting product with a colored marker. (*Note*: For each turn, a player may move only one of the factor markers.) Players continue alternating turns. The winner is the first player to cover four spaces in a row, horizontally, vertically, or diagonally.

**Notes:**

▶ Students should have facility with strategies for multiplication and division and some level of automaticity before playing this game.

▶ Relational knowledge for multiplication and division is important in this activity, as children might select two numbers to multiply or might have selected a number they would like to capture and must determine what factors could be used.

▶ In addition to the practice with multiplication and division, this activity is rich with underlying strategies for play. Over time children will develop strategies for blocking and for factor selection that limits their opponent's options.

**Materials:** Four's a Winner game board, (see Figure 10.17) game markers in two colors, two see-through markers for the factor strips.

| 64 | 20 | 9 | 16 | 48 | 4 | 54 | 14 | 25 |
|----|----|----|----|----|----|----|----|----|
| 49 | 32 | 36 | 10 | 32 | 81 | 42 | 35 | 12 |
| 21 | 63 | 7 | 15 | 63 | 20 | 45 | 24 | 16 |
| 14 | 72 | 18 | 8 | 35 | 28 | 12 | 40 | 8 |
| 2 | 56 | 12 | 27 | 4 | 18 | 8 | 24 | 36 |
| 15 | 6 | 72 | 30 | 16 | 9 | 42 | 6 | 40 |
| 30 | 18 | 36 | 48 | 27 | 56 | 24 | 3 | 54 |
| 12 | 28 | 21 | 6 | 24 | 18 | 10 | 5 | 45 |

FACTOR

| 1 | 2 | 3 | 4 | 5 | 6 | 7 | 8 | 9 |
|---|---|---|---|---|---|---|---|---|

×

| 1 | 2 | 3 | 4 | 5 | 6 | 7 | 8 | 9 |
|---|---|---|---|---|---|---|---|---|

FACTOR

**Figure 10.17** Four's a Winner game board

## ACTIVITY IA10.10: I Have … Who Has …

**Intended learning:** To use multiplication and division in determining products and factors.

**Description:** I Have/Who Has cards are distributed to the children (one per child). The teacher begins the round by posing the first task (*Who has …* ). All children work out the answer and check to see if the answer is on their card. The child who holds the card with the correct answer responds by reading their card (*I have … who has …*), posing a new task for the group. Play continues in this way until the teacher has the correct answer.

**Notes:**

▶ Students can be instructed to work out each item individually, record the answer on paper or whiteboard, and display to the teacher. This holds all children accountable for all task items and allows the teacher to assess an individual child's work.

▶ The teacher might need to assist some children to read the cards, as the written language for these concepts might prove difficult. The emphasis for this activity is on verbally based tasks.

▶ Certain cards can be assigned to specific children to match capabilities and allow for success.

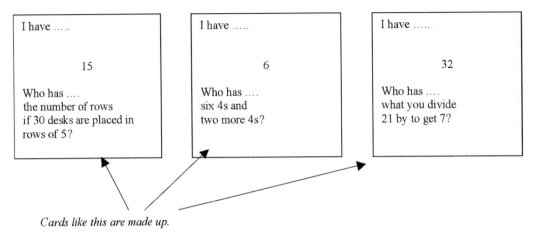

Cards like this are made up.

**Figure 10.18** I have ... who has ... cards

▶ I Have/Who Has can be played by the whole class or in small groups. When used in small groups, each child will be responsible for more than one card.
▶ Sets of I Have/Who Has cards can be created to work on a variety of topics and for a variety of levels.

**Materials:** I Have/Who Has cards for 2s, 3s, 4s, and 5s.

# PART III

# 11
# The Teacher as a Learner
## Penny Munn

### Summary

This chapter focusses on issues related to teacher professional development in early numeracy. This includes discussion of four examples of children's conceptual difficulties and four examples showing how teachers can use their intuition and creativity to support children's learning. Also explained are teachers' use of video-taped interviews of assessments to support their learning about children's conceptual development and, related to their use of videotaped interviews, the three stages of growth in teachers' reflective conversations with children. The chapter includes a set of six teachers' activities that can be the basis of a programme of school-based professional learning focussing on children's early numeracy knowledge. It concludes with a detailed discussion of the role of repeatability and differentiation in early number instruction.

How can class teachers begin to establish an inquiry-based approach in their classrooms? In our experience, good classroom teachers are well able to adapt their teaching to an inquiry-based approach for a whole class of young children. This chapter describes important aspects of the inquiry classroom under the headings of 'The Learning Teacher' and 'The Active Child', with suggestions on how to maximize these for teachers and children.

## THE LEARNING TEACHER

Classroom teachers tend to be skilled at a number of things done routinely – planning flexibly, thinking on their feet, reading the mood of a class, keeping tabs on the children's abilities, personalities, foibles and domestic backgrounds, to name but a few. So when we talk about the 'learning teacher' we do not mean to imply one who moves from knowing little to knowing much. On the contrary, the classroom teacher is competent in myriad ways and already has sophisticated knowledge of the children. The only thing we would want to add to this is a very specific knowledge of how the children develop mathematical understanding.

Most primary teachers have more interest in children than in academic subjects, and this is a great strength when working with young children. Young children do not confine themselves to narrow subject areas, they learn holistically and in context. This is well understood in the context of language and literacy, but most teachers find it hard to teach mathematics in a similar style. One of our aims is to help primary teachers (who might not to be mathematics experts) to become as skilled at teaching mathematics as they are at teaching language and literacy. Developmental mathematics teaching begins with the child, not with the mathematics. Skill in teaching mathematics to the whole child is one that we have helped many teachers to develop, but previously the process has been much more complex than can be contained in this book. We have used intensive programmes that allow teachers to be as creative with their mathematics teaching as they are with their language and literacy teaching. The key to these programmes is diagnosis of mathematical development – something that has been distributed through the teaching chapters of this book.

The difference between diagnosis of development and assessment of mathematical knowledge lies in our understanding of the progressions that underlie change. When teachers assess mathematics attainment they generally use as a yardstick the commonly understood progression of mathematical skills. These skills begin with counting and continue in a progressive fashion through multiplication and algebra to higher levels of mathematics. This is the progression that structures the curriculum, and it is tempting to believe that children will progress right along this line if only they are taught in the right sequence and drilled hard enough. Any experienced primary school teacher knows that things are not so simple. In every class there are children who just do not 'get' the mathematics lesson, and who struggle to solve problems. How can elementary mathematics be so hard? Let us examine why we are now much better at understanding young children's difficulties with mathematics.

## Understanding Why Young Children Find It Hard to do Mathematics

Research undertaken through the 1980s and 1990s has shown us in great detail how young children's number concepts develop. One of the realizations that has come with this knowledge is that schools routinely both underestimate and overestimate young children's understanding of mathematics.

We underestimate what young children know about number. We also underestimate their capacity to learn within this domain. When children come into school we rarely take time to understand the meanings that they hold for number, that is, to understand what their number system is. We also play down what they already know of 'our' number systems – that is, what the children understand about the meanings that we hold for number. School systems routinely underestimate young children's capacity to learn for themselves about the number system. Children are often held back according to what's on the schedule, and made to do repetitive activities because of a belief that this is the way to learn number. When some children do not learn number through these methods, the school system does nothing to revise its beliefs.

While school systems *underestimate* children's knowledge and their ability to manage their own learning, teachers usually *overestimate* children's mathematical concepts. This is because concepts generally grow after knowledge has increased, so children can give the appearance of having a particular aspect of knowledge well before the relevant concept has developed. Concepts give coherence and focus to mathematical activity and knowledge, and for this reason conceptual growth is crucial to a child's development as a mathematician.

Usually, the underestimation of learning ability and overestimation of conceptual underpinning comes about because schools use very superficial assessments of children's mathematics knowledge. Little attention is paid to the wider context of that knowledge, or to assessing the concepts that might underpin it. There are no objective techniques for assessing or judging these concepts. Teachers have to just rely on their intuition and experience to tell them whether a child's knowledge is well founded or not.

In order to assess children's concepts we need a different yardstick than the progression in the mathematics books. It is not that the progression is inaccurate, just that the timing of children's concept development follows an altogether different path than the logical sequence represented in the progression. It takes a very long time for children's concepts to unfurl. We now know that there are only four or five major conceptual transformations between simple counting and advanced multiplicative thinking. Each of these transformations can give rise to many different mathematical behaviors. It is our purpose in this book to help teachers 'read' mathematical behaviors and relate them to the underlying concepts that the children are developing. Our hope is that when teachers are able to do this, they will be as creative and broad-ranging with their mathematics education as they are with their language and literacy education.

## Understanding the Conceptual Foundations of Number Understanding

Once teachers understand the basic number concepts and their sequence of development, they find it easy to understand children's mathematical behavior.

---

*Child Example 1*
How come my children keep forgetting how many fingers they have on their hand? Do they not understand that they have five fingers on each hand?

---

Teachers of 5-year-olds often wonder why it is that some of the children in their class do not seem to know how many fingers they have. When these children add two lots of fingers together (say 5 and 2) they count 1, 2, 3, 4, 5, – 6, 7 each time. After a good year or more of counting to ten on their fingers you would think they would notice that they have five fingers on the first hand every time they counted. Why do they not save themselves some time and effort by counting 5, – 6, 7 and skipping numbers 1,2, 3, 4? They do not, even if you point this out to them. You need to take a developmental view to understand why children do this. These children are still at a stage where they understand number words as items in a sequence rather than as quantities. Later they will move to a more advanced concept where they realize that the number '5' is a quantity that incorporates all the number words that come before it. Until they have this initial number concept they will continue to count from one rather than using the 'count-on' strategy. Teachers often try to demonstrate the count-on strategy without realizing that it is not children's behavior that needs to change, but the meaning that the children attach to the number words they are using.

---

*Child Example 2*
Teachers of 5-year-olds often find it hard to teach them missing addends. If a child knows that 3 and 2 more makes 5, why can she or he not work out from that if you have 3 and add a hidden amount to make 5 in all, then the hidden amount must be 2.

---

This logic might be obvious to us, but it is not obvious to children who still think of 5 as a point in a sequence – those same children who do not know they have 5 fingers on each hand. These children are doing something that is not mathematical when they put their fingers up and model 2 + 3 makes 5. For them, '2' is the number word that lies between 1 and 3. They are not yet able to see '2' as the space between 3 and 5. To see 2 'as a space' is to share the common metaphor of numbers as points within a space. This metaphor is one of the grounding metaphors that defines concept development. Until children have concepts just like our own they will not grasp the logic of the missing addend.

## Teachers' Responses to Understanding the Conceptual Foundations

When teachers understand the sequence of developments in the early years, two things happen to their thinking. First, they stop feeling negative about what the children cannot do and they begin to notice evidence of these stages in the children they are teaching. They understand why the children are behaving as they do, and they begin to engage creatively with the children – they begin to create teaching encounters that will truly help their children. The second thing that happens is that the teachers begin to rely less on words and symbols and more on gestures when they engage with the children. By doing this they are using the children's own preferred mode of communication, and this allows the children to link their teacher's communication directly to their early number concepts.

After learning about developing number concepts, teachers go back to their classrooms with a clearer idea of the appropriate use of fingers. They stop trying to hurry the youngest children away from using their fingers to help with addition and subtraction. They engage the children in number play with finger patterns and gestures. The children's positive response to this appropriate level of communication can inspire teachers to creative insights into their teaching.

### Teacher Example 1

Amanda was trying out ways of using finger patterns to do number bonds with her 5-year-olds. The children enthusiastically learned how to raise and count their fingers for different ways of making 5. Then Amanda realized that she could introduce commutativity merely by crossing her hands over and reversing the order of the numbers. The children followed suit, and had a physical experience of 2 + 3 is the same as 3 + 2 – something far more appropriate to their level of development than the usual whiteboard sums. Since then, Amanda has felt no real need to follow the traditional route of writing sums on the whiteboard and then rewriting them in reverse to demonstrate commutativity.

## Teacher Thinking about Older Primary Children

It is not just in the early years that teacher thinking can be transformed by diagnostic assessment. The following examples show how teachers gained a better understanding of children's problems by thinking developmentally after a diagnostic assessment.

*Child Example 3*
Why do children make the classic 'buggy' error when doing subtraction?

52
17 –      52 – 17      50 – 10 = 40      7 – 2 = 5      40 + 5 = 45
45

This error has been much discussed and written about because it is an example of a learned procedure that has been subverted to a child's intuitions about number. This child thinks 'seven is bigger than 2 so I must take the 2 from the 7' and then proceeds to do two separate single-digit subtractions that are completely unrelated to the original problem.

The problem is not that children misremember the procedure; the problem is that they relate the sum to their intuitive knowledge of numbers 1 to 10 rather than to their intuitive knowledge of numbers 17 to 52. Children using this 'split' strategy have gone beyond the primitive (but commendable) strategy of counting up 17 units from 35 to work out that 35 + 17 is 52. The primitive strategy is very difficult to operate for subtraction, because it involves counting down and keeping track in a backwards direction. The typical error in Child Example 3 arises when children move to splitting the numbers into their component digits before they develop an intuitive sense of each number's quantity in relation to the other. Until children are able to think of the part and the whole simultaneously, they cannot split the numbers into their constituents while thinking about the quantity of the whole. Often, when they are taught the 'splitting' procedure at school, they learn to operate on digits without relating these operations to their wider knowledge of number. Worse, because they are working on large numbers using procedures that are isolated from their number intuitions, they do not build up a store of knowledge about larger numbers. While they are doing mathematics, they are not thinking – just calculating. The 'empty number line' (Chapter 8) techniques in mathematics teaching go some way to helping these problems, but it is still important that teachers are able to recognize children's individual stages and understand how children are using the strategies that they choose.

When teachers realize that children need to develop part–whole understanding after they have developed to the 'count-on' stage, then they tend to analyze the reasoning behind children's written sums.

## Teacher Example 2

Stephanie looked carefully at her 10- and 11-year-olds, and saw that even her most able children made the classic error on double-digit subtractions. She concluded that these errors were related to the way the chidren had been taught subtraction as a written procedure involving 'splitting' of tens and units. She was able to use her videotapes of children's erroneous reasoning, and her explanation of the developmental stages, to persuade her colleagues to approach subtraction differently in the future.

---

*Child Example 4*

Why do some children find it so hard to remember and apply their times tables?

Sam, asked to say what $8 \times 4$ makes, stares at the problem for a while, then smiles and moves his fingers very slightly. 'It's 16' he announces confidently. The interviewer backtracks, trying to understand why he thinks this. 'How did you get 16?'. Sam says, 'Well my teacher told me that times problems work both ways – you can turn them around. And I know my four times table, but I do not know my eight times table, so I turned that one around and I got 16 because 4 and 4 and 4 and 4 makes 16'.

---

Sam had remembered his teacher's well-intentioned advice, but he was still at the stage of doing multiplication by repeated addition. When he 'turned the sum around' he was leaving his intuitions about repeated addition behind, and he easily became confused. He was so sure that his teacher's simple rule had given him the right answer that he was astonished at the right answer when the interviewer laid out 8 bundles of 4 and invited him to check his answer.

## Teacher Example 3

Ros looked at videotapes of her 6- to 8-year-olds responding to diagnostic assesment items and realized that some of them were not able to think of part and whole simultaneously. The most able children had progressed to learning tables (basic facts), but often did not relate the multiplication facts to their intuitions about numbers. They were all still at the stage of doing multiplication as repeated addition. The least able children were still using count-by-ones strategies. There were a few who had not yet developed count-on strategies. She helped the first group of children to build up their intuitive knowledge of whole numbers to 200 by playing verbal number games. She arranged for the second group of children to work with arrays and verbal representations of numbers so that they could link multiplication facts with their number intuitions. She helped the third group of children to work with arrays, verbal representations and numerals, so that they could develop a sense of the relations among number and thus develop more advanced strategies. She helped the children who were struggling with number to develop a stronger sense of the number words, especially in the backward direction.

The four child examples illustrate the difficulties that children can have when their conceptual development does not quite match curricular expectations for their age. The three teacher examples show how teachers can use their intuition and creativity to support children's conceptual development in mathematics once they understand where the children are coming from. The assessment activities were clearly important in helping them understand the children's conceptual difficulties. However, it is important to realize that the videotapes of these assessments, and the opportunities for reflection that they provided, had a vital impact on the quality of the teachers' contribution.

## The Importance of Videotape

Teacher thinking changes when teachers understand the reasons for children's mistakes. It is important that teachers can map this 'reason why' onto their understanding of number development. All the teachers in the examples had developed their understanding of the stages of development through careful viewing of videotaped interviews. They had assessed the children in their class using conversational techniques to probe concepts and using videotape to record the interview. The use of videotape had a number of implications for the teachers' interactions with the children.

1. It meant there was no need for the teachers to write during the conversation. This allowed the teachers to devote their whole attention to their conversation with the child.
2. It provided a space for the teachers to reflect on what had passed during the interview.
3. It provided colleagues with an opportunity to offer their interpretations of the children's reasoning and explanations.
4. It provided a public record of the child's reasoning and of the teacher's insight.
5. It provided a powerful tool for communication with colleagues, parents and other professionals.

We have found that the best and quickest way for teachers to develop a clear understanding of children's conceptual development is for them to analyze and discuss videotapes of children's responses to verbally presented tasks such as those in the assessment suggestions. Initially, teachers' feelings about these verbal tasks can intrude on their perceptions and can affect the way they interact with children. Teachers are accustomed to working through the medium of written mathematics, and the close contact of verbal interaction can leave them feeling uncomfortable. In particular, they can feel awkward when a child clearly does not know something in the context of verbal interaction. The normal rules of teacher–pupil interaction dictate that the teacher must take responsibility for the child's ignorance, and a teacher's first instinct is to cover up the gap in the child's knowledge by intervening and filling in for the child. Where teachers use skillful leading questions and subtle cues, children can often give a scaffolded performance that covers up a total lack of understanding. In addition, teachers can feel very awkward and embarrassed about videotaping themselves. There are three distinct stages during which teachers develop a conscious control over the conversational rules that usually drive them in the classroom, and these stages are characterized by the growth of reflective conversations with children.

### Stage 1: Teacher as Interactive Leader, Focus on the Adult

In the first stage, the teachers' primary concerns are with their own role in the assessment. Teachers worry about how to manage the assessments, and about the resources needed to produce the tapes. They also worry about their own appearance on the tape. At this stage, teachers might feel uncomfortable about appearing on the video with the child. They regard the conversation as a test of the child's abilities rather than as a way of getting to know what teaching the child needs. They worry about the child's ability to cope with the presented task. When the child struggles, they might give the child some thinking time, but they generally show tension and anxiety. They often cut in to stop the child working too long or to show the child how to do the task. At this stage it is usual to see teachers using leading questions, subtle prompts and **scaffolding** children's responses in assessments to produce a performance that conforms to what the teachers think the child ought to know. A close examination of the videotape shows a great deal of tension and anxiety in both teacher and child.

### Stage 2: Focus and Responsibility Shifting to Child

In the second stage, teachers focus on the tasks that they are using with the children. They are preoccupied with resourcing and arranging the tasks for the child, and they focus on themselves to check the accuracy of their own actions. During this stage they become consciously aware of their own reflective capacity and often issue (silent) instructions to themselves to check their anxiety or suppress their instincts to intervene. It is common during this stage to see the child reacting to the change in the teacher with surprise, and with attempts to draw the teacher back into the usual role. The teacher's inactivity produces interesting examples of children's thinking, and their observation of these arouses their interest further, thus leading them into the third stage.

### Stage 3: Teacher Allowing Child to Take Responsibility, Focus on the Child

In the third stage, the teachers are wholly engaged with their impact on the children, and their focus has shifted from themselves to the child. In this final stage, teachers are focussed on the children's thinking, are close observers of the task from the child's viewpoint, and find it relatively easy to make notes on the children's understanding (as opposed to their own teaching). During this time teachers develop specific knowledge of the growth of number understanding, they develop the habit of reflecting critically on the children's interview responses and they become preoccupied with the way children understand and benefit from specific tasks. At this stage teachers are also interested in the child's thinking to prompt, lead or induce a 'performance'. The teacher is relaxed and able to tolerate any difficulty the children might have. The children are able to engage in uninterrupted thinking for a minute or more if need be. Although the children might be thinking hard, there is no social anxiety or tension – just involvement with the problem. Similarly, the teacher shows no negative feeling and communicates no negativity to the children. The teacher's engagement allows a distance from the children's struggle, and lets the children be at their current stage of cognitive development rather than wanting to cover over the gap and hurry the children through to the desired outcome.

### Developing Teachers' Thinking

Teacher thinking can be developed through these stages by engaging in structured tasks that will focus them on aspects of children's mathematics that they are not usually encouraged to notice in the classroom. Six teacher activities are described below. The first activity is designed to shift teachers into the third stage of focus on the child. Only at this third stage will teachers start to build their understanding of children's number knowledge. If you are working with a group of teachers you might find it necessary to repeat the first activity until they are clearly focussed on the children's thinking rather than on their own concerns. The main criterion for judging this focus is the teachers' videotaped responses to children's lack of knowledge. When they can remain still in the face of the children's struggles, they are focussed on the children's learning rather than on themselves. Activities 2 – 6 are designed to help teachers think through the difficulties that children might be experiencing and to choose activities appropriate to the children in their class.

## Activities to Help Teachers Develop their Thinking about Children's Mathematics

These activities can be done by teachers working alone to enhance their understanding of children's number, or they can be used as part of a whole-school plan to enhance assessment and teaching in number.

## TEACHER ACTIVITY 1

**Purpose:** To relate the assessment tasks to familiar classroom work.

**Equipment:** Videotapes of assessment tasks.

**Action:** Look through those portions of the tape where the teacher and child are working with written numerals. For each minute of these portions of the tape, code the teacher's ease and comfort on a scale of 1 to 3 where:

1 = very uncomfortable (voice pitch is high, body signals high tension, teacher moves around a lot, teacher fidgets uncomfortably, movements and verbal statements are very sudden, reactions to the unexpected from the child are sudden);
2 = not uncomfortable, but not particularly comfortable (voice pitch is moderate, tension is not very high, but teacher is not very relaxed); and
3 = comfortable (voice pitch is low, body posture communicates relaxation, teacher watches child steadily without intruding, interactions are slow and smooth).

Now look through those portions of the tape where the teacher is working with verbal interactive tasks. For each minute of these portions of the tape, code the teacher's ease and comfort on the same scale as above.

Average the ratings across all the minutes and compare the teacher's state during the tasks with written numerals as opposed to the tasks relying on verbal interactions. Is there a difference? Why?

**Table for coding teacher's ease**

| Minute number | Type of task (numeral based or purely verbal) | Rating of teacher's comfort |
|---|---|---|
|  |  |  |
|  |  |  |
|  |  |  |
|  |  |  |
|  |  |  |
|  |  |  |
|  |  |  |
|  |  |  |
|  |  |  |
|  |  |  |
|  |  |  |
|  |  |  |
|  |  |  |
|  |  |  |

## TEACHER ACTIVITY 2

**Purpose:** To develop a focus on the child being assessed.

**Equipment:** Videotapes of assessment tasks.

**Action:** Look through videotapes of verbal assessment tasks and write down times and durations of incidents where the child did not know something or was not able to complete a task. Use the table below to record each instance.

In the comment boxes write notes as follows:

▶   How do you think the teacher felt about the child not knowing?
▶   How do you think the child felt about not knowing?
▶   What was the response of the teacher on the video (for example, length of wait time, nature of intervention – did she or he repeat, clarify, or explain?)
▶   What do you think the teacher felt during the wait time?
▶   What do you think the child felt during the wait time?
▶   What do you think the teacher discovered about the child's learning during this incident (or what would the teacher have discovered if she or he had not intervened)?

**Table for times and durations of incidents**

| Incident and tape time | Comment box 1 – observations on teacher | Comment box 2 – observations on child |
|---|---|---|
|  |  |  |
|  |  |  |
|  |  |  |
|  |  |  |
|  |  |  |
|  |  |  |

## TEACHER ACTIVITY 3

**Purpose:** To help teachers understand the structure of children's number knowledge.

**Equipment:** Videotapes of about 12 children of various abilities and ages doing additive and subtractive tasks.

**Action:** Teachers look through the videotapes and makes notes on the children's responses using precise descriptions. Each child's response is put into a table with the following column headings:

Number range within which child responded well
Complexity (for example, screened/unscreened) of task to which child responded well
Number range within which child gave sensible answers
Observable techniques used (for example, fingers, vocalization).

## TEACHER ACTIVITY 4

**Purpose:** To help teachers understand the development of the number word sequence.

**Equipment:** Videotapes of about 12 children of various ages and abilities doing backward and forward number word sequence assessment tasks (including number word before and number word after).

**Action:** Teachers looks through videotapes and makes notes on the children's responses using precise descriptions. Teachers compile a table of the following information for each child:

Extent of forward number word sequence
Highest number to which child can give 'Number word after' without resorting to counting up to find the number word after
Numbers for which child had to resort to counting up to find number word after
Numbers on or around decade that child stumbles over when going backwards
Extent of backward number word sequence
Highest number to which child can give 'Number word before' without resorting to counting up to find the number word before
Numbers for which child had to resort to counting up to find number word before
Numbers on or around decade that child stumbles over when going backwards
Number words that child is confusing by focusing on the first or the last syllable – for example, four*teen* and for*ty; seven* and e*leven; twelve* and *twenty*.

## TEACHER ACTIVITY 5

**Purpose:** To help teachers understand the development of place value.

**Equipment:** Videotapes of about five 6–8-year-old children doing tens tasks, horizontal double-digit addition and subtraction, and working with arrays.

**Action:** Teachers look through videotapes and make notes on children's responses to these tasks. Teachers compile a table of the following information for each child:

Whether child can count in tens on the decade
Whether child can count in tens off the decade
Whether child can count in fives, fours, threes and twos
Whether child uses fives and tens information when working with arrays
Whether child uses jump, split, or count by ones strategies on horizontal sums.

## TEACHER ACTIVITY 6

**Purpose:** To help teachers understand the development of multiplicative concepts.

**Equipment:** Videotapes of about five 6–8-year-old children doing multiplicative tasks using screened and unscreened arrays and verbal presentations.

**Action:** Teachers look through videotapes and make notes on children's responses to these tasks. Teachers compile a table of the following information for each child:

Whether the child can solve multiplicative problems visually when these are screened
Whether the child can solve multiplicative problems visually when these are unscreened
Whether the child can solve multiplicative problems when these are presented verbally
Whether the child uses repeated addition to solve multiplicative problems
Whether the child has a concept of multiplication as the inverse of division.

The information gathered during Teacher Activities 3–6 should be used to reflect on each child's 'next steps' in number learning and to choose activities that will be most helpful for developing ideas around the gaps and misconceptions in each child's number knowledge. The next step for the teachers is to use one or more of the activities as appropriate with the children, and to record something about the variety of the children's responses to these activities.

## THE ACTIVE CHILD

Active children are just as important to the inquiry-based approach as are learning teachers. A teacher needs more than activities if the inquiry classroom is to have vibrant and active children. The children need to be purposefully engaged in these activities, and the quality both of the activities and of the teacher's implementation is crucial to this. The teacher needs to have a range of differentiation strategies, and the activity implementation needs to have a quality that we describe as 'repeatability'.

## Repeatability

### Taking Time to Develop a Skill

Becoming good at something requires that one spends time doing it. The person – adult or child – who can pick up a new skill almost instantly is very rare. Most of us need to stick at a thing until we develop some initial skill, and then stick at it some more to develop that skill. This is true of both mental and physical skills. This simple truth is unarguable, and accounts for a great deal of the diversity that one finds among human beings. Psychologists now talk about the way in which children 'pick niches' for themselves in their family and school environment, and slowly burrow away at their skills, practicing favored activities. In the teen and adult years they emerge variously as sportspeople, poets, playwrights, mathematicians, social supremos or simply themselves, with a broad smattering of many skills, and they often attribute their skills to patient teaching by parents, professionals, or siblings. However, the truth of the matter is that the sporty ones have spent thousands of hours working on their balance and flexibility. This might have looked to outsiders like 'mucking about' on a bicycle or a skateboard, but truly it was work. Similarly, the accomplished linguists spent hours working on their vocabulary and comprehension, and the socially accomplished spent much time working on their understanding of emotion. To outsiders, this might have looked like chatting to their mates, or partying, but really it was work. Human skill in anything is a complicated thing, it has a value beyond compare, and it begins with individuals engaging in activity for many hundreds or thousands of hours. Think about an orchestra playing a symphony and work out how many hours of human activity it took to produce – the hours that it took for each musician to learn their accomplishment, the hours that it took for each instrument-maker to learn their craft and produce the instrument, the hours that it took for the composer to learn his craft and produce the piece of music. By the time all these hours of effort are added together we have reached over a million hours, even by conservative estimates – or over a century of effort. Time spent on a task results in skill and any skill takes both time and effort to develop.

### Counting-by-ones and Mathematics Anxiety

Mathematics involves skill and it takes both time and effort to develop that skill. This was brought home to me very sharply the first time I went to our neighboring school with Jim Martland and a group of colleagues to try out the advanced assessment on some 7-year-olds. The school took children from the surrounding upper-middle class area, and these children tended to be well disciplined and accustomed to concentrating for long periods. I interviewed Luke, who was still using count-by-ones strategies, and when I got to the 'horizontal sentences' section and asked him to add 43 and 21 he did this by counting up from 43 in ones. This took him quite some time, and he concentrated hard on a spot behind my head while he did it, making small movements with his fingers all the while. Eventually he took his eyes away from the spot behind me, looked me in the eye and said '64' with some satisfaction. Novice interviewer that I was, I then went quickly on to the next item and asked him whether he could add 37 and 19. His satisfied look changed slowly to one of sadness and wearisome defeat. He looked at me silently for a number of seconds, and I could read the wordless look in the eyes as clearly as anything. It said, 'Well yes I *can* add 37 and 19, but I'd really rather not'. I am pleased to recall that I relented and stopped him at that point, but his look and his wordless plea had in an instant taught me everything I needed to know about how hard it is to learn number. I felt that in that moment I had looked into the face of mathematics anxiety and seen the hours of hard and tedious work that children (and adults) who are 'stuck' at count-by-ones strategies have to do. I understood completely why so many people hate mathematics, why it is so unpleasant for them and such hard mental work. I had also seen a vision of the means by which children can move to higher level strategies – by engaging both willingly and playfully in reflection on the strategies that they use, not, absolutely not, by engaging in a mindless and repetitive 'drill' that will cause them to flee from any real thought about number. Time on task is important for learning, but the quality of the time spent is more important than the quantity. Time spent on task while engaged, reflective or playful will result in fast learning. Time on task when the attention is not fully focussed will result in slow learning or no learning at all. It would not have helped Luke to spend wearisome hours counting up and down to do his sums. What he most needed was some quality time playing with powerful strategies to do these sums. However, for him to be properly engaged, these strategies would need to be his own, not ones that someone else had drilled him in.

## Activities with the Quality of Repeatability

We should always try to attend to the subjective quality of the time that children spend on task in mathematics work. By spending quality time on task they can get the maximum amount of learning out of the time that they spend doing mathematics. There is a big difference between simple repetition of an activity and engagement with an activity. Understanding this difference is the key to understanding the nature of the activities in Chapters 3 to 10. These activities have all been selected for their quality of 'repeatability'. By this, we mean the extent to which a class or group can repeatedly engage with the activity. If activities have 'repeatability' then groups will engage with them in a playful way over and over again. The children will not experience the activities as 'the same' each time they repeat them, and the activities will not become boring. Each time the class engages with the activity, the activity will provide a different experience, because the game and the experience will change even though the rules and the materials remain the same. To draw an analogy, a game of football is a unique and unpredictable event made up of the actions and interactions of the opposing teams, with a lot of chance events thrown in. The fact that each game of football has identical pitches, balls and rules is irrelevant to the players and the fans; it is *today's* game that engages them, not the abstractions that make this game similar to yesterday's or tomorrow's game. So it should be with mathematics activities. The children might well recognize the activity as the one they did yesterday, but their experience of it should not be the same as yesterday's, or they will not learn from it.

This difference between 'repetition' and 'engagement' is what we mean by 'repeatability' and it is the key to understanding the nature of the activities in Chapters 3 to 10. These activities have the characteristic of 'repeatability' if they are presented to a class in the right way and at the right time. The invitation should have the quality of playfulness if the children are to be persuaded to engage with the activity as a repeatable event.

### Engagement and Play in Mathematical Activities

Play has been downgraded in our culture, and usually gets treated as a childish and unimportant activity. However, the truth is that play is an attribute and not an activity in itself. You can do anything playfully, and often there is a large dose of pretense involved in a playful activity. Along with pretense and playfulness comes both enjoyment and a release from instrumentality. Playful actions do not have to have any purpose, except to be themselves. Playful actions are often highly communicative, and are often done in concert or in collaboration with others. Grown-ups play, of course, but we usually describe adult play with words like 'fun' and 'sport' to avoid the connotations of childhood and low status that the word 'play' has. 'Fun' is a rather dismissive way of referring to playfulness – something that is very important for children and adults.

Mathematics educators have been exhorting us to 'make mathematics fun' and peppering us with books with 'mathematics' and 'fun' in the title for many years now. However, the truth is that mathematics is not much fun for children still at Luke's stage of counting-by-ones, and 'fun' is not a characteristic that resides in an activity per se. 'Fun' exists in the children's minds, in their attitude towards the activity, in their relationship with their teacher, and in their experience of the activity. The teacher's input to the activity decides whether it is going to be a routine practice item or whether it will have a playful, engaging element. It is this playful engagement that will give the mathematics activities their quality of 'repeatability'. This quality will encourage the children to engage with the activities so that they create a different learning experience for themselves each time they engage.

## Differentiation

The element of individual engagement is important in understanding how these activities can be differentiated so that they can be used with large and diverse groups of children. Ideally, the children will engage with the activities at a variety of levels, and each child's learning experience will be unique. Traditional analyses of differentiation assume that the teacher must decide what each child is to learn. So for instance, work can be differentiated by content – more able children get higher-level exercises; by process – more able children use more complex processes; by role – more able children help other children; by group – more able children are grouped together, as are less able children; or by level of support – teacher gives more help to less able children.

### Differentiation and Social Interaction

Classroom teachers are probably using all these methods of differentiation in their other work, and should not find it hard to extend their current practices to the number activities in Chapters 3 to 10. However, if teachers take account of the importance of the children's subjective experiences, as outlined above, then there is yet another dimension to the differentiation that takes place daily in a diverse classroom. This dimension is one in which the teacher is not deciding what will be learned and assigning learning content, but noting the social dynamics of the classroom and using this knowledge to extend each child's experience of the number activities. This is quite different from the more traditional differentiation, where teachers provide learning experiences according to each child's apparent ability. In the social interactive version of differentiation, teachers note how the number activities engage with the children's individual and social characteristics, and then use what they know of the classroom context to maximize each child's learning. In the interactive differentiation, the teacher is contributing to the way in which the children construct their experiences of the number games, but is allowing an equal contribution from the children – who might have surprisingly different views of their own and other children's abilities with number.

### Teacher Example 4

Ros's class of 6–8-year-olds had a range of abilities. Some children had not yet developed an initial sense of number, while others were developing 'non-count-by-ones' strategies and understanding multiplication as repeated addition. Ros assessed the children and grouped them according to their conceptual level. She then devised activities for group-work, and to engage the whole class. In her previous class of 5-year-olds, simple whole-class number activities had shown her that the children's game strategies were often driven by the social relations in the class. Her 'Decades out!' game was designed to focus children's attention on the numbers before and after the decade number words. The whole class participated in a count-round, and game rules stipulated that each child decided whether to count one, two, or three numbers in the sequence and that every child that spoke a decade number was 'out' of the game. Ros found that the children would look along the row and plan for the decade number to fall on someone who was not their friend, or not in their group. In short, the social structure of the class was instrumental in getting the children to think about the number sequence they were playing with.

With this experience in mind, Ros introduced the games 'Century' and '99', with multiplying by 10 options to her 6–8-year-olds, and monitored their strategies. She noted that the children's strategies reflected both their social relationships and their individual characteristics. Robbie, for instance, was very able, and was also very competitive. He realized before starting '99' that if he used the multiplying option he would reach the target too soon, so he used this option very strategically. Scott was also competitive, but did not have Robbie's foresight so he used the multiplying option regardless of whether its powerful effects would 'bust' him. Stuart had Robbie's foresight but really was not concerned about winning, so he used this understanding to show the other children how to multiply strategically. Rafee, by contrast, only played the game once and was acutely aware of his lack of ability; he left the game because, although he enjoyed winning, he was not good at persevering when he did not win. Ros used her knowledge of the children, their characteristics, and their relationships with each other to introduce variations to the game and new games that would draw on their own and others' abilities and that would encourage them to play with numbers in cooperative and competitive contexts.

## SUMMARY AND CONCLUSIONS

Classroom teachers are already very skilled observers of children's social and intellectual abilities. It is possible to draw on these skills and align them with an understanding of number development to improve classroom numeracy activities. When teachers understand why some children have problems with number and begin to focus on the children's learning, rather than their own teaching, they usually begin to engage creatively with the children's number learning. A combination of learning teachers and active children will maximize this creative engagement. Videotape is an important tool for the learning teacher. Time on task is important for the active child, but it should be measured by engagement with an activity rather than by numbers of repetitions. The 'repeatability' of an activity will depend on the teacher's skill in engaging the class and monitoring their experience of activities. Use of activities with the whole class will depend on teachers' skills in differentiation, which can be accomplished in a number of ways, as well as by using knowledge of the social dynamics of the class to extend the children's experiences of number activities.

# Glossary

**Additive task.** A generic label for tasks involving what adults would regard as addition. The label 'additive task' is used to emphasize that children will construe such tasks idiosyncratically, that is, differently from each other and from the way adults will construe them.

**Arithmetic rack.** An abacus-like instructional device consisting of two rows of 10 beads. In each row the beads appear in two groups of five, that is, using two different colors for the beads.

**Backward number word sequence (BNWS).** A regular sequence of number words backward, typically but not necessarily by ones, for example, the BNWS from ten to one, the BNWS from eighty-two to seventy-five, the BNWS by tens from eighty-three.

**Color-coding.** Using color to differentiate different parts of an instructional setting (a collection of 6 red counters and a collection of 3 green counters).

**Commutative.** Addition is said to be a commutative operation because, for any two numbers, the order of adding does not change the result, for example, $7 + 4 = 4 + 7$. Multiplication is also a commutative operation whereas subtraction and division are operations that are not commutative.

**Counting-back-from.** A strategy used by children to solve Removed Items tasks, for example 11 remove 3 – 'eleven, ten, nine – eight.' Also referred to as counting-off-from or counting-down-from.

**Counting-back-to.** Regarded as the most advanced of the counting-by-ones strategies. Typically used to solve missing subtrahend tasks, for example, have 11, remove some, and there are eight left – 'eleven, ten, nine – three.' Also referred to as counting-down-to.

**Counting-by-ones.** Initial or advanced arithmetical strategies which involve counting-by-ones only. Examples of initial counting-by-ones strategies are perceptual and figurative counting, which involve **counting-from-one.** Examples of advanced counting-by-ones strategies are counting-on, counting-back-from and counting-back-to.

**Counting-on.** An advanced counting-by-ones strategy used to solve additive tasks or missing addend tasks involving two hidden collections. Counting-on can be differentiated into counting-up-from for additive tasks and counting-up-to for missing addend tasks. Counting-on is also referred to as counting-up.

**Counting-up-from.** An advanced counting-by-ones strategy used to solve additive tasks involving two hidden collections, for example, seven and five, is solved by counting up five from seven.

**Counting-up-to.** An advanced counting-by-ones strategy used to solve missing addend tasks, for example, seven and how many make twelve, is solved by counting from seven up to twelve, and keeping track of five counts.

**Difference.** See Minuend.

**Digit.** The digits are the ten basic symbols in the modern numeration system, that is '0', '1', … '9'.

**Early number.** A generic label for the number work in the first three years of school and learned by children around 4 to 8 years of age. Also known as 'early arithmetic'.

**Empty number line (ENL).** A setting consisting of a simple arc or line which is used by children and teachers to record and explain mental strategies for adding and subtracting.

**Facile.** Used in the sense of having good facility, that is, fluent or dexterous, for example, a facile counting-on strategy, or facile with the backward number word sequence.

**Figurative.** Figurative thought involves re-presentation of a sensory-motor experience, that is a mental replay of a prior experience involving seeing, hearing, touching, and so on. Figurative counting may be figural, in which visualized items constitute the material which is counted, motor, in which movements constitute the material which is counted, or verbal, in which number words constitute the material which is counted.

**Five-wise pattern.** A spatial pattern for a number in the range 1 to 10 made on a ten frame (2 rows and 5 columns). The five-wise patterns are made by progressively filling the rows. For example, a five-wise pattern for 8 has a row of 5 and a row of 3, a five-wise pattern for 4 has a row of four dots.

**Flashing.** A technique which involves briefly displaying (typically for half a second) some aspect of an instructional setting, for example, a ten frame with 8 red and 2 green counters is flashed.

**Forward number word sequence (FNWS).** A regular sequence of number words forward, typically but not necessarily by ones, for example the FNWS from one to twenty, the FNWS from eighty-one to ninety-three, the FNWS by tens from twenty-four.

**Jump strategy.** A category of mental strategies for 2-digit addition and subtraction. Strategies in this category involve starting from one number and incrementing or decrementing that number by tens or ones.

**Knowledge.** A collective term for all of what the child knows about early number. The term 'knowledge' is sometimes juxtaposed with 'strategies' and in that case refers to knowledge not easily characterized as a strategy (for example, knowing the names of numerals).

**Mathematics Recovery (MR).** A programme originally developed in schools in New South Wales which has been implemented widely in schools in the UK and the USA. The programme focusses on intensive teaching for low-attaining children and an extensive programme of specialist teacher development.

**Micro-adjusting.** Making small moment-by-moment adjustments in interactive teaching which are informed by one's observation of student responses.

**Minuend.** In subtraction of standard form, for example $12 - 3 = 9$, 12 is the minuend, 3 is the subtrahend and 9 is the difference. Thus the difference is the answer obtained in subtraction, the subtrahend is the number subtracted and the minuend is the number from which the subtrahend is subtracted.

**Missing addend.** A subtractive task posed in the form of addition with one addend missing, for example 12 and how many make 15?

**Non-canonical.** The number 64 can be expressed in the form of 50 + 14. This form is referred to as a non-canonical (non-standard) form of 64. Knowledge of non-canonical forms is useful in addition, subtraction, and so on.

**Non-count-by-ones.** A class of strategies which involve aspects other than counting-by-ones and which are used to solve additive and subtractive tasks. Part of the strategy may involve counting-by-ones but the solution also involves a more advanced procedure. For example, 6 + 8 is solved by saying 'six and six is twelve – thirteen, fourteen'.

**Notating.** Writing which relates to numbers and numerical reasoning.

**Number.** A number is the idea or concept associated with, for example, how many items in a collection. We distinguish between the number 24 – that is, the concept, the spoken or heard number word 'twenty-four'– the numeral '24', and the read or written number word 'twenty-four'. These distinctions are important in understanding children's early numerical strategies.

**Number word**. Number words are names or words for numbers. In most cases in early number, the term 'number word' refers to the spoken and heard names for numbers rather than the read or written names.

**Numeral**. Numerals are symbols for numbers, for example, '5' and '27'.

**Numeral identification**. Stating the name of a displayed numeral. The term is used similarly to the term 'letter identification' in early literacy. When assessing numeral identification, numerals are not displayed in numerical sequence.

**Numeral recognition**. Selecting a nominated numeral from a randomly arranged group of numerals.

**Numeral sequence**. A regularly ordered sequence of numerals, typically but not necessarily a forward sequence by ones, for example the numerals as they appear on a numeral track.

**Numeral track**. An instructional device consisting of a sequence of numerals and for each numeral, a hinged lid which can be used to screen or display the numeral.

**Numerosity**. The numerosity of a collection is the number of items in the collection.

**Pair-wise pattern**. A spatial pattern for a number in the range 1 to 10 made on a ten frame (2 rows and 5 columns). The pair-wise patterns are made by progressively filling the columns. For example, a pair-wise pattern for 8 has four pairs, a pair-wise pattern for 5 has two pairs and one single dot.

**Partitioning**. An arithmetical strategy involving partitioning a small number into two parts without counting, typically with both parts in the range 1 to 5, for example partitioning 6 into 5 + 1, 4 + 2, and so on.

**Perceptual**. Involving direct sensory input – usually seeing but may also refer to hearing or feeling. Thus perceptual counting involves counting items seen, heard or felt.

**Quinary**. This term refers to the use of five as a base in some sense, and typically in conjunction with, rather than instead of, ten as a base. The arithmetic rack may be regarded as a quinary-based instructional device.

**Scaffolding**. Actions on the part of the teacher to provide support for student learning during interactive teaching.

**Screening**. A technique used in the presentation of instructional tasks which involves placing a small screen over all or part of a setting (for example, screening a collection of 6 counters).

**Setting**. A physical situation used by a teacher in posing numerical tasks, for example collections of counters, numeral track, hundreds chart, ten frame.

**Split strategy**. A category of mental strategies for 2-digit addition and subtraction. Strategies in this category involve splitting the numbers into tens and ones and working separately with the tens and ones.

**Strategy**. A generic label for a method by which a child solves a task. A strategy consists of two or more constituent procedures. A procedure is the simplest form of a strategy, that is, a strategy that cannot be described in terms of two or more constituent procedures. For example, on an additive task involving two screened collections a child might use the procedure of counting the first collection from one and then use the procedure of continuing to count by ones, in order to count the second collection.

**Subitizing**. The immediate, correct assignation of a number word to a small collection of perceptual items.

**Subtractive task**. A generic label for tasks involving what adults would regard as subtraction. The label 'subtractive task' is used to emphasize that children will construe such tasks idiosyncratically, that is, differently from each other and from the way adults will construe them.

**Subtrahend**. See Minuend.

**Symbolizing**. Used in a very broad sense – developing or using symbols in the context of numerical reasoning.

**Task**. A generic label for problems or questions presented to a child.

**Temporal sequence**. A sequence of events that occur sequentially in time, for example, sequences of sounds or movements.

**Ten frame**. A setting consisting of a $2 \times 5$ rectangular array which is used to support children's thinking about combinations to 10 (for example, $7 + 3$) and combinations involving 5 (for example, 7 is $5 + 2$).

# Bibliography

Anghileri, J. (2000) *Teaching Number Sense*. London: Continuum.

Anghileri, J. (ed.) (2001) *Principles and Practices of Arithmetic Teaching*. Buckingham: Open University Press.

Beishuizen, M. (1993) Mental strategies and materials or models for addition and subtraction up to 100 in Dutch second grades, *Journal for Research in Mathematics Education*, **34**: 394–433.

Beishuizen, M. and Anghileri, J. (1998) Which mental strategies in the early number curriculum? A comparison of British ideas and Dutch Views, *British Education Research Journal*, **34**: 519–38.

Bobis, J. (1996) Visualisation and the development of number sense with kindergarten children, in J. Mulligan and M. Mitchelmore (eds), *Children's Number Learning: A Research Monograph of MERGA/AAMT*. Adelaide: Australian Association of Mathematics Teachers. pp. 17–34.

Bobis, J., Clarke, B., Clarke, D., Thomas, G., Wright, R., Young-Loveridge, J. and Gould, P. (2005) Supporting teachers in the development of young children's mathematical thinking: three large-scale cases, *Mathematics Education Research Journal*, **16**(3): 27–57.

Cameron, A., Hersch, S.B., and Fosnot, C.T. (2004) *Young Mathematicians at Work: Constructing Number Sense, Addition, and Subtraction: Working with the Number Line, Grade 2: Mathematical Models (CD)*. Portsmouth, NH: Heinemann.

Carpenter, T.P., Fennema, E., Franke, M.L., Levi, L. and Empson, S.B. (1999). *Children's Mathematics: Cognitively Guided Instruction*. Portsmouth, NH: Heinmenann.

Clements, D. and Sarama, J. (eds) (2004) *Engaging Young Children in Mathematics*. Mahwah, NJ: Lawrence Erlbaum.

Cobb, P. (1991) Reconstructing elementary school mathematics, *Focus on Learning Problems in Mathematics*, **13**(3): 3–33.

Cobb, P. and Bauersfeld, H. (eds) (1995) *The Emergence of Mathematical Meaning: Interaction in Classroom Cultures*. Hillsdale, NJ: Lawrence Erlbaum.

Cobb, P. and Wheatley, G. (1988) Children's initial understandings of ten, *Focus on Learning Problems in Mathematics*, **10**(3): 1–36.

Cobb, P., McClain, K., Whitenack, J. and Estes, B. (1995) Supporting young children's development of mathematical power, in A. Richards (ed.), *Proceedings of the Fifteenth Biennial Conference of the Australian Association of Mathematics Teachers*. Darwin: Australian Association of Mathematics Teachers. pp. 1–11.

Cobb, P., Wood, T. and Yackel, E. (1991) A constructivist approach to second grade mathematics, in E. von Glasersfeld (ed) *Radical Constructivism in Mathematics Education*. Dordrecht: Kluwer. pp. 157–76.

Cobb, P. Yackel, E. and McClain, K. (eds) (2000) *Symbolizing and Communicating in Mathematics Classrooms: Perspectives on Discourse, Tools, and Instructional Design*. Mahwah, NJ: Lawrence Erlbaum.

Copley, J. (ed.) (1999) *Mathematics in the Early Years*. Reston, VA: National Council of Teachers of Mathematics.

Dowker, A.D. (2005). *Individual Differences in Arithmetic: Implications for Psychology, Neuroscience and Education*. Hove: Psychology Press.

Fosnot, C. and Dolk, M. (2001) *Young Mathematicians at Work: Constructing Number Sense, Addition and Subtraction*. Portsmouth, NH: Heinemann.

Fountas, I.C. and Pinnell, G.S. (1996) *Guided Reading: Good First Teaching for All Children*. Portsmouth, NH: Heinemann.

Fuson, K. (1988) *Children's Counting and Concepts of Number*. New York: Springer-Verlag.

Fuson, K.C., Wearne, D., Hiebert, J., Human, P., Olivier, A., Carpenter, T. and Fenema, E. (1997) Children's conceptual structure for multidigit numbers and methods of multidigit addition and subtraction, *Journal for Research in Mathematics Education*, **38**: 130–63.

Gravemeijer, K.P.E. (1994) *Developing Realistic Mathematics Education*. Utrecht: CD-B Press.

Gravemeijer, K.P.E., Cobb, P., Bowers, J. and Whitenack, J. (2000) Symbolizing, modeling, and instructional design, in P. Cobb, E. Yackel and K. McClain (eds) *Symbolizing and Communicating in Mathematics Classrooms: Perspectives on Discourse, Tools, and Instructional Design*. Mahwah, NJ: Lawrence Erlbaum. pp. 335–73

Gray, E.M. (1991) An analysis of diverging approaches to simple arithmetic: preference and its consequences, *Educational Studies in Mathematics*, **33**: 551–74.

Hiebert, J., Carpenter, T.P., Fenema, E., Fuson, K.C., Wearne, D., Murray, H., Oliver, A. and Human, P. (1997) *Making Sense: Teaching and Learning Mathematics with Understanding*. Portsmouth, NH: Heinemann.

Kamii, C. (1985) *Young Children Reinvent Arithmetic*. New York: Teachers College Press.

Kamii, C. (1986) Place value: an explanation of its difficulty and educational implications for the primary grades, *Journal of Research in Early Childhood Education*, **1**: 75–86.

McClain, K. and Cobb, P. (1999) Supporting children's ways of reasoning about patterns and partitions, in J.V. Copley (ed.), *Mathematics in the Early Years*. Reston, VA: National Council of Teachers of Mathematics. pp. 113–18.

Mix, K., Huttenlocher, J. and Levine, S. (2002) *Quantitative Development in Infancy and Early Childhood*. Oxford: Oxford University Press.

Mulligan, J.T. and Mitchelmore, M.C. (1997) Young children's intuitive models of multiplication and division, *Journal for Research in Mathematics Education*, **28**: 309–30.

Steffe, L.P. (1992) Learning stages in the construction of the number sequence, in J. Bideaud, C. Meljac and J. Fischer (eds), *Pathways to Number: Children's Developing Numerical Abilities*. Hillsdale, NJ: Lawrence Erlbaum. pp. 83–8.

Steffe, L.P., and Cobb, P. (with E. von Glasersfeld) (1988) *Construction of Arithmetic Meanings and Strategies*. New York: Springer-Verlag.

Steffe, L.P., von Glasersfeld, E., Richards, J. and Cobb, P. (1983) *Children's Counting Types: Philosophy, Theory, and Application*. New York: Praeger.

Stephan, M., Bowers, J., Cobb, P. and Gravemeijer, K. (2003) *Supporting Students' Development of Measuring Conceptions: Analyzing Students' Learning in Social Context*, *JRME Monograph #12 (Vol. 12)*. Reston, VA: National Council of Teachers of Mathematics.

Streefland, L. (ed.) (1991) *Realistic Mathematics Education in Primary School*. Utrecht: CD-B Press.

Thompson, I. (1994) Young children's idiosyncratic written algorithms for addition, *Education Studies in Mathematics*, **36**: 333–45.

Thompson, I. (ed.) (1997) *Teaching and Learning Early Number*. Buckingham: Open University Press.

Thompson, I. (ed.) (1999) *Issues in Teaching Numeracy in Primary Schools*. Buckingham: Open University Press.

Thompson, I. (ed.) (2003) *Enhancing Primary Mathematics Teaching*. Buckingham: Open University Press.

Tolchinsky, L. (2003) *The Cradle of Culture and What Children Know about Writing and Numbers before Being Taught*. Mahwah, NJ: Lawrence Erlbaum.

Van de Walle, J.A. (2004) *Elementary and Middle School Mathematics: Teaching Developmentally (5th edition)*. Boston, MA: Pearson.

Van den Heuvel-Panhuizen, M. (1996) *Assessment and Realistic Mathematics Education*. Utrecht: Freudenthal Institute, Utrecht University.

Van den Heuvel-Panhuizen, M. (ed.) (2001) *Children Learn Mathematics: A Learning–teaching Trajectory with Intermediate Attainment Targets*. Utrecht: Freudenthal Institute, Utrecht University.

Von Glasersfeld, E. (1982) Subitizing: the role of figural patterns in the development of numerical concepts, *Archives de Psychologie*, **50**: 191–318.

Von Glasersfeld, E. (1995). *Radical Constructivism: A Way of Knowing and Learning*. London: Falmer.

Vygotsky, L.S. (1963) *Mind in Society: The Development of Higher Psychological Processes*. Cambridge, MA: Harvard University Press. (Translator M. Lopez-Morillas, original work published 1934.)

Wheatley, G. and Reynolds, A. (1999) *Coming to Know Number*. Tallahassee, FL: Mathematics Learning.

Worthington, M. and Carruthers, E. (2003) *Children's Mathematics: Making Marks, Making Meaning*. London: Paul Chapman Publishing/Sage.

Wright, R.J. (1989) Numerical development in the kindergarten year: a teaching experiment. Doctoral dissertation, University of Georgia [DAI, 50A, 1588; DA8919319].

Wright, R.J. (1991a) An application of the epistemology of radical constructivism to the study of learning, *Australian Educational Researcher*, 18(1): 75–95.

Wright, R.J. (1991b) The role of counting in children's numerical development, *Australian Journal of Early Childhood*, 16(2): 43–8.

Wright, R.J. (1991c) What number knowledge is possessed by children entering the kindergarten year of school? *Mathematics Education Research Journal*, 3(1): 1–16.

Wright, R.J. (1992) Number topics in early childhood mathematics curricula: historical background, dilemmas, and possible solutions, *Australian Journal of Education*, 36: 125–42.

Wright, R.J. (1994a) Mathematics in the lower primary years: a research-based perspective on curricula and teaching practice, *Mathematics Education Research Journal*, 6(1): 23–36.

Wright, R.J. (1994b) A study of the numerical development of 5-year-olds and 6-year-olds, *Educational Studies in Mathematics*, 36: 35–44.

Wright, R.J. (1996) Problem-centred mathematics in the first year of school, in J. Mulligan and M. Mitchelmore, *Research in Early Number Learning: An Australian Perspective*. Adelaide: AAMT. pp. 35–54.

Wright, R.J. (1998) Children's beginning knowledge of numerals and its relationship to their knowledge of number words: an exploratory, observational study, in A. Olivier and K. Newstead (eds), *Proceedings of the 22nd Conference of the International Group for the Psychology of Mathematics Education*. Stellenbosch, South Africa: PME. Vol. 4, pp. 201–8.

Wright, R.J. (2001) The arithmetical strategies of four 3rd-graders, in J. Bobis, B. Perry and M. Mitchelmore (eds), *Proceedings of the 25th Annual Conference of the Mathematics Education Research Group of Australasia*. Sydney: MERGA. Vol. 2, pp. 547–54.

Wright, R.J., Martland, J. and Stafford, A. (2000) *Early Numeracy: Assessment for Teaching and Intervention*. London: Paul Chapman Publishing/Sage.

Wright, R.J., Martland, J., Stafford, A. and Stanger, G. (2002) *Teaching Number: Advancing Children's Skills and Strategies*. London: Paul Chapman Publishing /Sage.

Young-Loveridge, J. (1989) The development of children's number concepts: the first year of school, *New Zealand Journal of Educational Studies*, 34(1): 47–64.

Young-Loveridge, J. (1991) *The Development of Children's Number Concepts from Ages Five to Nine*. Hamilton: University of Waikato. Vol. 1 and 3.

# Index

2-digit addition and subtraction: jump
  strategies, 120–143,
  assessment tasks, 126–133
  instructional activities 134–143
2-digit addition and subtraction: split
  strategies,144–148
  assessment tasks, 148–150
  instructional activities 151–154
2-digit numbers,
  difficulty with names, 31
2-digit numerals, 10, 23, 43
3-digit addition and subtraction, 146
3-digit numbers, 23
3-digit numerals, 31, 43

Abstract composite unit see Multiplication and
  division
Adding through five, 67 see also Strategies
Addition,
  beginning through counting, 48
  from 49, 138
  from a decade, 126–127
  higher decade, 144–145
  using doubles, fives and tens, 108
  to a decade, 127–128
  with spatial patterns in the range 1 to 10, 72
  with 11, 137
  see also Counting, advanced
Additive tasks, 49
  two screened collections, 86
Arithmetic rack, 98–110
  see also Numbers 1 to 20
  adding two numbers on the, 101–102
  progressing to mental strategies, 103–104
  subtraction on the, 102–103
Arrays, use of, see Multiplication and division
Arrow cards, 43
Assessment,
  individualized, 22
  observational, 21
  videotaped interviews, 22
  written, 21
Assessment task, 6
  adaptations, 21
  as instructional activities, 22

as a source of teachers' learning, 22
  format, 21 groups, 2, 20–21
  in early counting and addition, 51–54
Automatized knowledge, 67

Backward Number Word Sequences (BNWSs),
  14
  assessment task, 35
  by 10s on and off the decade, 126, 141–142
  facility with, 30
  instructional activities, 40–41, 90, 95
Bead bar see Bead string
Bead board, 118–119
Bead string, 92
  with ten catcher, 136
Block scheduling, 5, 13
Bunny ears, 73–74

Calculator challenge, 138–139
Classroom Instructional Framework for Early
  Number (CIFEN), 5, 8–9,
Combining and partitioning, 20
  approaches to teaching, 64
  doubles to 10, 64
  doubles to 20, 64
  instructional activities, 43
  involving 2-digit numbers, 149
  involving non-canonical forms, 149
  partitioning numbers 2 to 5, 64
  partitioning numbers 6 to 10, 64
  small numbers, 64
  using spatial patterns, 65
  without using counting-by-ones, 64–65
Commutativity, 104, 160
Comparative subtraction see Subtraction
Compensating, see Strategies
Conceptual foundations of number
  understanding, 179–180
Counting,
  advanced assessment tasks,86–89
  advanced instructional activities, 90–97
  coordinating words and items, 49
  early, 47–48, see also Early counting
    assessment tasks
emergent, 50

figurative, 49–50
importance of, 47
instructional activities, 44, 55–63
levels of sophistication in, 47, 50
perceptual, 48–50, 85
Counting-by-ones, *see* Strategies
advanced, *see* Strategies
Counting-back-from, *see* Strategies
Counting-back-to, *see* Strategies
Counting-forward-from-one-three-times, *see*
Strategies
Counting-from-one, *see* Strategies
Counting-on, *see* Strategies
instructional activities, 60–61
Counting-on-from, *see* Strategies
Counting-on-to, *see* Strategies
Counting-up-from, *see* Strategies
Counting-up-to, *see* Strategies

Decade numbers,
sequencing, 43
Difference between, 97
Differentiation, 191–192
Digits, 29
Domino patterns *see* Spatial patterns
Doubles, 104
Double ten frame, 98–99, 111–118
Dropping back to one, 30, 33

Early counting assessment tasks
additive tasks involving two screened
collections, 54
comparing small collections, 51
counting and copying temporal sequences and
temporal patterns, 54
establishing a collection of specified
numerosity, 53
establishing the numerosity of a collection,
52, 59, 61–62
establishing the numerosity of two collections,
53
increase and decrease in the range 1 to 6, 52
Early counting instructional activities, 55–63
Early multiplication and division, *see*
Multiplication and division
Early number knowledge, 7
Early arithmetical strategies. 30
Empty Number Line (ENL), 16–18, 94, 121–122

Facile, 19
Finger patterns 64–65
adding two numbers in the range 1 to 5, 65
and advanced count–by-ones strategies, 84–85
assessment tasks, 68–72
numbers in the range 1 to 5, 65, and 68–69
numbers in the range 6 to 10, 69
numbers in the range 6 to 10 using 5 as a
reference, 65
why and when, 65
Five-frame, 65
Five as a reference point, 65–66, 118–119
*see also* strategies
Five-wise patterns on a ten frame, 71, 78–79
naming and visualizing, 71, 105–108
Formal algorithms, 27
Forward Number Word Sequences (FNWSs), 14
assessment task, 33
by 10s on and off the decade, 126, 141–142
facility with, 30
instructional activities, 40, 90, 95
in multiples, 167 *see also* Skip Counting
Five and ten structure of numbers, 64

Guiding principles for classroom teaching
(GPCT), 5, 6

Incrementing and decrementing 2-digit
numbers, 123–124
Incrementing and decrementing by 10s on and
off the decade, 128–129
Incrementing and decrementing by 100s, 146
Incrementing flexibly by 10s and ones, 129–131
Instruction,
designing, 13
organizing, 9
Instructional activities, 22
Instructional procedures, 7
Instructional sequences, 8
Inverse operations, 160

Jump strategies *see* Strategies

Locating numbers in the range 1 to 100,
assessment task, 39

Minuend, 72
Missing addend tasks, 16, 82, 86–88

Missing subtrahend tasks, 81, 88–89, 97
Multiplication and division,
    abstract composite unit, 159
    assessment tasks, 162–166
    determining products and factors,174–176
    early, 155–176
    instructional activities 167–176
    relational thinking, 165–166
    repeated equal groups, 155–158, 162–164,
        170–171
    division as sharing or measuring, 155, 158
    skip counting, 157, 162, 168–169
    use of arrays, 155, 159–161, 164–165, 171–173
    word problems, 165

Near doubles, 104
Non-count-by-ones Strategy, 49
    5 and 10 as a reference point, 120
    adding to 10, 49
    adding through 10, 49
    bridging to 10, 49
    doubles, 120
    see also Jump strategies
Numbers, 29
Numbers 1 to 20,
    making and reading on the arithmetic rack,
        99–100
Number clothes line, 14
Number knowledge, 6
Number Line see Empty Number Line
Number words, 29
    to 1000,146
Number word after, 30
    assessment task, 33
    teen/decade confusion, 33
    instructional activities, 45
Number word before, 30
    assessment task, 35
Number word sequences, 30
Numeral Identification,
    assessment task, 36
    instructional activities, 42
Numeral Recognition,
    assessment task, 36
    instructional activities, 42
Numeral track, 45–46,
    activities, 95–97
Numerals, 7, 29
    from 1 to 10, 30

    from 11 to 20, 31
    from 20 to 99, 31
    identifying, 30
    learning about, 30
    naming, 30
    reading, 30
    recognise, 30
    sequences, 30
    write, 30
Numeration system, 29
Numerosity, 48

One hundred square activities, 91
Ordering numerals, 38
    instructional activities, 44, 58

Pair-wise patterns on a ten frame, 70, 78–79
    naming and visualizing, 70, 105–108
Place value, 23
    additive sense of, 26
    alternative view, 25
    difficulties, 24
    teaching through addition and subtraction, 25
    traditional view, 25
Perceptual counting see Counting
Perceptual replacements, 85
Professional development,177

Quinary pattern see Five-wise patterns

Removed items task, 83, 88
Repeated equal groups see Multiplication and
    division
Repeatability, 189–191

Screened collections versus word problems,
    83–84
Sequencing numerals, 37–38
    assessment task, 37
    instructional activities, 40, 44
    non-sequential, 41–42
Sharing, see Multiplication and division
Skip counting, see Multiplication and division
Spatial patterns, 64
    domino patterns, 70, 79–81
    five and ten frame flashes, 77–78
    partitions of 5 and 10, 71
    subitizing, 65, 75–76
    see also Five-wise patterns

*see also* Pair-wise patterns
Split strategy *see* Strategies
Strategy, 14
Strategies,
  adding through five, 67
  compensating, 132–133
  counting-by-ones, 20, 49
    advanced, 20, 66, 82, 98
    advanced in the range 20–100, 84
  counting-from-one, 49
  counting-back-from, 66, 82–83, 93
  counting-back-to, 66, 82–83
  counting-forward-from-one-three-times for
    addition, 83
  counting-forward-from-one-three-times for
    subtraction, 83
  counting-on, 49, 57, 66, 82, 92–93
  counting-on-from, 66
  counting-on-to, 66
  counting-up-from, 82
  counting-up-to, 82
  five as a reference point, 65–66
  fostering the development of, 124–125
  informal, 27
  jump, 27, 120–143
  non-count-by-ones, 49
  split, 27–28, 121–123, 144–154
  ten as a reference point, 65–66
  transforming, 132–133
Structuring Numbers,
  in the range 1 to 10, 64–81
  assessment tasks, 68–72
  instructional activities, 73–81
Structuring Numbers,
  in the range 1 to 20, 98–119
  assessment tasks, 105–110
  instructional activities, 111–119

Subitizing *see* Spatial patterns
Subtractive tasks, 82
Subtraction,
  2-digit, 120–125
  comparative subtraction, 89–90
  from 49, 138
  from a decade, 127–128
  higher decade, 144–145
  to a decade, 126–127
  using doubles, fives and tens, 108
  with 11, 137
  with spatial patterns  in the range 1 to 10, 72
  *see also* Counting, advanced
Symbolising numbers, 29

Teaching,
  problem based, 6
Teaching and Learning Cycle, 5, 13–14
Teaching number,
  emerging approaches, 22–24
  traditional approaches, 22–24
Teens, 31
Temporal patterns *see* Early counting assessment
    tasks
Temporal sequences *see* Early counting
    assessment tasks
Ten as a reference point, 65–66 *see also* Strategies
Ten-frames, 10, 65
Tens and ones structure of teen numbers, 25–26
Transforming, *see* Strategies

Verbally based strategies, 7
Videotaping, 177
  importance of, 182

Zone of proximal development, 7